The Czech Republic

Postcommunist States and Nations

Books in the series

Belarus: A denationalized nation
David R. Marples

Armenia: At the crossroads
Joseph R. Masih and Robert O. Krikorian

Poland: The conquest of history
George Sanford

Kyrgyzstan: Central Asia's island of democracy?
John Anderson

Ukraine: Movement without change, change without movement
Marta Dyczok

The Czech Republic: A nation of velvet
Rick Fawn

Uzbekistan: Transition to authoritarianism on the silk road
Neil J. Melvin

Romania: The unfinished revolution
Steven D. Roper

The Czech Republic

A NATION OF VELVET

Rick Fawn

harwood academic publishers
Australia • Canada • France • Germany • India • Japan
Luxembourg • Malaysia • The Netherlands • Russia
Singapore • Switzerland

Amsteldijk 166
1st Floor
1079 LH Amsterdam
The Netherlands

British Library Cataloguing in Publication Data

A catalogue record for this book is available from the British Library.

ISBN: 90-5823-044-9 (softcover)

TABLE OF CONTENTS

CHRONOLOGY

1918
28 October   'Bloodless revolution' when the Czechoslovak Committee announced the separation from Austria-Hungary of the Czech and Slovak lands.
11 November   Proclamation of the Republic of Czechoslovakia.

1935
      Treaties of Mutual Assistance signed separately with France and the Soviet Union; Beneš succeeded Masaryk as President.

1938
September   Munich Agreement; Sudetenland given to Germany.

1939
March   Bohemia and Moravia annexed to Germany; independent Slovakia proclaimed.

1944
August   Slovak national uprising.

1945
5 April   Košice Programme set postwar agenda.
29 June   Carpathia transferred to USSR.

1946
16 May   Communists won 38 percent in free election.

1948
25 February   Communists in power and date after which seizures of property were restituted in post-communist Czechoslovakia.
9 May   New constitution proclaimed Czechoslovakia a 'people's democracy'.

1949–1952
      Intensified political persecution, including 'show trials' of leading communists such as Slánský.

1953
March   Gottwald's death follows Stalin's; Novotný became KSČ leader; Zápotocký President.

1968
5 January   Reformist Communists in power, led by Dubček.
April   Action Programme launched; called for revisions to socialism in practice.
August   Warsaw Pact intervention.

1969
1 January   Czechoslovakia became federal political system when the only Prague Spring reform to be retained was implemented.
16 January   Philosophy student Jan Palach immolated himself to protest end of Prague Spring.
17 April   Dubček formally removed as KSČ leader; replaced by Husák.

1977
1 January   Charter 77 signed by Czechoslovak dissidents such as Havel; several arrested as they attempted to post the document to government officials.

1987

April	Gorbachev visited Prague.
December	Husák succeeded by Jakeš as KSČ leader.

1988

21 August	Unsanctioned protests marked 20th anniversary of Warsaw Pact intervention.

1989

January	Unsanctioned commemoration of death of Jan Palach broken up by police; many arrested, including Havel who was again sentenced to prison.
17 November	Officially sanctioned student march attacked by police; injuries and rumours of a student death brought people out in support; peaceful protests of hundreds of thousands follow; umbrella opposition groups Civic Forum and Public Against Violence formed.
21 November	PM Ladislav Adamec opened nominal talks with opposition.
27 November	Two-hour orderly general strike involving millions.
29 November	Federal Assembly annulled KSČ's monopoly of power.
3 December	Adamec's proposal of communist-dominated coalition government rejected.
10 December	Coalition government formed; 13 of 21 posts held by non-communists, although new Prime Minister Marian Čalfa was still KSČ member, he left the party in January.
28 December	Dubček elected speaker of Federal Assembly.
29 December	Havel elected President by Federal Assembly.

1990

19 April	Czechoslovakia officially renamed the Czech and Slovak Federative Republic.
8–9 June	First fully free elections after communism; Civic Forum and Public Against Violence won majority and created broad coalition government of all major parties, except Communist.
5 July	Havel re-elected President by the new parliament.
September	Parliament's 'November 17 Commission' established to investigate the Velvet Revolution and connections of MPs to the previous regime; start of the 'lustration' process.
22 September	Czechoslovakia admitted to IMF.
December	Power-sharing agreement between federal government and republics passed by federal parliament.
December	Central Bank devalued Czechoslovak crown, made it internally convertible.

1991

1 January	Price liberalization; trade with former socialist countries to be conducted hereafter in hard currency.
February	Civic Forum split into Klaus's centre-right Civic Democratic Party and Dienstbier's centre-left Civic Movement.
March	Pro-independence demonstrations in Slovakia; Havel attacked by protestors in Bratislava; Mečiar made new faction within Public Against Violence called Public Against Violence — for a Democratic Slovakia.
May	Movement for a Democratic Slovakia (HZDS) registered as new political party; a founding Congress was then held in June.
13 June	Large-scale privatization begun.

21 June	Last Soviet soldier left Czechoslovakia, ahead of the agreed end of June deadline.
1 July	Warsaw Pact formally disbanded itself at a meeting in Prague.

1992

12 February	'Milovy Agreement' for common state.
May	First wave of coupon privatization begun.
June	Elections resulted in continued coalition of ODS, KDU-ČSL and ODA.
June	Čalfa's federal government resigned; interim government established under Jan Stráský.
3 July	Havel did not secure re-election as President; further attempts failed.
20 July	Havel resigned as President.
23 July	Klaus and Mečiar concluded agreement for separation of state, including a requirement of 60 percent majority vote in each republic's parliament.
13 November	Law on the separation of the Federation passed; included provisions for the division of federal property between the two constituent republics.
16 December	Czech Constitution adopted.
19 December	Czech National Council rejected filling new Czech Senate with sitting Czech members of the Federal Parliament; Senate to be empty until January 1997.
20 December	The Czech Republic entered Central European Free Trade Area with Poland, Hungary and Slovakia.

1993

1 January	Czech Republic officially in existence.
26 January	Havel elected President of the Czech Republic; sworn in a week later.
8 February	Czech Crown introduced.
22 June	Prague Stock Exchange expanded from dealing in bonds to trading of company shares from first wave of voucher privatization.
30 June	The Czech Republic entered the Council of Europe.
4 October	Association Agreement signed with EU replacing previous agreement signed with Czechoslovakia.

1994

10 March	Czech Republic signed Partnership for Peace.
9 May	Czech Republic gained Associate Membership of WEU.
September	New law stipulated that Czech citizenship obtainable with two years' residence and five years without a criminal record.

1995

1 February	Czech Republic became an EU associate member.
1 March	Shares from second wave of voucher privatization began trading on Prague Stock Exchange.
27 September	Parliament affirmed the formation of the Senate.
1 October	Crown became generally convertible, including for current account transactions.
28 November	Czech Republic became the first post-communist country to gain full OECD membership.

1996

17 January	Czech Republic applied for EU membership.
31 May–1 June	Minority government of 99/200 seats formed by Klaus's ODS with ČSL and ODA; ČSSD's Zeman made parliamentary speaker. 15–16, 22–23 November First elections to the Senate.

1997

27 May	Czech Crown floated; lost over 10 percent of its value that day; the second, and more severe, austerity budget in two months followed the next day.
9 July	NATO Madrid Summit issued membership invitations to the Czech Republic, Poland and Hungary; entry likely in 1999.
15 July	European Commission's Agenda 2000 criticized Czech developments but recommended it, with Poland, Hungary, Estonia, Slovenia and Cyprus, for detailed EU accession negotiations.
Summer	Substantial flooding in Moravia and eastern Bohemia.
Summer	Czech Romanies sought political asylum in Canada, then Britain and France.
23 October	Zieleniec resigned as Foreign Minister and Deputy ODS Chairman in protest against Klaus party leadership style.
7 November	New cabinet ministers sworn in; Havel became ill during ceremonies.
30 November	Klaus resigned as Prime Minister to go into 'constructive opposition'.

1998

2 January	Central Bank Governor Tošovský sworn in as Prime Minister.
17 January	Freedom Union founded by breakaway faction of Klaus' ODS.
20 January	Havel re-elected President.
March	Accession negotiations with the EU begun.
May	Czechs shocked that Canada imposed visas on all Czechs resulting from the summer 1997 arrival of Czech Romanies.
19–20 June	ČSSD won 74 and ODS 63 of 200 parliamentary seats in elections; a month of negotiations followed.
17 July	Zeman appointed Prime Minister according to the 'opposition agreement' by which Klaus became Parliamentary speaker and pledged not to allow defeat of Social Democrat minority government.
19 August	Zeman's minority government won confidence vote after, according to the 'opposition agreement', ODS MPs walked out of Parliament to avoid voting.

1999

12 March	Czech Republic, with Poland and Hungary, joined NATO.

PREFACE

The fledgling Czech Republic emerged from the vast, rich history of Czechoslovakia. Foremost this is a history of experimentation and innovation; the contemporary Czech nation issues from its Czechoslovak predecessor and builds on a heritage that has been called a "museum of the major political options of the twentieth century" and a "laboratory for social change".[1] Interwar Czechoslovakia was called the most democratic country in Central Europe; its supposed multicultural polity and ethos made it the Switzerland of the region; the appellation extended beyond domestic politics to be an adept indicator of its relative wealth and prosperity. Even within the restraints of communism Czechoslovakia was pioneering, advancing perhaps the most articulate and refined ideological revisions to the creed that governed the states of the Soviet bloc. The anti-communist outcry of November 1989 toppled a fierce, stalwart regime peacefully and with humour, and gave the world the phrase 'Velvet Revolution'. Thereafter Czechoslovakia led the post-Soviet world in many of its economic reforms, in a process, in this case, admiringly styled the 'Velvet Transformation'. The split of the country between June and December 1992 generated, at least theoretically, a new model for negotiated and peaceful dissolutions for countries worldwide; and it, too, was characterized as the 'Velvet Divorce'.

While Czechoslovakia can be deemed pioneering and innovative, the paradoxical flipside of this is that the Czechs and Slovaks were fundamentally dissatisfied with their economic and political identities, and indeed also with their national identity and cultural and geographic locale.

Despite flirtations with pan-Slavism in the nineteenth century, in the twentieth century the Czechs have perceived themselves overwhelmingly as western-oriented Europeans. But it was throughout this century that the Czech ambition to be—or, more accurately, to remain 'western'—was derailed or even hijacked, either by outside forces or by choices made internally, if later to be regretted. The Czechs have never been closer to fulfilling their western yearning since the birth of the Czech Republic in January 1993.

Newborn states and societies have missions. When it was created, the Czech Republic also had a mission. But unlike the history of its people or its predecessor-state, Czechoslovakia, the ultimate aim of the new entity was profoundly mundane: to be an 'ordinary' country.

This project consisted in creating a normal, particularly 'European', society and nation, in which the economy functioned, albeit with allowances for cyclical changes, and politics was benevolently routinized. In view of the communist legacy, achieving the mundane was, and remains, an arduous task; it is one shared by all post-communist countries committed to market and democratic reform. But it is an aim that the Czech Republic has pursued atypically, with alacrity, vigour and singularity. The Czech nation would distinguish itself by attempting to become *extraordinarily* ordinary.

This book will trace the practices initiated to achieve what is a strikingly difficult task. It seeks both to show and to interpret what the Czechs have wanted since 1989 but especially since 1993; for, as is argued here, the Czech Republic is a new entity. The book will not hide a certain Czechophile disposition. Anyone familiar with the Czech nation cannot feel some sense of the specificity, indeed the attraction, of Czech culture and of the sad betrayal that contours much of its history. This does not imply, particularly with hindsight, that Czech historical actions have not been misguided. The book will also be critical of aspects of Czech life. Indeed, part of the necessary critical assessment is that the Czech velvet is, in various areas of the development of the new Czech society, thinning or patchy.

The future success of the Czech Republic rests substantially on its history. The defining process for the Czech Republic is its twentieth-century history, a period for most of which the pre-eminent identity for the Czech was the hybrid 'Czechoslovak'. Many Czechs devoted considerable political, cultural and intellectual energy throughout this century to fostering that identity. Now they are embarking on the creation of a new one.

Extensive material is now available on the Czech nation, in English as well as in Czech. This volume hopes to provide the contours of developments in the Czech Republic, to advance and substantiate certain observations, and to provide some indication of the literature available, while refraining from unduly burdening the reader with extensive referencing and parenthetical discussions. Two notes, however, may be of benefit. First, the term 'postcommunist' is occasionally used in other literature to mean 'ex-communist'; in this volume it strictly denotes developments that succeed the Velvet Revolution of 1989. Thus, reference to Václav Havel as a post-communist president does not suggest that he ceased to be a commun-ist (he never was one) but that he secured the position after the end of the communist monopoly on power. Second, on a technical note, diacritical marks are used when in the original; Czech names or authors who are cited or give themselves without these marks appear here in their anglicized form.

Lastly, my thanks are due to Jaroslav Brada, Jan Čulík and Kieran Williams who kindly commented on individual chapters and to Karen Henderson and George Sanford who helpfully commented on a full draft. The staff of Harwood Academic Publishers also provided their assistance and Petr šilhánek has supplemented my Internet access to Czech newspapers with a supply of the hard copy. Needless to say, all errors of fact and interpretation are my own.

---

1. Carol Skalnik Leff, *National Conflict in Czechoslovakia: The Making and Remaking of a State, 1918–1987* (Princeton: Princeton University Press, 1988), p. 3; Jaroslav Krejčí and Pavel Machonin, *Czechoslovakia, 1918–1992: Laboratory for Social Change* (London: Macmillan, 1995).

GLOSSARY OF ABBREVIATIONS

CEFTA	Central European Free Trade Area
CFE	Conventional Forces in Europe
CMEA	Council for Mutual Economic Assistance
CSFR	Czech and Slovak Federative Republic
ČSSD	*Česká strana sociálně demokratická*, Czech Social Democratic Party
DTI	Department of Trade and Industry
EBRD	European Bank for Reconstruction and Development
EU	European Union
HSD-SMS	*Hnutí samosprávné demokracie-Společnost pro Moravu a Slezsko*, Movement for Self-Governing Democracy-Society for Moravia and Silesia
IMF	International Monetary Fund
KDH	*Křest'ansko-demokratické hnutí*, Christian Democratic Movement
KDS	*Křest'anská demokratická strana*, Christian Democratic Party
KDU-ČSL	*Křest'ansko-demokratická unie-Československá strana lidova*, Christian Democratic Union-Czechoslovak People's Party
KŠC	*Komunistická strana Československa*, Communist Party of Czechoslovakia
KSČM	*Komunistická strana Čech a Moravy*, Communist Party of Bohemia and Moravia
NATO	North Atlantic Treaty Organization
ODA	*Občanská demokratická aliance*, Civic Democratic Alliance
ODS	*Občanská demokratická strana*, Civic Democratic Party
OECD	Organization for Economic Cooperation and Development
OF	*Občanské fórum*, Civic Forum
OH	*Občanské hnutí*, Civic Movement
OSCE	Organization for Security and Cooperation in Europe
PfP	Partnership for Peace
SDL	*Strana demokratické levice*, the Party of the Democratic Left

SNS	*Slovenská národná strana*, Slovak National Party
SPR-RSČ	*Sdružení pro republiku-Republikánská strana Československa*, the Republican Party
StB	*Státní bezpečnost*, [Communist] Czechoslovak state secret police
UNPROFOR	United Nations Protection Force
US	*Unie Svobody*, Freedom Union
VPN	*Veřejnosti proti násilí*, Public Against Violence
WEU	West European Union
WTO	Warsaw Treaty Organization

Map of Czech Republic

Chapter 1

THE LEGACIES OF HISTORY: FROM THE FOUNDATION TO THE VELVET REVOLUTION AND THE VELVET DIVORCE

In September 1938, British Prime Minister Neville Chamberlain expediently proclaimed Czechoslovakia to be a faraway country of which people knew nothing. Nevertheless, the history of Czechoslovakia is now well-travelled. Its history is very much the history of Europe, and, similarly, is replete with ambiguity and controversy. This chapter seeks to offer an outline of Czechoslovak and Czech history while also acknowledging the varying interpretations of that history and inviting the reader to further judgement.

CREATING CZECHOSLOVAKIA

The birth of Czechoslovakia in 1918 resulted from the skilful statesmanship of Czech and Slovak intellectuals, the mobilization of émigré communities in North America and the coincidence of their aims with that of the victorious Allies. This product, however, was less of a concert between Czech and Slovak populations themselves. Under the aegis of Tomáš G. Masaryk, an intellectual born in the southern Moravian town of Hodonín, the 30 May 1918 Pittsburgh Agreement called for the union of the Czechs and Slovaks in their own independent state. The Agreement intimated that the Slovaks would enjoy autonomy in the new state. The justifications for the creation of Czechoslovakia were ambiguous, and that ambiguity was a harbinger for the viability and durability of the country, particularly as it replicated the multiethnic nature of the Austro-Hungarian empire from which it had extricated itself.

Czechoslovakia moved towards reality when, on 28 October 1918, the National Committee that had campaigned for independence during the war announced the separation from Austria-Hungary of the Czech and Slovak lands. Key figures in the Czechoslovak independence movement, including Masaryk, Eduard Beneš and Milan Štefánik, were not even present in Prague when the pronouncement was made. A 'bloodless revolution' followed, in which Habsburg officials willingly ceded administrative control. The most audacious act of this peaceful revolution was the removal of public signs bearing the double-eagle emblem of the Habsburg empire.[1]

The formal Proclamation of the Republic of Czechoslovakia was made on 11 November. The creation of Czechoslovakia was foremost underwritten by pragmatism. For the Western Allies, the principle of national self-determination also justified the creation of a series of independent states forming a *cordon sanitaire* between defeated Germany and emasculated but revolutionary Russia. In addition, the proposed Czechoslovakia had what were considered natural frontiers, particularly a series of low mountains surrounding Bohemia and Moravia. Such topographical features added to the perceived defencibility of the country, which in turn increased the logic of Czechoslovakia as a country.

A nationality had to be created in order to fulfil the principle of national self-determination. The Czechs constituted barely half of the population while Germans constituted the second largest ethnic group, outnumbering the Slovaks. An ethnic fusion of the Czechs and Slovaks would generate an indisputable majority nation, thereby confirming its right to national self-determination. The higher Slovak birthrate was also expected over time to help reinforce the Slavic preponderance in the new country.

Linguistic and cultural reasons might have suggested that the Czechs and Slovaks were fraternal nations and their fusion was natural. But they had disparate historical experiences; the Czechs rose to cultural importance in Europe when Charles IV ascended the throne of the Holy Roman Empire. The Czechs lost their independence to the Austrians following the Battle of White Mountain of 1620 during which its nobility was destroyed, contributing to a national belief thereafter that the Czechs were an egalitarian people. By contrast, the Slovaks were under Hungarian tutelage for nearly a millennium. So absorbed into the Hungarian realm was Slovakia that St Martin's Cathedral in Bratislava was the site of the enthronement of Hungarian kings. The development of a possible Slovak elite was pre-empted by intensive Magyarization and cooption. Religion also differentiated the Czechs and Slovaks. While Protestantism was important in Slovak culture and political life it was much more dominated by Catholicism than in the Czech Lands where the religious ethos was contoured by the Hussite-secular protest tradition. What similar heritage the two peoples shared did not make for a natural fusion. Rather, like many peoples around them, the Slovaks had undergone a national revival in the mid- and late-nineteenth century; and in 1918 they were asked to cede an identity that, while not fully enshrined as a popular ethos, was still strong enough to present an obstacle to the installation of a successor.

The fusion, then, was expedient, and expedience became an enduring feature of Czechoslovakia. As one commentator observed, the 'full meaning of the political union of Slovaks and Czechs in 1918 was nebulous and difficult for the Czechs to grapple with or even understand. Prior to 1917 such a union had been given hardly any real consideration'.[2] As another writer notes, 'Czechoslovak unity was still a vessel to be filled with content and purpose in 1918'.[3]

Several features of the new country suggested that it would be strong and successful: its economic prowess, democratic credentials and accommodation of ethnic diversity. The country inherited a great economic legacy: Bohemia had been the industrial powerhouse of the Austro-Hungarian empire. The new Czechoslovakia constituted only a fifth of the territory of the defunct empire but held over half its industrial capacity, nearly half of its industrial workers and alone was responsible for 70 percent of its industrial production.[4] Even with agrarian Slovakia, Czechoslovakia ranked as one of the world's ten most industrialized countries.[5]

This industrial base was complemented by Czechoslovakia's extensive arable land and forests. Agriculture was therefore an important economic sector and although its farming was not as technologically advanced as in Western Europe, productivity in many crops exceeded the European average. By Austrian calculations, per capita income in the Czech Lands between 1911 and 1913 exceeded that of Austria by 21 percent.[6] Economically viable, the country also provided wide-ranging social insurance. While this was not thoroughly organized in the Republic's initial years, it represented a general principle of Czechoslovak social life. The new republic introduced economic measures to ensure Czechoslovak control over the economy and also to insulate it from Austria's post-war economic problems. Steps taken by the first half of 1919 included the launch of a separate Czechoslovak currency and the establishment of Czechoslovak banks and the Prague Stock Exchange. While its neighbours went through economic crisis and even socialist coups, Czechoslovakia enjoyed a relatively prompt economic recovery from the Great War. These successes inspired Czechoslovakia's post-communist economic architects, and Václav Klaus and Tomáš Ježek referred in 1989 to the post-World War I era as part of a Czech liberal economic tradition.[7]

It was not only for its economic success but also for its multiethnic composition that Czechoslovakia earned the nickname of the Switzerland of the east. According to the first official census, conducted in 1921, 66 percent of the total Czechoslovak population was Czech and Slovak; 23.4 percent was German and a further 5.6 percent Hungarian, while the smaller minorities of East Slavs, Russians, Ukrainians and especially Ruthenians totalled 3.5 percent.

The laws of the fledgling country made provision for its ethnic diversity, with extensive legal and political provisions for its minorities, which were particularly enshrined in the Bill of Rights. In addition, a Supreme Administrative Court was established to hear cases of infringements of political rights. The education system was strong and also made provision for minority language education. Czech teachers were despatched to Slovakia to expand its education system. By 1930, 96 percent of Slovaks, as well as 97 percent of Germans and 93 percent of Hungarians, were receiving schooling in their native tongues.[8] Major cities had parallel Czech and German universities or technical schools. The 1920 Constitution also entrenched equality among the country's diverse ethnic groups and offered minority rights, including the use of minority languages in conducting government business in areas where they comprised at least a fifth of the population.

Both the Germans and Slovaks found grounds for dissatisfaction with the new country. The German minority, which had resided on the territory that had become Czechoslovakia for centuries, believed that its rights were curtailed and its interests underrepresented. The proposals of the Pittsburgh Agreement, including a Slovak assembly, were stalled after 1918 and then superseded by the Constitution of 1920, which created a highly centralized, unitary state.

Masaryk believed that as much as fifty years and certainly at least a generation was required for the Czechs and Slovaks to merge into a common nation.[9] In the interim the young Czechoslovak state sought to strengthen the roots of Slovak identity and therein strengthened the Slovak sense of distinctiveness. Negligible industrial development was undertaken in Slovakia during the interwar period, save for modest military projects in the 1930s. What industry had been developed under the Austro-Hungarian empire (and it was the most industrial part of Hungary's domain) was forced to compete, and generally unsuccessfully, against its Czech counterparts after 1918. At least the comprehensive education system in Slovakia, often run by Czechs sent to redress the region's dearth of teachers, erased the effects of Magyarization. But the linguistic and cultural reinstatement of Slovak identity also had political consequences. Soon into the life of the young republic Slovaks began to believe that they were deprived of autonomy in the centralized state, particularly as they saw the central government, as well as their own local offices, overwhelmingly staffed by Czechs. Politically conscious Slovaks were divided between those who supported the idea of Czechoslovakia and those who classed themselves as Czecho-Slovaks, the latter most notably represented by the Slovak People's Party of Andrej Hlinka. The Czecho-Slovaks approached the electoral strength of their competitors in Slovakia in only one of the four elections held in the First Republic.[10]

Nevertheless, the interwar parliamentary system was intended to include all ethnic and political interests. Proportional representation gave rise to a broadly based multiparty system that covered the political spectrum and the ethnic composition of society. A striking indication of the liberal, tolerant ethos of Czechoslovak politics was that, unlike elsewhere in the region, the Czechoslovak Communist Party (KSČ) was legally established in 1921 and allowed to operate openly throughout the interwar period. Party politics was a prevalent feature of political life. This was a result of the Constitution, which mandated proportional representation. Fifty parties ran in the interwar elections, with fifteen generally represented. Securing just eight percent of the popular vote allowed a party the possibility of entering a governing coalition. Because of the fragmentation of votes, at least five parties were needed to form a coalition,[11] and this grouping became known as the *Pětka* (The Five). As would be the case in post-communist Czechoslovakia and then in the Czech Republic, parties operated on the basis of a list of candidates, and those candidates sat in parliament.

The centrality of political parties to Czechoslovak politics was highlighted by the relative impotence of the President, who possessed limited power and was elected by Parliament. But Masaryk enhanced the powers of his post through his moral and intellectual prestige, as Havel would do seven decades later. Known as '*Tatíček*', or Daddy, the scholarly Masaryk contrasted with other interwar Central European leaders, who tended to be military figures and inclined to centralized rule, such as Poland's Marshall Piłsudski or Hungary's Admiral Horthy, or the autocratic monarchs of south-eastern Europe.

International circumstances would not favour interwar Czechoslovakia. The Depression of the late 1920s affected Czechoslovakia particularly badly. As a trading nation, protectionism crippled its exports. The economic downturn exacerbated ethnic relations. The Slovak economy, which trailed European standards of growth throughout the interwar period by forty years, suffered significantly and charges were levelled against Czech financial circles for manipulating the Slovak economy.

The efforts to accommodate Sudeten Germans in Czechoslovakia decreased as the Depression worsened. Invitations to the Sudeten Germans to participate in the government and the provision of education, and in the German language, that was superior to that received by their co-ethnics in Germany,[12] failed to alleviate the effects of the economic crisis. The economic welfare of Czechoslovak Germans was already dented by the economic redistribution programmes of the post-1918 Czechoslovak government. But because of the extensive industry in the Sudetenland and its disproportionate employment of the Czechoslovak Germans, the fall in industrial production and exports affected their livelihoods especially profoundly. These circumstances offered fertile ground for the pro-Nazi National Front Party led by Konrad Heinlein. In May 1935 his party won almost two-thirds of the Sudeten German vote and he began advocating the federalization of Czechoslovakia. Thereafter, with backing from Hitler, he made increasing demands on Prague for German rights which ultimately meant secession and which were therefore incompatible with the integrity of the Czechoslovak state. The National Front Party also became increasingly totalitarian, seeking to mimic its successful fraternal party in Germany by commanding the full loyalty of its members, and that of all Sudeten Germans. Consequently it pressured, even with violence, moderate Czechoslovak-German political parties into joining with it. By 1938 it was effectively the only voice for Germans in Czechoslovakia.

CZECHOSLOVAKIA DISMEMBERED

Unlike its neighbours, democratic rule in Czechoslovakia was subverted not by developments from within but forces from without. While the Sudeten Germans carry some responsibility for the destruction of Czechoslovakia, they acted in an environment fashioned by Hitler, and Hitler had claims on Czechoslovakia. At his trial in 1924 Hitler inverted the concept of self-determination and proclaimed that the Germans were disenfranchised from regrouping their co-nationals and enjoying the right of self-government: 'Self-determination, but self-determination for every negro tribe, and Germany does not count as a negro tribe'.[13]

As the international turbulence of the 1930s increased Czechoslovakia vigorously sought to secure itself through a combination of what can be called 'good international citizenship' and through recourse to standard measures of self-defence. Czechoslovakia was a strong advocate of international law, the League of Nations and international legal control over the use of force. Indeed, throughout his career as Czechoslovakia's Foreign Minister and, after 1935, as President, Eduard Beneš was known and respected as a key figure in the League system. Detractors of Czechoslovakia would simply argue that, as a beneficiary of the Versailles order, it was upholding a self-serving status quo. It was against the revisionist powers of Germany and Hungary that Czechoslovakia also undertook to defend itself through more than moral persuasion. By May 1935 Prague secured two separate, but reinforcing, Treaties of Mutual Assistance with France and the Soviet Union. Czechoslovakia also participated in the 'Little Entente' with two other states that risked revisionist claims against them: Romania and Yugoslavia. In addition to these international agreements, Czechoslovakia used its advanced military industries to increase stockpiles of arms and to construct internal defences. Foremost in this planning was a Czechoslovak version of the French Maginot line along its borders with Germany, although only one-quarter of the intended installations were completed, and many of those would never be armed. So committed was Prague to the security of the country that defence spending climbed from 17 percent of government expenditure to 44.5 percent in 1938.[14]

Despite these efforts, Czechoslovakia was defeated and dismantled without the exchange of either shots or rhetoric. After the Munich Conference of September 1938, attended by Britain, France, Germany and Italy but not by the country in question, the four powers agreed to cede the Sudetenland to Germany. Given no option, Prague consented on 30 September. The incorporation into Germany of this wide band of territory, extending around three sides of the Czech lands, ensured that the remainder of Czechoslovakia was undefendable. In addition, with the surrender of the Sudetenland, Germany gained 1,213 aircraft, 2,253 pieces of artillery, 501 anti-aircraft guns and 1,966 anti-tank guns; 810 tanks; nearly two million pieces of small arms; more than one billion rounds of small arms ammunition and three million artillery shells. Ironically, 'Czechoslovak equipment exacted a heavy toll from the Allies' in the course of the coming war.[15]

While the justification for the transfer of the Sudetenland was the lofty principle of national self-determination, in this case, as Alfred Cobban observed, 'national self-determination gives way to national self-determination'. Thus Munich also fuelled the territorial aspirations of Czechoslovakia's other neighbours. Poland reasserted its claim to Těšín, seized by Czechoslovakia in 1920 during the Polish-Soviet war, while revisionist Hungary demanded southern Slovakia and Carpathia.

While the territorial changes permitted by Munich were justified by the principle of national self-determination, the result was at least as ambiguous as before. Now Czechs became minorities in Germany and Poland. In addition, German-Italian arbitration in November 1938 awarded Hungary southern Slovakia and Carpathia, only half the population of which was Hungarian.[16]

The remainder of Czechoslovakia was reconstituted as the 'Second Republic' and referred to as Czecho-Slovakia, the historical significance of which would reappear in the post-communist debate on renaming the country. Slovakia and Carpathia gained a margin of autonomy. By October, however, the nationalist Slovak People's Party, first led by Hlinka and, after his death in 1938, by Father Josef Tiso,[17] had secured power in Slovakia and articulated demands for autonomy. Meanwhile, revisionist Hungary fulfilled its aims of reabsorbing the remainder of Carpathia.

Unsatisfied with possession of only the Sudetenland and encouraged by Anglo-French appeasement, Hitler clamoured for more of Czechoslovakia. Accusing rump Czechoslovakia of being a 'dagger' which stabbed at the heart of Germany, he threatened Czechoslovakia's new Prime Minister, Emil Hacha, with German air raids on Prague. Hacha capitulated and on 15 March 1939 the Czech lands were militarily occupied and annexed into the German Reich as the Protectorate of Bohemia and Moravia. Not only was Czechoslovakia dead, but its remains were also gnarled. Polish forces occupied the Těšín area while Hungary seized southern Slovakia.

As he increased pressure on Prague, Hitler proposed to Tiso that he would support a Slovak bid for independence. But, Hitler threatened, if Slovakia did not accept this path immediately, Germany would leave Slovakia to fend for itself. This was hardly an enticing situation for an independent Slovakia because it was clear that Hungary wanted Slovak territory. Thus, one day before the German occupation of the Czech lands, Slovakia declared full independence on 14 March, and became closely allied to the Axis powers. Czechoslovakia came to an end.

The Czech Lands and Slovakia had separate experiences during the war, and these would shape post-war attitudes and perceptions of each nation towards the other. Bohemia and Moravia were annexed into the Reich as a Protectorate while Slovakia became an independent but servile vassal state. Both populations were used as a workforce. Estimates of those taken to Germany as forced labour range between 200,000 and 1,000,000, with the Slovaks supplying twice as many workers as the Czechs. At home Czech industry and its workforce were mobilized for the German war effort. Bohemia and Moravia alone produced between 9–12 percent of Germany's total wartime industrial output, proportionately higher than any other part of the German empire.[18]

A qualitative distinction arose from the type of survival each nation undertook during the war. The German Reich had definite plans to reshape the Czech population by 'extinguishing all vestiges of Czech culture and political values'.[19] Czechs interpreted Slovak assistance to Germany as 'treason' while Slovaks viewed Czech work for the Reich as slavery.[20] Their resistance to Fascism also differentiated the two nations, particularly in historical and political discourse after the war. The Czechs, while occupied, were often viewed as indifferent to the occupation, leading frugal and frightened but otherwise normal lives; the novels of Josef Škvorecký set during the period, depicting jazz and romance, tend to lend at least literary credence to that view. But acts of Czech resistance, notably the 27 May 1942 assassination of the German responsible for the Protectorate, Reinhard Heydrich, received disproportionate retribution. The Bohemian town of Lidice was razed two weeks later; the male inhabitants were summarily executed, the women despatched to concentration camps, and the children either gassed or seized and Germanized. The 365,000 Jews of both the Protectorate and Slovakia were marked for extermination. Only a single-digit percentage of the prewar Czechoslovakia's Jewish population returned from German concentration and death camps. Albeit under Nazi tutelage, the Slovak National Council nevertheless voted for the deportation of Slovak Jews. This act encouraged the view among at least some Czechs that the Slovaks were not only undemocratic but even fascist.

While Czech national resistance during the Second World War has been called a 'failure' even by sympathetic historians,[21] Slovak efforts at resistance became part of their national identity. The Slovak National Council led an uprising of combined communist and non-communist forces in August 1944 to liberate Czechoslovakia. Its aims, however, extended further, to the construction of a federal country. This aspiration was pursued to some degree by the post-war government, such as with the establishment of individual National Committees for the Czechs and Slovaks, but the prospect of self-rule was ended with the communist takeover in 1948. The experience of wartime independent Slovakia remained in memory, with its leaders controversially commemorated by some post-communist Slovak politicians after 1989, despite associations with the deportation of Slovak Jews.

Czechoslovakia's foreign policy between 1945 and 1948 was conditioned by the experience of Munich. Beneš' government distrusted Britain and France for their betrayal of Czechoslovakia and his government was much more sympathetic to the Soviet Union than other governments-in-exile from the region. While, for example, relations between the Polish government-in-exile and the Soviet Union ruptured entirely, Beneš' exiled government signed the Czechoslovak-Soviet Treaty in 1943. Since the Munich *Diktat* Czechoslovak political leaders, including Beneš, had pronounced that the Soviet Union was in fact prepared to assist the country. To what extent this is true remains debatable; but Czechoslovak Communist leader Gottwald 'was most determined to turn the alleged willingness of Moscow to assist Czechoslovakia in 1938 into a tool of political struggle'.[22] Throughout the war the Beneš' government-in-exile engaged in diplomacy to achieve a favourable post-war outcome for Czechoslovakia. This included overtures to Stalin, and Beneš' may have given Carpathia to the USSR on 29 June 1945 in order to secure his favour.

Prague was reassured of Soviet intentions as the Red Army withdrew from Czechoslovakia (as did the US Army from Western Bohemia) in late 1945, in contrast to another allied country, Poland, where Soviet forces remained indefinitely. Certainly good relations with the USSR translated into Soviet support for the expulsion of the three million Sudeten Germans from Czechoslovakia, an act sanctioned in principle by Winston Churchill even before the war ended.

As the British Prime Minister explained to the House of Commons on 15 December 1944: 'expulsion is the method which, so far as we have been able to see, will be the most satisfactory and lasting. There will be no mixture of populations to cause endless trouble....A clean sweep will be made. I am not alarmed by these large transferences, which are more possible in moderns conditions than they ever were before'.[23]

Despite Churchill's expectation of a tidy transfer of minorities, the expulsion of the Germans from Czechoslovakia provoked great difficulties which plagued Czech-German relations to the present. Each party disagrees on what happened and the language that should be used to describe those events. Sudeten Germans tend towards *Vertreibung*, denoting an aggressive and unjust act, whereas Czechs refer to *odsun*, or transfer, a more tidy and legal process. Expulsions of the half-million Hungarian minority from southern Slovakia were planned, and some expelled, but the process was stopped by Czechoslovak-Hungarian negotiation.

The expulsions had demographic implications within Czechoslovakia. Some two and a half million people were rehoused, many of them Gypsies, or Romanies, brought from rural Slovakia to live in properties vacated by the Sudeten Germans. The Sudeten German explusion also elevated the Slovak proportion of the population from under one-fifth to over a quarter of the total Czechoslovak population.

In politics, initially the post-war period was one of relative consensus, although the number of political parties was limited and right-wing parties were disallowed, having been blamed for the country's pre-war demise. Nevertheless, the distribution of power within parliament closely resembled that of the First Republic. Interwar democrats returned from the London-based government-in-exile; Beneš resumed the office of Prime Minister while Tomáš Masaryk's son Jan became Foreign Minister.

A general agreement was struck between Beneš' non-communists and the Czechoslovak Communists. This took the form of the Košice Programme, launched on 5 April 1945. Politically, the Košice Programme dictated that all political parties participate in a coalition government; but, initially, the KSČ cooperated with other parties of its own accord. And in addition to stipulating the confiscation of property belonging to wartime collaborators, the Programme articulated a wide-ranging policy of nationalization.

A coalition government was established in October 1945, with the communists holding eight Cabinet posts, including the sensitive Ministries of Information and the Interior. The government enacted nationalization, the first law of which was scheduled to coincide with the 27th anniversary of the foundation of the Republic. Major industries and financial services were affected, and over half the country's industrial workforce was transferred from the private to the nationalized economy. By early 1947, nationalized enterprises accounted for 80 percent of employment and two-thirds of production.[24] The government introduced other measures to equalize wealth, including high progressive taxes, the confiscation of large personal savings, and caps on higher salaries. Most significantly, the National Front government introduced its 'Two-Year Plan for the Renewal and Reconstruction of the Czechoslovak Economy'. Not only was this significant for following the Soviet model, but it was also the first to be enacted outside the USSR and the first by a democratic market economy.

Unlike in neighbouring countries, where Soviet occupation forces impeded the efforts of non-communist parties,[25] the KSČ enjoyed what is generally considered to be genuine support among the population. The KSČ won 38 percent of the vote in the May 1946 elections, the highest of any party.[26] This success gave it predominant influence in the coalition government, and a ninth cabinet post. KSČ leader Klement Gottwald became premier.

The KSČ was well organized, having developed organizations throughout society, including trade unions and some student movements. It also undertook measures to secure authentic support and gained advantage by having its members hold economically important Cabinet posts, including Agriculture and Education, as well as others that secured levels of public control, namely the Ministry of Interior. But even though the KSČ enjoyed much popular support, it did not refrain from using tactics typical of communist parties throughout East Europe after the war. Quite simply, the KSČ began a march to power, combining legal and astute measures with subversive ones, throughout benefiting from Soviet assistance.

Quite apart from indigenous Czechoslovak communist designs on power, Stalin was intent on thorough control of Eastern Europe and, accordingly, began to demand tighter communist control of Czechoslovakia. This included his unwillingness to have Czechoslovakia (as well as Poland) participate in the Marshall Plan and his objections to Czechoslovak membership of nascent post-war international institutions, of which Czechoslovakia was a founding member. When Masaryk returned from meeting Stalin in 1947 he proclaimed that he went to Moscow as the foreign minister of a sovereign state but returned as a stooge of Stalin.

The presence of Soviet forces throughout Eastern Europe, the sub-version of pro-Western indigenous governments by Moscow-backed communists, and the liquidation of non-communist political movements ensured Stalin's control of the region by 1948. Czechoslovak democratic parties were neither prepared for communist tactics nor sufficiently responsive and events pushed the communist and non-communist repre-sentatives to confrontation, particularly as the KSČ sought even more extensive nationalization and financial penalties against the wealthy.

Communists proceeded to use their government positions to para-chute party loyalists into posts, particularly in the police. Democratic cabinet ministers responded to such communist subversion by resign-ing, believing that a moral act would force a proper outcome. Instead, the Communists took advantage of the democratic withdrawal. They also organized massive public demonstrations, particularly through their trade and youth movements, of popular support for their gover-nance. Even though Beneš had accepted the resignations he became intent on resisting the communists. On 23 February 1948 he pro-claimed: 'I will act as I did in September 1938. I shall not give up, be sure of that'. Two days later, however, he accepted a KSČ demand for the appointment of still more Communists and Communist sympathiz-ers to the Cabinet. Beneš' concession may have been due to poor health; foremost, however, the outcome was predetermined by the pre-ponderance of Communist power in Czechoslovakia and of Soviet power in Central Europe.

The Communist ascent to power had been variously called a 'coup', a 'subversion' or a 'passive revolution'.[27] Regardless of the interpreta-tion of February 1948, the Czechoslovak Communists gained pre-eminent power and went about consolidating their hold on the country. While many Czechs and Slovaks genuinely welcomed the advent of communist rule, their idealism would soon clash with the realities of their rule. On the wintery day of 28 February 1948, Gottwald proclaimed socialism from a balcony over Wenceslas. His Communist colleague Vladimír Clementis put his own hat on Gottwald's bare head. Later, Clementis would be denounced as an enemy of the people and airbrushed from the photo of the proclamation every Czechoslovak would come to possess. Only his hat remained.[28]

COMMUNIST CZECHOSLOVAKIA, 1948–1968

The foremost aim of the Communists after the coup of February 1948 was to replicate Stalinism in Czechoslovak politics and economics. The government was run by a coalition of left-wing parties, including the Communist Party, which was called the National Front. This was a 'front' in another sense, providing a veneer of institutional pluralism to mask the communist monopoly of power. The true practice was to eliminate all competing sources of power. Even left-wing parties were subject to coercion and the Social Democrats were forced to merge with the KSČ.

The openly anticommunist Jan Masaryk was found dead on 10 March below his apartment window. The communists asserted that he had committed suicide (revising their verdict to accidental death) but non-communists at home and abroad were convinced he was murdered. As part of their consolidation of power, the communists rewrote the Czechoslovak constitution and thereby proclaimed Czechoslovakia a 'People's Democracy', Stalin's terminology for new socialist regimes that had not yet achieved the maturity of the Soviet Union. The National Front won unfree elections in late May and early June whereupon Beneš resigned as President and Gottwald promptly took his place. Beneš died shortly thereafter.

Society was to be atomized and then reconstituted under communist control; independent organizations, political and otherwise, were either disbanded, converted into or absorbed by official communist structures. Censorship was introduced, and religious persecution was begun. This process intensified under 'High Stalinism'. Religious leaders were arrested; and then leading communists themselves were tried in political show trials, with former KSČ leader Rudolf Slánský and other important figures sentenced to death. In total, some 180 political figures were executed and thousands of private citizens were unjustly accused and punished with sentences of forced labour or imprisonment. Monuments in towns across former Czechoslovakia now commemorate these victims.

Slovak communists found themselves in an ironic situation. While their wartime resistance was meant to translate into political favour under communism, support for communism was stronger in the Czech Lands and 'the case for keeping the power of state centralised and in Czech hands appeared obvious'. Slovak communists therefore had to 'accept a role subordinate to that of the traditional Communist Party of Czechoslovakia within which Slovak aspirations would be more easily contained. The fact that the Slovak Communist Party had no counterpart in a Czech Communist Party was an anomaly which, however, proved convenient for the centralising of the Czech communists'.[29]

The new regime sought to replicate Soviet economics. Nationalization, already appropriating the bulk of the economy before 1948, was intensified, while wide-ranging land reform was introduced. Czechoslovakia's first Five-Year Plan was launched on 27 October 1948. It stressed heavy industrialization, particularly for Slovakia. Part of this programme diverted resources to military production. The currency reform of 1 June 1953 wiped out savings and reduced the bulk of the population to a uniform economic level.

Czechoslovakia mimicked the Soviet Union in international affairs as in domestic life. Whereas between 1945 and 1948 the Soviet Union redirected Czechoslovakia away from new international institutions, after 1948 it was enmeshed in new socialist bloc mechanisms. The first was the Council for Mutual Economic Assistance, established in 1949, which would allow the further centralization of all East European economies under one plan. In 1955 the Warsaw Treaty Organization (WTO) was enacted, in part to counter the rearming of West Germany and its entry into NATO. The WTO facilitated the integration and centralization of command of East European armed forces. This served both external security needs, ostensibly deterring attack from the West, but also enhanced Soviet leverage over indigenous armed forces. Such regional mechanisms were particularly useful to the Soviets in the case of Czechoslovakia because, unlike in Poland, Hungary, East Germany and, before 1958, Romania, the official Soviet military presence in Czechoslovakia had been withdrawn. The extent of Soviet penetration was revealed in August 1968 when Czechoslovak reform leaders discovered that their Soviet counterparts often knew more about the Czechoslovak security services and military than they.

With Czechoslovak communists firmly in power, a small nod to reform was made by the KSČ after Soviet leader Nikita Khrushchev's 'Secret Speech' of 1956 condemned aspects of Stalin's rule. But no softening of communist rule or socioeconomic experimentation was permitted in Czechoslovakia, even though such occurred in Poland and Hungary. For a time it seemed that the economic situation in Czechoslovakia was favourable, with increasing foreign trade and initial signs of a 'consumer society'.[30]

The original hardline of the KSČ continued after the death of Gottwald in 1953, just nine days after that of Stalin. This intolerance was illustrated by the violent repression of a moderate protest in Plzeň in June 1953 over price increases. Later the same year the country's two senior posts of President and KSČ First Secretary, both of which had been held by Gottwald, were reassigned. Antonín Zápotocký became the former, Antonín Novotný the latter. Through these leadership changes the Party remained wedded to its original programme. Indeed, the Communists continued to turn on themselves. Some Slovak Communists were arrested in the early purges of 1949–50 because they had been 'home communists' during the war and therefore deemed politically unreliable; thereafter other Slovak communists were charged with 'bourgeois nationalism', including the future KSČ First Secretary Gustáv Husák who was arrested in 1951 and sentenced in 1954.

With Zápotocký's death in 1957, Novotný also became President. But because of his personal involvement in Czechoslovak crimes, he ensured that the findings of the Investigation and Rehabilitation Commission, established by the KSČ in 1955, were negligible. Even after Khrushchev's Secret Speech Czechoslovakia underwent little of the 'thaw' experienced in neighbouring Poland and Hungary. Czechoslovakia remained a hardline communist regime.

While political life was centralized under the communists, perhaps the most significant post-war political development resulted from the expulsion of Germans and some Hungarians and the granting of Carpathia to Stalin: Czechoslovakia was now decidedly a binational country, with a small Hungarian minority remaining. Stemming from the Košice Programme, an expectation continued among some Slovaks of greater autonomy for Slovakia and more access to the decision-making process. But instead of increased autonomy, Slovaks suffered severely under the post-1948 political repression. The many organizations that existed to represent Slovak interests, often not having cognates in the Czech Lands, were subordinated to national communist structures, including the Slovak Communist Party. The stifling of Slovak political hopes became one of the many sources for change in the 1960s that led to the reform movement.

Economic policy meant the thorough absorption of private property and self-governing economic entities into a centrally planned system. Similarly, throughout the 1950s, private plots of lands were appropriated by the state and amalgamated into collective farms. By 1960 over

90 percent of farmland in the country was collectivized.[31] The Communist regime employed legal pretexts such as tax evasion, although exaggerated or falsified, to nationalize smaller enterprises so that nationalization went much further than was ever envisaged after the war. Severe limitations were imposed on family inheritance.

Foremost in the communist plan was heavy industrialization. The country's successful consumer goods industries were converted to heavy industry. The agrarian areas were to be transformed, and with them their peoples. Interwar Czechoslovakia's least developed region, Carpathia, was shed to the USSR; efforts were concentrated on Slovakia. Particularly because of its location—sufficiently removed from the East-West faultline but close to the Soviet heartland—it was designated for arms production. For Czechoslovakia the industrialization of Slovakia was one of the most important legacies of the Soviet era: the transformation of a primarily agrarian population into an industrial one, who had to rely on inefficient industry for their livelihoods. The result, however, was that by 1968 the industrial lag between the Czech Lands and Slovakia was reduced from 50 to 20 years.[32] Equality was achieved, according to official Communist Czechoslovak statistics, in what became the final year of communist rule.[33]

The communist economic programme was not strictly for production; it sought to redesign people and society. As in all Soviet-type systems, the intention was to generate a large proletarian working class and, at least before the communist notional egalitarian society was achieved, to invert the social hierarchy. Party affiliation rather than merit determined advancement, as did class background. Those classified as children of the bourgeoisie—shopkeepers, professionals—were barred from higher education. Such a fate befell the future dissident playwright and post-communist president Václav Havel. Those that came from un- or under-educated backgrounds filled universities and technical schools. A new cadre of the politically correct was created, but its expertise and skills were by no means guaranteed. This social revolution occurred rapidly enough that by the early 1950s, half of the personnel in party administration, state bureaucracy and economic management lacked education commensurate with their work requirements.[34] As a major post-communist Czech reassessment of the 1960s attests, understanding Czechoslovak society and politics of that era rests on appreciating the simultaneous stratification of society and the egalitarian and bureaucratic tendencies that ran alongside it.[35]

The Communist programme did not deliver popular goods. In the 1950s the country had already suffered an economic downturn. Further currency devaluation and abolition of savings reduced economic well-being across the population and provoked industrial action and the Plzeň uprising. Despite these economic problems, Czechoslovakia was in a relatively privileged economic position in communist Eastern Europe. It was largely undamaged by the Second World War and did not have to rebuild to the same extent as war-ravaged Poland; it could also draw on Bohemia's advanced industries. But this legacy masked deep-seated problems, ones which communist rhetoric sought to hide even more.

The new Constitution of 11 July 1960 heralded Communist Czechoslovakia's successes by renaming the country the Czechoslovak Socialist Republic and announcing that it had achieved 'really existing socialism'. This was an ideological landmark as Czechoslovakia became the first country, after the Soviet Union itself, to gain the title of 'socialist'. Socialism in its egalitarian sense may have been attained in Czechoslovakia, but only in a crude and unintended fashion: the bulk of the population was now economically 'equal'. But instead of advancing the economic status of the many, it achieved a lowest common denominator which impoverished many more people than it had elevated.

Despite official statements to the contrary, Czechoslovakia continued to brew an economic crisis. In 1961–63 economic growth stopped altogether, an unprecedented occurrence for the communist bloc. The fall of national income in 1962 and 1963 was accompanied by a paucity of consumer goods. The regime responded to these indicators by attributing the economic decline to the (limited) decentralization permitted in 1958, which it then tried to reverse at the 1962 Party Congress. During this time Novotný succeeded in removing some Stalinists from senior posts and proposing modest reforms. But these measures were a palliative; those who wanted greater reform remained unsatisfied and the continuing fall in productivity became evident to all as the use of street lights was curtailed to conserve electricity.

Under the third Five-Year Plan which covered the period 1961–65, national income was to rise by 42 percent, industrial production by 56 percent, and agricultural output by 22 percent. The results, however, were substantially less, with national income increasing only by 10 percent, industrial output by 29 percent and agriculture actually contracting by 0.4 percent.[36] The economic situation both called for and permitted wider, more free economic discussion and important economic studies emerged from this debate. More than providing solutions to the economic malaise, these studies amounted to attacks on specific policies in Czechoslovakia and on tenets of Soviet-bloc socialism. Throughout the arts and social sciences alternatives to Czechoslovakia's unmitigated socialism were being quietly contemplated. Wrote one Western observer, 'in their contributions to cultural weeklies and in scholarly journals and conferences, in the daily round of lectures and discussions, in books' Czechoslovaks were conducting 'an intellectual revolution'.[37]

Alternative thinking particularly emerged in the economic and social sciences. Economists like Ota Šik contemplated significant modifications of the socialist economy,[38] while a substantial team of researchers produced the far-ranging study entitled *Civilization at the Crossroads: Social and Human Implications of the Scientific Technological Revolution*. First published in 1966, the study attempted to demonstrate that it was in keeping with Communist Party practice. In explaining their methodology, the collective of authors wrote 'we are now able to draw on the first steps in a Marxist approach to the scientific and technical revolution, contained in the Programme of the CPSU'. They also pronounced that American studies failed to confront the 'sociological and anthropological dimensions' of the scientific and technological revolution; this may have been a genuinely-felt observation, but it was also one that could serve to appease ideological scrutineers in the Czechoslovak or Soviet Communist Parties.[39]

The whole reform movement amounted, especially in its cultural aspects, to a departure from Soviet norms and 'a return to Europe'. So momentous was the reformers' thinking that, as one commentator put it, 'the goals, thus conceived, had no precedent'.[40] Pressure for change mounted within and without the Communist Party, and ran through society. While 1968 saw social protest in several countries, Czechoslovakia was unique in the cross-generational character of its movement.[41]

THE PRAGUE SPRING AND SOVIET INVASION

Divisions within the communist leadership over such liberalization concluded with the establishment of a reform-minded leadership. Alexander Dubček replaced Novotný as First Secretary in January 1968. Dubček had solid political credentials, his father was a co-founder of the KSČ who had taken his family to live in the Soviet Union during the decade preceding Munich. Dubček was active in the wartime communist resistance. The National Assembly then elected General Ludvík Svoboda President on 30 March 1968, while shortly thereafter reformist economist Šik was made Deputy Prime Minister.

The reforms were codified and launched publicly on 5 April as the Action Programme. It largely ended censorship and opened lively discussion on the possibilities for political life and on sensitive historical questions, particularly the 1950s show trials. It sought initiatives from society rather than top-down directives from the Party. In its first section, the Action Programme concluded that the implementation of socialism in Czechoslovakia had had harmful consequences. It attributed the problems to centralised control and decision-making, which resulted because 'socialist democracy was not expanded in time, [so that the] methods of revolutionary dictatorship deteriorated into bureaucracy and became an impediment to progress in all spheres of life in Czechoslovakia'.[42]

In addition, the Party, according to the Action Programme, removed the contribution of individual opinion from society. The Action Programme seemed to challenge Lenin's notion of the dictatorship of the proletariat by writing: 'In the past, the leading role of the Party was often conceived as a monopolistic concentration of power in the hands of Party bodies. This corresponds to the false thesis that the Party was the instrument of the dictatorship of the proletariat'. The Action Programme declared 'this harmful conception weakened the initiative and responsibility of the State, economic and social institutions and damaged the Party's authority, and prevented it from carrying out its real function'. The role of the Party, it elaborated, 'is not to become a universal "caretaker of the society, to bind all organizations and every step taken in life by its directives"'. Instead, the mission of the Party lay 'primarily in arousing socialist initiative, in showing the ways and actual possibilities of communist perspectives, and in winning over all workers for them through systematic persuasion'.[43]

The combination of popular initiatives and a Party document rolling back its own authority risked giving the impression that the Party had lost control over society. This was increased with the publication of Ludvík Vaculík's '2,000 Words' which attacked the corruption and self-service of the Communist Party. Moscow was irate, but Dubček refused Soviet leader Brezhnev's demand that he renounce the Action

Programme. The Soviet Union and its allies continued to signal to the Czechoslovak leadership, including through Warsaw Pact meetings in March and April, that its reforms were unacceptable and even jeopardizing the integrity of the bloc. By June, the warnings had turned into Warsaw Pact exercises being conducted on Czechoslovak territory. But the Czechoslovak communists never believed that their reforms amounted to 'counterrevolution', seeing them as still within the ambit of socialist thinking and never intending them as a rejection of it. The Dubček leadership was also cautious in its reforms, avoiding statements of an outright withdrawal from the WTO such as Hungarian reform-leader Imre Nagy had fatally proposed in 1956. Never did the Dubček government propose an end to the KSČ's monopoly on power. The phrase most associated with the Czechoslovak reforms, 'socialism with a human face', captured Western imaginations, especially among the European left, as a viable form of socialism. It later became a catch-phrase for the 'third way', and came, if ill-fatedly, to be associated with Gorbachev's reforms in the Soviet Union in the late 1980s.

Despite the seemingly benign nature of the reforms and the level of international sympathy, the Warsaw Pact continued to press Prague to change its course. Soviet-Czechoslovak talks commenced at the end of July 1968 while the largest post-war movement of Soviet forces began in Czechoslovakia's three neighbouring socialist states. Dubček left the talks still believing that Czechoslovak sovereignty was secure. Throughout the night of 20–21 August military forces from five Soviet bloc countries overran Czechoslovakia and Dubček and his entourage were taken forcibly to Moscow. In September the Soviet newspaper *Pravda* carried an article that proclaimed the obligation of socialist states to intervene to protect socialism. This principle would become known as the 'Brezhnev Doctrine'.

Various interpretations of the Soviet motivations for the intervention have been advanced, including that it was based on a strategic calculation of the risks posed to the integrity of the Warsaw Pact, the danger of ideological non-conformity within the bloc, or the dissemination of political or even nationalist sentiments in East European states such as East Germany or Soviet republics such as Ukraine.[44] Ultimately, it may be that Dubček could not convey his intentions in suitable language and was unable to show the Soviet leadership sufficient 'political love'.[45]

Dubček and other senior reform leaders were taken to the Soviet capital where they were forced to sign the Moscow Protocol on

26 August. After pleading with Soviet officials in Moscow, Svoboda secured the release of Dubček. Public displays of support for him upon his return to Prague deferred Dubček's ouster, but the presence of Soviet military forces and increasing Soviet penetration of the Czechoslovak government undermined his position. There was some resistance, often noted as 'passive', which manifested itself in removing roadsigns to impede the movement of Soviet military forces. Of particular significance was the self-immolation of philosophy student Jan Palach in January 1969. Others fled the country, or did not return if abroad, including some notable figures of the Czech cultural world.

One enduring legacy of the intervention was that whatever genuine sympathy and support Czechs and Slovaks had held for the Soviet Union and for communism evaporated and was replaced by fierce anti-communism. But an equal legacy was that the current generation of Czechoslovaks would overwhelmingly become passive and accepting of Soviet domination and of communist entrenchment in Czechoslovakia. The Soviets were able to call upon another faction within the KSČ leadership and initiate a process euphemistically called 'normalization' to weed out reformers and to solidify hardline communist rule.

'NORMALIZATION'

Normalization began at the pinnacle of Czechoslovak leadership. Already politically humiliated and denuded, Dubček was finally removed from office in April 1969. His successor was Gustav Husák, who ironically was imprisoned by his fellow communists in the 1950s on charges of Slovak nationalism. Normalization sought to penetrate deeply into society. Some 500,000 Czechoslovaks, representing almost one third of the Party, resigned, were expelled or 'deleted' from the KSČ.[46] This affected, by extension, millions, as party membership carried with it family privilege such as access to education. People both within and outside the Party were forced to give written denunciations of friends and colleagues who had participated in the Prague Spring or refused themselves to engage in denunciation. A few individuals, such as Havel, opted not to accept this collective act of falsification and became isolated and persecuted dissidents. The regime reimposed strict control over the media, and those who refused to conform to the dictates of the regime met with police surveillance, telephone tapping, coercion and prison sentences.

All reforms of the Prague Spring, save one, were reversed. Retained was the federalization of the country, which was introduced as a constitutional amendment in October 1968 and formally implemented on 1 January 1969. As a result, a federal parliament was complemented by the establishment of Slovak and Czech republics, each with its own parliament, prime minister and executive. In addition, the federal parliament was made bicameral, with a House of Nations and a House of the People. The latter was simply representational by direct election throughout the country, but the former was constituted on the basis of 75 MPs elected separately from each of the two republics. These substantial governmental changes could be construed as a deliberate and genuine effort to recognize and enshrine Slovak national interests in the political policy process. Routine legislation required a simple majority in each House, but major bills, including constitutional amendments, required a three-fifths majority of all those elected, not just those present. The Slovak and Czechs MPs would be counted separately in the House of the Nations and each group would have to return a majority vote in order to enact legislation. As few as 31 members of the House of Nations could, therefore, veto key legislation; this was a structural legacy destined to become pivotal to the future of Czechoslovakia in 1991.[47]

Indeed this was exceptional, with Western scholars noting that they knew of 'no democratic government anywhere in which comparable minorities of legislative bodies have as much blocking power'.[48] Slovaks seemed to receive greater representation in general political life as well. Normalization affected Czechs disproportionately more than Slovaks, but Slovaks were elevated in the political system. Foremost was the ascent of Husák, but fellow Slovak Vasil Bil'ak assumed responsibility for the important posts of Ideology and International Affairs. Husák was then seen to provide disproportionate state and party employment to Slovaks. While these promotions may have dismayed Czechs they did not necessarily satisfy Slovaks either as they tended to dismiss co-ethnics who moved to Prague for federal posts as having become 'Czechs'. This was often the view held of the Slovak post-communist Czechoslovak Prime Minister Marián Čalfa.

The Slovak economic situation continued to improve, both in absolute terms and relative to the Czechs. Sociological studies determined that proportionately more Slovaks lived in private houses, with more rooms per family and in superior condition than the Czechs. While this was partly due to Slovakia having been less urbanized than the Czech Lands before communism, it also suggested overall that Slovaks enjoyed an improving standard of living. In addition, very notably, Slovakia received substantial subsidies and continued its industrialization. Even if the gap was not entirely filled, by the end of the 1980s 'the Czech Lands constituted the stagnating part of the federation, whilst Slovakia the progressing one'.[49] The rapidity and thoroughness of industrialization and of the raising of the standard of living in Slovakia under communism has even been called 'an economic miracle'.[50]

The tremendous irony was that Slovaks would come to feel that they were run by Prague and stymied in their attempts to secure true self-rule. The Czechs meanwhile viewed the post-1968 constitutional changes, political appointments and economic subsidies of Slovakia as evidence that the Slovaks had managed to seize the country.

The post-1968 leadership was fortunate that the economic situation in Czechoslovakia picked up and that it did not suffer real setbacks until the 1980s. (This can be compared to Hungary and especially Poland where deteriorating economic conditions spawned social discontent.) Many simply engaged in what became known as 'inner migration': avoiding politics in exchange for a modest standard of living.

There was one group that consciously did not accept this withdrawal. The most striking literary expression of the rejection of this thinking was Havel's 'The Power of the Powerless'. His essay centred metaphorically around a greengrocer who, unconsciously, followed central instructions to place among his vegetables a sign proclaiming 'workers of the world, unite'. While the slogan meant nothing to the greengrocer, it signalled his robotic compliance with the regime and contributed to a public aura of acceptance of the regime's creed. Havel called upon people to empower themselves by rejecting the masquerade of supporting the regime and to 'live in truth'.[51]

State persecution helped to concentrate the limited opposition that existed. The trial of the underground rock group 'Plastic People of the Universe', so named to mock the quality of the country's political leadership, united and made more public what opposition there was. The core of Czechoslovakia's independent thinkers coalesced during the 1970s. On 1 January 1977, Charter 77 was launched, being a loose grouping of independently-minded citizens. Its leading members were arrested even as they posted an open declaration of their cause to the Czechoslovak President and other officials.[52]

Dissent in the form of Charter 77 certainly provided an important intellectual core. Its membership included three distinct groups: Catholics, or religious advocates; independent intellectuals; and former or 'reform' Communists. This seemed, therefore, to be a broad grouping. But in reality, its scope and influence was limited. It never achieved the mass membership of Poland's independent Solidarity trade union, having 231 original signatories (of whom only two were Slovak) and its membership never exceeded 2,000. More importantly, however, it probably served as a national conscience and certainly, when the protests began on 17 November 1989, it provided a nucleus and structure for maximizing opportunity and carrying through the Revolution. While dissent was important, impetus for change came from elsewhere.

GORBACHEV: THE WINDS OF CHANGE?

Elected General Secretary of the Communist Party of the Soviet Union in March 1985, Mikhail Gorbachev slowly inaugurated reforms in his country. His policy pronouncements on Soviet bloc relations in the first two years of his leadership indicated that he wanted to retain and even intensify the mechanisms of control that bound the East European satellites to the Soviet Union. By late 1986 and early 1987 Gorbachev was embarking on substantial reforms at home and pronouncing policy changes for Eastern Europe. The hardline Czechoslovak regime greeted Gorbachev's reforms with hesitation for fear that they might disrupt its firm control over the country. The Czechoslovak population was also sceptical of both Gorbachev's intentions and his ability to institute them. A contemporary joke compared his reforms to Dubček's in 1968, and asked the difference between the two reformers, intimating the fate that befell Dubček. The answer ran 'none—but Gorbachev doesn't realize it yet'.

Modest economic proposals were advanced in January 1987, including a nod to planning decentralization and increasing the scope of enterprises, but there was no mention of any political reform.[53] Rather, the proposals could be seen in the light of Husák's efforts to deflect the winds emanating from Moscow. In early 1987, in advance of Gorbachev's Prague visit in April 1987, Husák began referring to *přestavba*, the Czechoslovak equivalent of *perestroika*. Change came in December 1987, not necessarily for the worse but equally not for the better, when Husák was succeeded as First Secretary by Miloš Jakeš.

But unlike in Poland or Hungary, there was no faction in the Czechoslovak leadership intent on serious reform or on accommodating the interests and demands of the opposition. Timothy Garton Ash describes these two countries as undergoing 'refolution', whereby change resulted from both inclination towards reform from above, the regime, and from pressures from below, the revolutionary population.[54] The context in Czechoslovakia was very different. Instead of seeking a negotiated compromise, the regime continued its crackdown on dissent.

The regime responded to the few demonstrations with violence and imprisonment, such as with the March 1988 Bratislava rally for religious expression and the protests to mark important national anniversaries, including the foundation of the Republic in 1918 (generally ignored by the regime), and the twentieth anniversaries of the Soviet intervention and Palach's death. It was during the latter that Havel was again arrested and jailed.

Events moved swiftly in summer 1989. Poland enjoyed elections in which some seats were contestable. With Solidarity's victories, the dissident Tadeusz Mazowiecki became Prime Minister. The reformist Communist government in Hungary removed part of its barbed wire border with Austria. The East German government, as a modest concession to its people, had eased visa requirements allowing its citizens to vacation in Hungary. Holidaying East Germans took advantage of the opened border to flee the Eastern bloc. As East Germans haemorrhaged to the West in greater numbers even more East Germans began protesting for change at home. Faced with continuous, sustained mass protests in 7 major cities in early November 1989, the East German regime consented on 9 November to open all of its border crossings, including the most famous at the Berlin Wall. This harsh regime effectively ebbed away as jubilant crowds enjoyed freedom of movement.

'VELVET REVOLUTION' IN 1989

Czechoslovaks were moved by developments in East Germany but remained defeatist. Students in particular pursued the view 'it won't happen here' and stated that the Czech national mentality differed from the German, Polish or even Slovak. Similarly, even after the resignation of the East German leadership, Czech academics expressed their pessimism, exclaiming 'but here we have Jakeš! Nothing changes'.[55] For its part, the Czechoslovak regime remained steadfast. A small demonstration commemorating the foundation of Czechoslovakia was dispersed. It would be an officially sanctioned march on 17 November, marking the fiftieth anniversary of the murder by occupying Germans of a Czech student, that sparked Czechoslovakia's regime change. The march became a pro-democracy protest; police responded by beating students. Rumours that one student had been killed fuelled popular support and eventually hundreds of thousands filled the main streets and squares of Prague. On 19 November dissidents formed Civic Forum (OF) in Prague and Public Against Violence (VPN) in Bratislava, and called for fundamental changes.

Junior parties of the National Front broke with the KSČ and proposed discussions with the opposition, which Communist Prime Minister Ladislav Adamec undertook on 21 November. Meanwhile, Dubček addressed a small crowd in Bratislava, making his first public appearance since the defeat of the Prague Spring, and then, with Havel, addressed the larger crowds in Wenceslas Square. A two-hour nation-wide strike was held on 27 November to underscore popular support for the opposition. The KSČ then surrendered its leading role but Adamec proposed a new government composed overwhelmingly of communists. Havel rejected this concession and the continued popular protests and strikes demonstrated the unity and determination of the opposition. On 7 December Adamec resigned and Jakeš was expelled from the KSČ. On 10 December the communist regime buckled entirely; Husák resigned, and a Government of National Understanding was established in which non-communists predominated. The Prime Minister, Marian Čalfa, was still a member of the Communist Party, although he left it a few weeks later. By the close of December two senior positions went to opposition figures. On 28 December Dubček was elected Chairman of the Federal Assembly (speaker of the federal parliament) and one day later Havel was elected by the Parliament, still seating communists, as state President.

In November 1989, the Czechoslovaks illustrated how through non-violent, popular protest a fierce regime could be ousted. The Czechoslovaks contributed the term 'Velvet Revolution' to the political dictionary and the English language.

Whether the Velvet Revolution was truly a revolution remains a matter for discussion; it did result in a change in the country's political and economic system, and it also changed the way people thought, acted and lived. The new government would undertake a wholesale restructuring of society; but it faced immense challenges in doing so, some of which would ultimately result in the dissolution of the country itself.

Post-communist Czechoslovakia set about to repluralize all aspects of domestic society and to reintegrate itself into the world. Details of this transformation, such as economic policies, are considered in the following thematic chapters. This last section of the current chapter travels the path from the Velvet Revolution to the Velvet Divorce, examining how the post-communist political order led the way to the second, and final, rupture of Czechoslovakia.

The prospects of Czechoslovakia's transition from communism to liberal democracy and market economy were exceedingly good. Consensus politics at the top of society aided the repluralization of society. By the end of February 1990 'round table' talks among existing political parties and the opposition movements resulted in arrangements for the first contested election since 1946. Legislation returned fundamental freedoms to the population, culminating in the January 1991 Bill of Rights. Official party and state organizations proclaimed themselves independent. This was also evident in the media, in which censorship was lifted and communist newspapers extricated themselves from party and state to become autonomous.

The first fully free elections since 1946 were held on 8–9 June 1990, with a resounding 95 percent turnout of eligible voters. The plurality of Czechoslovak politics was evidenced by the fact that 23 parties contested them. Some were staple-issue or sectoral parties, such as the Party of Women and Mothers; others were light-hearted, like the Friends of Beer Party. However, it was Civic Forum that swept the elections in the Czech Lands, securing just over 51 percent of the vote. Its Slovak counterpart, Public Against Violence, secured a plurality in Slovakia with slightly over one-third of the ballots. These two civic movements together represented 56 percent of the electorate. The KSČ, however, gathered the second highest number of votes. The consensus politics born in the Velvet Revolution nevertheless continued. The two civic movements, along with the Christian Democratic Movement and some people unaffiliated to political groupings, formed a government on 27 June. Čalfa, having since become a member of VPN, was again made Prime Minister. A week later the new parliament re-elected Havel to a two-year presidential term.

Czechoslovakia's political and democratic credentials were endorsed when it became the first post-communist state to enter the Council of Europe on 21 February 1991. This organization provided a hallmark of European democratic maturity; membership was contingent on fully free elections and the rule of law. As a result of the requirement of entirely free elections, Poland's negotiated transition from communism meant that only some of its parliamentary seats had been contested in 1989 and the country consequently could not gain entry to the Council until after Czechoslovakia.

But repluralization of political life also signalled the re-emergence of nationalism in Slovakia. In August 1990, despite concern from Prague, some Slovak nationalists began commemorating the wartime government of Josef Tiso. Several Slovak political parties began calling not simply for autonomy but outright independence. Popular support grew for a new language law that would openly discriminate against non-Slovaks. Even when, in October 1990, the Slovak National Council proclaimed Slovak to be the Republic's official language, Slovak nationalists remained dissatified because this measure was seen to be too permissive towards minority languages, especially Hungarian.

From early in 1990 federal politicians undertook what they believed were measures to accommodate Slovak interests within the Federation. These steps, however, proved counterproductive. The post-communist government sought to remove the last vestiges of communism, including from the official name of the country: the Czechoslovak Socialist Republic. But this change opened up a larger debate on the name of the country. Slovaks argued that 'Czechoslovak' presupposed the existence of such a hybrid ethnic entity; in addition, they had long noted that 'Czechoslovak' was often shortened abroad, with the result that ethnic Slovaks, like Dubček, were inappropriately called 'Czech'. Discussion regarding the name of the country crystallized in Parliament in what became known as 'the hyphen debate' after one proposal suggested 'Czech-Slovak'. In April 1990, after acrimony, the country's name was changed to 'the Czech and Slovak Federative Republic' to signal the existence of two separate peoples. Not only names were changed but new legislation was also introduced: on 12 December 1990 the Federal Parliament devolved power to the two republics. Proposals were agreed among political parties thereafter to make a new constitution that recast Czechoslovakia as consisting of two republics in a voluntary federation.

After the fragmentation of Civic Forum its Slovak counterpart VPN expressed its willingness to continue working with its successors. But VPN was facing difficulties itself, both from without and within. Following the June 1990 elections VPN had nominated Vladimír Mečiar as Prime Minister of Slovakia. But his increasing opposition to market reforms and 'authoritarian and aggressive style of leadership' endangered relations with the Czechs and even democracy in Slovakia.[56] Tension between Mečiar and moderate members of VPN increased. Mečiar attempted to gain control of the organization at its February 1991 conference but was defeated by former dissident Fedor Gál who warned against commandeering the organization for personal ambition.[57] Undeterred, in March he created a breakaway faction within the movement called Public Against Violence—For a Democratic Slovakia. In April 1991 Mečiar was removed as Premier on charges of incompetence and misuse of secret police files, and was succeeded by Christian Democratic Movement (KDH) leader Ján Čarnogurský. Undeterred, in June Mečiar registered his faction as a separate political group, now called the Movement for a Democratic Slovakia (HZDS).

Economic differences exacerbated national differences and could not be resolved by political solutions alone; instead, economic issues led to the end of consensus politics and to the undoing of the federation. Czechoslovakia's post-communist political consensus, typified by the non-political party ethos of Civic Forum, was overly idealistic and proved short-lived. Divisions within OF over the pace of economic reform led by 1991 to a split that produced the centre-right Civic Democratic Party (ODS), headed by Finance Minister Klaus, and the centre-left grouping of the Civic Movement (OH), led by Foreign Minister Dienstbier. In addition, some the leftist OF members joined the Social Democratic Party. Even with the demise of Civic Forum, centrist politicians and parties in the Czech Republic still cooperated in running the government. The situation in Slovakia would become different.

Economic problems added to the divide between Czechs and Slovaks. Even in 1990, Klaus was frank about the benefits of achieving a successful economy and political system in two smaller units spared the problems caused by diverging nationalist interests. Klaus' commitment to full marketization for the country was reinforced in principle by Article 4 of the 1990 constitutional amendment that declared 'that there is to be a uniform Czechoslovak market integrating the economies of the two republics'. Slovak resistance to the economic reforms, however, should not have been surprising. Even in communist Czechoslovakia in the 1960s 'certain Slovaks began to cultivate a stance supportive of a separate Slovak economy, insulated from the more advanced Czech economy: two nations, two economies'.[58] After communism, Slovak aspirations for autonomy intensified, while Bratislava's control over its own economy was increasingly challenged by reforms undertaken in Prague. Through redirected investment, the Slovak economy had caught up with the Czech by 1989. But the Slovak economy also had several weaknesses, including persistent Slovak republican budget deficits. By mid-1991, with price liberalization initiated and the small and large privatization programmes launched, market forces were clearly tending to reshape society. The heavy industry bequeathed by communism to Slovakia and employing much of its population now became a burdensome legacy in a market environment. Slovakia's communist-era arms industry, relying on the export of tanks and aircraft to undemocratic former socialist countries and the developing world, was a liability to Prague's moral foreign policy. The economic reforms gave greater impetus for decentralization of the federation as Slovak leaders sought thereby to regulate the rate and impact of the transition. As one commentator wrote of the mood in the region, 'many Slovaks saw themselves as victims of shock therapy—all shock and no therapy'.[59]

For two Slovak sociologists (one of whom was a senior adviser to Havel), Slovak nationalist leaders also deliberately undercut in their rhetoric the benefits of the federal government's economic reforms:

> As a result of anti-federal brainwashing in which practically the entire political opposition (except for the Hungarian parties) had participated, the citizens of Slovakia failed to appreciate the existing economic prosperity could best be achieved through the existing economic reform programme and within a common Czech-Slovak state, provided that state remained a 'strong federation'.[60]

Ironically, in June 1990 as few as five percent of Czechs and eight percent of Slovaks sought entirely independent states.[61] But politics became deadlocked on constitutional issues, particularly on how a referendum on the future form of the country could be invoked. The Referendum Law passed in July 1991 enabled either the Federal or a Republic Parliament to initiate a referendum on secession from the federation. Criticized by some for being oblivious to Slovakia's aspirations—or demands—Havel became increasingly concerned with inter-republican relations. In December 1990 he unsuccessfully sought emergency powers from the Federal Parliament to thwart the country's rupture. Thereafter he offered various amendments to the federation, including a revised constitution, but he was marginalized from discussions, often held among political parties, and his proposals were defeated. Mečiar in particular referred to Havel's involvement in talks as 'unfortunate interventions'.[62]

In addition to being politically marginalized on these core issues, Havel was even attacked by demonstrators during a visit to Bratislava in March 1991. On the second anniversary of the Velvet Revolution, Havel made an emotional speech in which he equated finding a solution of the federal crisis as decisive to whether the country would evolve into a civilized European democracy or a zone of persistent conflict. He proposed making the republics truly equal by ensuring that no constitutional change could be made without majority support of both republics. As one analyst observed, Havel 'intended to meet a crucial point of the Slovak demand with a new compromise on the issue of subsequent ratifications, which the Czechs continued to oppose'.[63] Havel also proposed that half a million Czechs and a quarter of a million Slovaks could demand a referendum, and he further suggested that the president be able to initiate a referendum.

As elections approached in 1992, representatives of all major political parties and several federal ministers, but not Havel, met in the Moravian town of Milový between 3–8 February 1992. The agreement retained a common state, and foreign and defence policy would remain a strictly federal responsibility. Otherwise, however, each republic recognized the sovereignty of the other and each had equal representation in the Federal Assembly. While that may have been viewed as a large concession by the more populous Czechs, the Slovak National Council narrowly rejected the measure on the grounds that it contained too many concessions.

The future of the federation would be fought out in the elections of 5–6 June 1992. The elections suggested that Czechoslovak pluralism was vibrant: 40 parties ran, 13 more than two years earlier. But this pluralism was constrained and would determine the future of the country. Aside from the Communist Party, no other party truly operated across the Federation; instead, the election was waged across one or the other republics. Post-communist Czechoslovakia's second democratic elections spawned a plurality of incompatible, even non-negotiable political agendas.

TABLE 1.1 1992 ELECTION RESULTS[64]

PARTY	VOTES (%)	SEATS
Czech National Council		
Civic Democratic Party/		
Christian Democratic Party	29.73	76
Left Bloc	14.05	35
Social Democratic Party	6.53	16
Republican Party	5.98	14
Christian Democratic Union	6.28	15
Liberal Social Union	6.52	16
Civic Democratic Alliance	5.93	14
Society for Moravia		
And Silesia	5.87	14
Slovak National Council		
Movement for a Democratic		
Slovakia	37.2	74
Party of the Democratic Left	14.7	29
Slovak National Party	7.93	15
Christian Democratic Movement	8.88	18
Coexistence/Hungarian		
Christian Democratic Movement	7.42	14

Public opinion immediately before the elections showed overwhelming support for the retention of the federation. While many polls were conducted, results showing 81 percent of Czechs and 63 percent of Slovaks opposed to separation were common. The election—a *de facto* referendum on the future shape and even the continuation of the country—saw about an 85 percent voter turnout. Neither Klaus nor Mečiar won a majority of votes in the country; they failed even to secure a majority of votes in their respective republics. At best, they each won a plurality, with Klaus garnering nearly half of the Czech votes and Mečiar one third of the Slovak. But both men would have to rely on others to govern, and the broader distribution of votes suggested an irreconcilable stalemate. As Table 1.1 shows, in the Czech Republic the centre-right parties of the ODS, the Civic Democratic Alliance and the Christian Democratic Union-People's Party received 29.73, 5.98 and 6.28 percent of the Czech vote, respectively, giving them a working majority. These parties would push for further market reforms, thereby heightening Slovak grievances. In Slovakia a majority of the electorate could, arguably, have been seen to vote for some form of autonomy. 45 percent of Slovaks supported the two parties that advocated autonomy, while a further 15 percent backed the former communist Democratic Left, which moved towards independence. But it was only the Slovak National Party that had unambiguously supported independence. Of Slovak-based parties, the Hungarian alone forthrightly backed the continuation of the federation.

On 8 June representatives of ODS and HZDS met to discuss the future of the state. Klaus emerged from the session stating that there were substantial differences. He said shortly after that if an agreement could not be reached then he would choose to split the federation. Unable previously to agree, within two weeks Klaus and Mečiar had agreed to separation, setting 30 September as the date by which procedures were to be in place. This elite deal, especially with the lack of popular support for an end to the federation, led to a common view that the breakup resulted from power politics and specifically of 'politicians abusing national differences to pursue their own ends'.[65] Mečiar and Klaus were sworn in as Prime Ministers of their respective republics; but political arrangements in the federal capital were not as smooth. What was clearly a temporary cabinet under Jan Stráský was installed.

With the decision taken by two politicians to dissolve the federation, Havel stood for re-election as President. He required a three-fifths majority to be re-elected by Parliament, a majority large enough to ensure that Slovak deputies had a veto. He was stymied when Slovak deputies in both Houses withheld the necessary votes. He warned Czechoslovak citizens of the dangers of self-interested politicians who put power above the interest of the federation. But he and the federal powers that he represented were now under siege from both Czechs and Slovaks. In a sense, his position was comparable to that of Soviet leader Gorbachev, facing secessionist threats from outside the centre, only to find that the centre itself, the Czech government, like Boris Yeltsin's independence-minded Russia, also wanted independence from the Union.

The final unravelling probably started in Slovakia, and was codified when the Slovak National Council voted on 17 July for what it called 'sovereignty'. Doubtless personally dismayed by the Slovak vote and unable to stop the centrifugal forces, Havel announced his resignation on that day and ceased to be President three days later, even though his term would have officially ended on 5 October.

Having rejected Havel, the Federal Parliament attempted in vain to secure other viable candidates. But that process revealed the Assembly's general paralysis and Klaus and Mečiar, in their republican power bases, became the driving force of politics. If their discussions in the summer determined anything, it was that separation was becoming inevitable. Klaus opted to push for further market reforms irrespective of the costs to the federation; in so doing, Klaus surprised Mečiar who ironically began a rearguard fight to retain certain benefits of the federation. Instead, Klaus proved 'a ruthless negotiator', and maneuvered Mečiar into agreeing a timetable for the dissolution of the country.[66]

Thus while the federal centre was imploding of its own accord, Klaus put a definitive end to the federation by rejecting further negotiations and killing off any chance of a revised federal system: 'in the final act it was actually the Czechs who short-circuited the negotiations and torpedoed the joint state project'.[67]

Many federal politicians still tried to arrest the breakup of the country, and as if showing the hesitation of its delivery, the Czech Republic almost did not come into existence. On 1 October, the Federal Assembly not only defeated a bill ending the federation but also passed a plan to create a Czech-Slovak Union. But Klaus and Mečiar responded five days later by dismissing the continuation of the federation in any form and thereafter accelerated the formalization of post-federation republican relations with a Czech-Slovak Customs Union. A resolution to disband the federation was only passed on 25 November 1992 and was opposed by both the far left and far right, as well as the main party of the Slovak Hungarian minority and the Slovak Christian Democratic Movement.

The specific plans for division were achieved as an elite bargain without public consultations; they were, at least, accomplished peacefully and efficiently. This was aided by the fact that, unlike in Yugoslavia or parts of the Soviet Union, the Czech and Slovak republics were home to relatively few of each other's co-ethnics. Neither had territorial claims on the other. Federal assets, from the national debt to military aircraft, were agreed to be divided in a 2:1 ratio in keeping with the population proportions of the Czechs to the Slovaks.

Neither the Czech nor the Slovak peoples decidely wanted separation; but once separation became an accepted fact, the Czechs adapted very quickly and made a success of the circumstance. Without Slovakia, they would develop a new political system and ethos, complete and then unravel their economic experiment, achieve foreign policy successes that would be closed to Slovakia, and through these processes, construct a new national identity. This book examines each of these developments in the chapters that follow.

1 Zbyněk Zeman, *The Masaryks: The Making of Czechoslovakia* (London: I. B. Tauris, 1990 [1976]), pp. 114–15.

2 Edita Bosák, 'Slovaks and Czechs: An Uneasy Coexistence', in H. Gordon Skilling (ed.), *Czechoslovakia, 1918–88: Seventy Years from Independence* (London: Macmillan, 1991), p. 66.

3 Carol Skalnik Leff, *National Conflict in Czechoslovakia: The Making and Remaking of a State, 1918–1987* (Princeton: Princeton University Press, 1988), p. 41.

4 Alice Teichova, *The Czechoslovak Economy* (London and New York: Routledge, 1988), p. 3.

5 Leff, *National Conflict*, p. 12.

6 Based on Jan Vachel, *Postavení československého hospodářství ve světě letech 1918–1965*, cited in Teichova, *Czechoslovak Economy*, p. 26; and A. Kausel *et al.*, 'Österreichs Volkseinkommen 1913–1963', in *Monatsberichte des österreichen Institut für Wirtschaftsforschung* (Vienna, 1965), p. 31, cited in Jaroslav Krejčí and Pavel Machonin, *Czechoslovakia, 1918–92: A Laboratory for Social Change* (London: Macmillan, 1996), p. 57.

7 Václav Klaus and Tomáš Ježek, 'Social Criticism, False Liberalism, and Recent Changes in Czechoslovakia', *East European Politics and Societies* (Vol. 5, No. 1, Winter 1991), p. 27.

8 Teichova, *Czechoslovak Economy*, p. 15.

9 Leff, *National Conflict*, p. 138; and Josef Korbel, *Twentieth-Century Czechoslovakia: The Meaning of Its History* (New York: Columbia University Press, 1977), p. 87.

10 Eugen Steiner, *The Slovak Dilemma* (Cambridge: Cambridge University Press, 1973),

11 Leff, *National Conflict*, pp. 48–9.

12 J. W. Bruegel, 'The Germans in Pre-War Czechoslovakia', in V. S. Mamatey and Radomír Luža (eds), *A History of the Czechoslovak Republic, 1918–1948* (Princeton, NJ: Princeton University Press, 1973), pp. 184–5.

13 Alfred Cobban, *The Nation State and National Self-Determination* (London: Collins, 1969), p. 94.

14 Milan Hauner, 'Military Budgets and the Armaments Industry', in Michael Kaser and E. A. Radice (eds), *The Economic History of Eastern Europe, 1919–1975*, Vol. II (Oxford: Clarendon Press, 1986).

15 Korbel, *Twentieth-Century Czechoslovakia*, p. 158.

16 Theodor Prochazka, 'The Second Republic, 1938–1939', in Mamatey and Luža, pp. 235–70.

17 Yeshayahu Jelinek, *The Parish Republic: Hlinka's Slovak People's Party* (Boulder, CO: East European Monographs, 1976).

18 Teichova, *Czechoslovak Economy*, p. 84.

19 Wolchik, 'Czechoslovakia in the Twentieth Century', in Joseph Held (ed.), *The Columbia History of Eastern Europe in the Twentieth Century* (New York: Columbia University Press, 1991), p. 128. Recent studies of this have been undertaken in Václav Kural, *Místo společenství konflikt: Češi a Němci ve Velkoněmecké říši a cesta k odsun (1938–1945)* (Praha: Ústav Mezinárodních Vztahů, 1994).

20 See Leff, *National Conflict*, p. 165.

21 Vojtěch Mastný, *The Czechs Under Nazi Rule: The Failure of a National Resistance* (New York: Columbia University Press, 1972).

22 Igor Lukes, *Czechoslovakia between Hitler and Stalin: The Diplomacy of Edvard Beneš in the 1930s* (Oxford: Oxford University Press, 1996), p. 257.

23 Hansard, cited in Thomas S. Musgrave, *Self-determination and National Minorities* (Oxford: Clarendon Press, 1997), pp. 127–8.

24 Krejčí and Machonin, *Czechoslovakia*, p. 79; and Teichova, *Czechoslovak Economy*, p. 102.

25 See generally, T. T. Hammond (ed.), *The Anatomy of Communist Takeovers* (London: Macmillan, 1975).

26 Zdeněk Suda, *Zealots and Rebels: A History of the Ruling Communist Party of Czechoslovakia* (Stanford: Hoover Institution Press, 1980), pp. 195–201.

27 François Fejtö, *Le coup de Prague 1948* (Paris: Editions du Seuil, 1976); Hubert Ripka, *Czechoslovakia Enslaved: The Story of the Communist Coup d'état* (London: V. Gollancz, 1950); Josef Korbel, *The Communist Subversion of Czechoslovakia, 1938–1948* (Princeton:

Princeton University Press, 1959); and Jon Bloomfield, *Passive Revolution: Politics and the Czechoslovak Working Class, 1945–8* (London: Allison and Busby, 1979).

28 Paraphrased from Kundera's *Kniha smíchu a zapomnění* (Toronto: Sixty-Eight Publishers, 1981), p. 9.

29 Krejčí and Machonin, *Czechoslovakia*, pp. 41–2.

30 Martin Myant, *The Czechoslovak Economy, 1948–1988* (Cambridge: Cambridge University Press, 1989), pp. 74–5.

31 Wolchik, in Held (ed.), *Columbia History of Eastern Europe*, p. 132.

32 Tecihova, *Czechoslovak Economy*, p. 98.

33 For an indication of general economic parity, see Sharon L. Wolchik, 'Regional Inequalities in Czechoslovakia', in Daniel Nelson (ed.), *Communism and the Politics of Inequalities* (Lexington, MA: Lexington Books, 1983).

34 L. Kalinová, *K proměnám sociální struktury v. Československu 1918–1968* (Praha: ÚSPV FSV UK, 1993), p. 113, cited in Krejčí and Machonin, *Czechoslovakia*, pp. 162–3.

35 Pavel Machonin, *Sociální struktura Československa v předvečer Pražského jara 1968* (Prague: Univerzita Karlova, 1992), p. 81.

36 Vladimir Kusin, *The Intellectual Origins of the Prague Spring: The Development of Reformist Ideas in Czechoslovakia, 1956–1967* (Cambridge: Cambridge University Press, 1971), p. 88.

37 H. Gordon Skilling, *Czechoslovakia's Interrupted Revolution* (Princeton: Princeton University Press, 1976), p. 91.

38 In English, see Ota Šik, *Plan and Market Under Socialism* (White Plains, NY: International Arts and Science Press, 1967).

39 Radovan Richta and a research team, *Civilization at the Crossroads: Social and Human Implications of the Scientific and Technical Revolution* (Prague: International Arts and Sciences Press Inc., 1968), pp. 16 and 14.

40 Kusin, *Intellectual Origins*, pp. 100–1.

41 Jan Urban, 'The Forgotten Season', *Transitions* (Vol. 5, No. 5, May 1998), p. 44.

42 Action Program, p. 10, in Paul Ello (ed.), *Dubcek's Blueprint for Freedom: His Original Documents Leading to the Invasion of Czechoslovakia* (London: William Kimber, 1969), p. 132.

43 *Ibid.* p. 22, in *ibid.*, p. 144.

44 Jiří Valenta, *Soviet Intervention in Czechoslovakia, 1968: Anatomy of a Decision* (Baltimore: Johns Hopkins University Press, 1979); Karen Dawisha, *The Kremlin and the Prague Spring* (Berkeley: University of California Press, 1984); and Grey Hodnett and Peter J. Potichnyj, *The Ukraine and the Czechoslovak Crisis* (Canberra: Australian National University, 1970).

45 Kieran Williams, *The Prague Spring and its Aftermath* (Cambridge: Cambridge University Press, 1997).

46 Bernard Wheaton and Zdeněk Kavan, *The Velvet Revolution: Czechoslovakia, 1988–1991* (Boulder: Westview Press, 1992), p. 7; and Gordon Wightman and Archie Brown, 'Changes in the Levels of Membership and Social Composition of the Communist Party in Czechoslovakia, 1945–1973', *Soviet Studies* (Vol. 27, No. 2, July 1975), pp. 396–417.

47 Karen Henderson, 'Czechoslovakia: The Failure of Consensus Politics and the Break-up of the Federation', *Regional & Federal Studies* (Vol. 5, No. 2, Summer 1995), pp. 111–33.

48 Lloyd Cutler and Herman Schwartz, 'Constitutional Reform in Czechoslovakia: E Duobus Unum?', *Chicago Law Review* (Vol. 58, 1991), p. 549.

49 Krejčí and Machonin, *Czechoslovakia*, pp. 207–8.

50 Ales Capek and Gerald W. Sazama, 'Czech and Slovak Economic Relations', *Europe-Asia Studies* (Vol. 45, No. 2, 1993), p. 218.

51 A standard English translation is included in Václav Havel, *Living in Truth* edited by Jan Vladislav (London & Boston: Faber & Faber, 1986).

52 For an account, see H. Gordon Skilling, *Charter 77 and Human Rights in Czechoslovakia* (London: Allen and Unwin, 1981), pp. 1ff.

53 Myant, *Czechoslovak Economy*.

54 Timothy Garton Ash, *We the People: The Revolutions of 1989* (London: Granta, 1990).

55 Michael Andrew Kukral, *Prague 1989: Theatre of Revolution: A Study in Humanistic Political Geography* (Boulder: East European Monographs, 1997), pp. 39 and 46.

56 Gordon Wightman, 'The Development of the Party System and the Break-up of Czechoslovakia', in Gordon Wightman (ed.), *Party Formation in East-Central Europe: Post-communist Politics in Czechoslovakia, Hungary, Poland and Bulgaria* (Aldershot: Edward Elgar, 1995), p. 65.

57 Abby Innes, 'The Breakup of Czechoslovakia: The Impact of Party Development on the Separation of the State', *East European Politics and Societies* (Vol. 11, No. 3, Fall 1997), pp. 408–9.

58 Leff, *National Conflict*, p. 238.

59 Leff, *Czech and Slovak*, p. 136.

60 Zorá Bútorová and Martin Bútora, 'Political Parties, Value Orientations and Slovakia's Road to Independence', in Wightman (ed.), *Party Formation*, p. 118.

61 Vladimir V. Kusin, 'The Road to the Current Debate', *Report on Eastern Europe* (5 October 1990), pp. 5–6.

62 *Pravda*, 26 June 1991.

63 Eric Stein, *Czecho/Slovakia: Ethnic Conflict, Constitutional Fissure, Negotiated Breakup* (Ann Arbor, MI: The University of Michigan Press, 1997), p. 142.

64 Adapted from Jiri Pehe, 'Czechoslovakia's Political Balance Sheet, 1990 to 1992', RFE/RL Research Report (Vol. 1, No. 25, 19 June 1992), p. 27.

65 Leff, *Czech and Slovak*, 137–8.

66 Judy Batt, *Czecho-Slovakia in Transition: From Federation to Separation* (London: Royal Institute of International Affairs Discussion Paper 46, 1993), p. 23. See also David Olson, 'Dissolution of the State: Political Parties and the 1992 Election in Czechoslovakia', *Communist and Post-Communist Studies* (Vol. 26, No. 3, September 1993), pp. 301–40.

67 Leff, *Czech and Slovak*, p. 131.

Chapter 2

FRAMING VELVET: THE INSTITUTIONAL ARENA AND RULES OF THE GAME IN CZECH POLITICS

With the birth of the Czech Republic on 1 January 1993 a new political system and ethos had also to be nurtured. The success and personality of the state would hinge on its politics and, as would be demonstrated by 1997, to a degree on its domestic integrity and international reputation also.

The Czech Republic was blessed with capable and intellectual leaders. From the outset, these leaders were intent on building a particular type of political community even though they disagreed on some of its philosophical tenets. Part of this was a continuity with interwar Czechoslovakia, part a continuation of the reforms of 1990–92, themselves linked to the First Republic, and part a new entity in its own right. This new conception was a blend of neoliberalism and conservatism that predated the centrist social democratic governments that would sweep into power across Western Europe in the late 1990s under the name of the 'third way'. The Czechs, however, might be enraged to hear such an appelation applied to them. Indeed, a gulf has existed between the aims of the Czech intellectual leadership and the aspirations of the population.

This chapter examines the political society that the new Czech Republic sought to create, beginning with the ideas on which it was to be based, before turning to its political institutions and parties. It will then look at the drama and denouement of Czech politics, including the elections of 1996, the downfall of the Klaus government in November 1997 and the elections of June 1998.

THE IDEALS OF NEW CZECH POLITICAL LIFE

Political life in the Czech Republic has been more substantive and philosophical than a mere struggle to enact policy preferences. The creation of the political structures and ethos of the Czech Republic must be construed as a philosophical experiment. This experimentation is in itself part of the nature of Czech political life. This stems mainly from the political antecedents of the country, its political culture and particular personalities.

Czechoslovakia, as suggested in the preceding chapter, was not only politically experimental but also a frontrunner in political developments in Eastern Europe, with its interwar democracy and innovation in communist ideology. Political innovation extended beyond the government; during the communist era Czech and Slovak dissident intellectuals engaged in intensive debates on the nature, meaning and practical application of civil society. The importance of such thinking, and indeed the figures behind it like Havel, were fundamental to the success of the Velvet Revolution. A remarkable number of Czech dissidents entered politics after 1989, and Czechoslovakia was noted in post-communist Eastern Europe for the disproportionately high number of such 'independent intellectuals' in public life after the regime change. Even though some, like the priest Václav Malý, did not participate, Czech political life benefitted from the diversity of the Czech dissident movement. Timothy Garton Ash has written of the 'fairy tale' in which dissidents were elevated to high public office following the Velvet Revolution.[1] Those dissidents who were defeated in electoral arenas, such as Jiří Dienstbier who lost his parliamentary seat in the June 1992 elections, remained active in political life. Similarly, Petr Pithart, Premier of the Czech Republic in the life of the post-communist Czechoslovak Federation but then sidelined, remained a prominent political commentator and returned to other posts such as that of Chairman of the Senate. Of course the most famous example is Havel himself who claimed that he never wanted public office, although he successfully stood for president of both Czechoslovakia and the Czech Republic. The presence of such personalities in Czech political life meant that politics would be infused with some debate and not simply be a clinical exercise in the grafting of Western political institutions and practices onto the Czech body politic. Havel's reconceptualization of politics was typified by his statement that the most useful asset in politics was not a degree in political science but 'good taste'.

Havel was profoundly concerned with reinvigorating moral values. Much as Masaryk's thinking could be summarized as 'never lie' so Havel's was to 'live in truth'. In his New Year's address on 1 January 1990 Havel ascribed collective guilt to the population: everyone was complicit in the communist regime. He spoke frankly about how rotten the country had become, morally as well as economically and institutionally, and of the sacrifices all citizens would have to make to rebuild it. Havel continued these themes in his presidency of the Czech Republic. In his inaugural speech as President of the new Republic he underlined the kind of community he wanted to build. His project was multifaceted and he called for Czechs to:

> revive healthy coexistence within the family, the village, at the workplace and in the national community. We must cultivate mutual relations and newly set our scale of life's values and a truly ethical foundation for all rules of civic and economic life including solidarity with the weak and the helpless.[2]

While he was concerned to reconstruct economic life, and Havel clearly supported the principles of a market economy, he also believed that economics was not sufficient to create a moral nation. Most Czechs, however, feel Havel's tenets are unrealistic and possibly unobtainable.

A second feature of Czech political life derives from the centrality given to the notion of civil society. It was a concept that gave rise to the most serious contestation of Havel's approach to political life, namely that from Klaus. That such basic concepts of political life could be challenged is indicative of the centrality of political sensibility to Czech society. This debate has implications beyond the borders of the Czech Republic. The divergent interpretations of the meaning and utility of 'civil society' presented in the Czech context have wider relevance for the study of politics, as evidenced by the debate between Havel and Klaus being featured in prestigious Western academic journals.[3]

For Havel, civil society was fundamental and was the only way to reconstitute Czech society. In his New Year's address of 1994 Havel called for a robust 'civil society' of independent organizations and associations that would mediate between the state and the individual. Havel's thinking almost suggests that he believes these grassroots entities can replace state services. Klaus, by contrast, rejected decentralization of the state and the creation of independent and non-profit organizations. Klaus' values are indicated in the phrases he and a colleague quote, such as 'the market is based on the liberty of the people' and 'by following his own interests the individual can contribute the most to the welfare of other individuals'. Klaus then adds, coyly, that these phrases are not from Adam Smith but rather from the programme of the post-communist Czechoslovak government.[4]

Generally prudent in his political commentaries, Havel was overtly critical of the Klaus government for its reliance on the market to reconstruct societal values. As demonstrated in his communist- and post-communist-era writings, Havel sought a highly pluralistic society. He envisaged a strong civil society and even called for the government to reduce its presence to allow non-governmental activities more prominence. While Havel wanted a market economy, he saw the Klaus government as too deeply concerned with economics and the management of government.

Klaus, by contrast, stressed liberal economics: in a democratic context, the market was a sufficient safeguard of political rights and freedoms. His view was that if self-interest is permitted to be fulfilled a harmony of interests would be achieved. But, as will be detailed in the chapter on economics, Klaus was practical enough to cushion his rhetoric on the necessity of unbridled capitalism, and his policies in fact sought to soften the effects of economic transition. (This thinking was subsequently discredited when people saw that Klaus government policies allowed poor bank regulation and general asset-stripping, which in turn impoverished the individual Czech.) In sum, Klaus dismissed Havel's conception of civil society and believed that a functioning market economy would fulfil post-communist Czech society's needs.

The difference in approach to Czech politics and political life advocated by the 'two Václavs' came to the fore at a number of points. During his 9 December 1997 speech to a joint session of Parliament, Havel reproved Klaus, although not by name, for over-emphasizing macroeconomics and neglecting morality and decency. Klaus replied specifically that not only was Havel confrontational but that he also entirely misunderstood the market economy and the society within which it operated. While the Czech debate on civil society has been largely academic, with people complaining that politicians remain arrogant and unaccountable, grass roots civil society has been developing, especially in local communities.

Post-communist Czech society was meant to have an ethos of reconciliation and inclusion. As in most other Central European countries, a broad-based umbrella group led the Czech and Slovak revolutions of 1989. Even after the coalition government of 10 December 1989, the Republic was led by a mix of unaffiliated technocrats, Communists expelled from the Party under normalization, KSČ members who left the Party following the Velvet Revolution and joined the new government, and true anti-communist intellectuals.

The inclusive and reconciliatory nature of Czech politics extended to Havel granting large-scale amnesties to prisoners, including those that were common criminals. After the amnesty the murder rate soared; that for common crimes increased as much as three times. Havel's amnesty may have been motivated solely by his sense of morality, or enhanced by his four-and-a-half years' personal experience of Czechoslovak jails. At best, the population accepted the results of this amnesty as a 'tax for democracy' but many also saw it as but one expression of the too-lofty idealism of the country's new intellectual leadership.

A striking feature of the new political creed, then, was the forgiveness shown to the communist past; but these efforts at inclusiveness and forgiveness were also ambiguous. Creating particular disagreement was the policy of *lustrace*, which has been translated into English as 'lustration'. Following the word's Latin meaning of illuminating and purifying, the process of lustration was meant to identify collaborators in the communist system and to remove them from public office, the military, state bureaucracy, higher education and the media for a period of five years. The law, however, was not applied to all KSČ members but only to those who had served in the district administration and higher, members of the secret police, the StB, or had been informers of the secret police, or had been members of the People's Militia.

While the provisions of lustration were meant to be lenient—only affecting those who were seen to have had a distinct and deliberate role in maintaining the repressive aspects of the communist regime—it nevertheless identified specific people as responsible for wrongdoing. This practice contradicted Havel's notion that all Czechs and Slovaks bore some responsibility and was also criticized in Agenda 2000, the European Commission's assessment of EU accession candidates, for its discriminatory nature. The principle of lustration aside, its application was also uneven. In some areas of public life Communists were removed, such as in the military where lustration, as well as standard retirements from senior military posts resulted in the General Staff consisting of only post-communist appointees by 1996. Otherwise, very few Communists were removed from senior posts with 'exclusions' granted by Ministers; even fewer were actually punished. Some confirmed former StB collaborators even sit in the current parliament as members of the Communist Party. The inequalities of lustration led former dissident Petruška Šustrová to compare the Czechoslovak situation to the absurdity of Salem-style witch-hunts in which no one had ever seen a witch yet women were burned to death. She noted that not only did the Czechoslovak secret police and their collaborators generally evade punishment but they also retained their posts and privileges.

In other cases, members of Civic Forum challenged the efficacy of its investigation of communist corruption, as did Petr Pithart over communist managers in southern Moravia in summer 1990 for using their communist-era power and privilege to block democratic reform.[5] In a leading case in September 1997, a lower court found communist leaders Miloš Jakeš and Jozef Lenárt innocent of treason with regard to the 1968 invasion. When the Supreme Court overturned that decision in January 1998, it said that insufficient investigating had been done. In other cases insufficient evidence nevertheless led to public censure. Jan Kavan returned from exile in Britain in 1990, from where he aided the Czechoslovak dissident movement by publishing *samizdat* literature, to be elected a Federal MP in the first post-communist parliament. When he was accused of collaborating with the secret police during his exile his parliamentary colleagues voted unanimously for his resignation despite a lack of evidence. Even though nothing was proven against him, suspicion still lingered over him even when he was appointed Foreign Minister in the ČSSD government nine years later. Kavan's case illustrates the lack of a presumption of innocence in lustration; subsequent evidence also suggests that the charges were politically motivated.[6]

The first government of the independent Czech Republic continued to have an ambiguous policy towards the communist past. In May 1993 it introduced draft legislation that called the Communist Party that had ruled between 1948 and 1989 'a criminal organization' and condemned its regime. This included the reformist Prague Spring and Dubček personally, even though the period engendered great sympathy at home and abroad and Dubček served as speaker of the federal parliament after the Velvet Revolution. While the legislation sought to lift any statute of limitations on political crimes perpetrated under communism so that its officials could be tried, the post-communist political environment nevertheless allowed the Czech Communist Party to continue in existence, and rather comfortably. The Party distinguished itself in the region among other Communist Parties by not removing 'Communist' from its name, by adhering to its old programme, and by refusing to reassess, let alone apologize for, any of its historical record.

Czech politics set high standards for itself. By January 1994 Havel said that regrowth had begun; but in March 1998 he said that even with eight years of freedom, Czech political culture remained 'primitive'.[7] On the ninth anniversary of the Velvet Revolution Havel said that he was unhappy with political and social development in the country, but that the new generation of Czech youth that had not been corrupted by the experience of communism left him optimistic.[8] Nine years of post-communism, and only five of an independent Czech Republic, is little time in which to reconstruct political institutions, values and norms. Still, there has been opportunity for some development. More significantly, setting high standards is a feature of Havel's conception of politics; and, as in the domain of Klaus' economic reforms, it is these high standards that distinguish the Czech transformation from post-communist transition in other countries and by which the transformation of the Velvet Nation must be measured.

THE STRUCTURE OF POLITICS IN PRINCIPLE

In principle and in their pronouncements the leadership of the Czech Republic sought to install political institutions and practices to ensure political representation and the necessary checks and balances of representative democracy. The practice, however, would be somewhat different. This section first establishes the arena and players of Czech politics and then proceeds to the system in practice. It is in the practice that we see how Klaus' government should have fallen but managed to endure considerably longer than expected, before ushering in a new era in politics for the Czech Republic and even the wider post-communist order.

Institutionally, the Czech Republic emulated—cynics would say only simulated—the political system of the First Republic,[9] with an elected legislature, which then elected the president. As we shall see, there were parallels in practice, as well, particularly in the nature of the president, the presidency, the political parties and the balances they made among themselves.

PRESIDENT

The importance of electing a president was paramount to the fledgling Czech Republic. It assumed precedence over the constitutional necessity of establishing the Senate, which was to participate in the election of the president. The Czech Constitution of 16 December 1992 established the requirements, limitations and responsibilities of the Czech President. The candidate is required to be a citizen of the Czech Republic and over the age of 40, and is limited to two consecu-tive five-year terms. The President is elected through a joint session of the two chambers of parliament.

Formal presidential powers concentrate around appointing, dismissing, and accepting the resignations of, senior officials, including the Prime Minister, the Executive and the judges of the Constitutional Court and Supreme Court. The President convenes and, in certain circumstances, can dissolve the Lower House of Parliament and can call elections. While the Czech, as opposed to the Czechoslovak President, can no longer propose legislation, the office's greatest power lies in signing laws and exercising a veto, although again that power is limited to non-constitutional legislation. Most presidential acts require the agreement of the Prime Minister.

The President signs legislation that is passed by both Houses, having an effective veto. In cases of veto bills are returned to Parliament with an explanation for their rejection but the President is not empowered to make amendments. Parliamentary amendments to vetoed legislation require a parliamentary majority. In practice, Havel has rarely employed this option but the Presidential veto can be said to have a 'preventative effect',[10] ensuring that a sufficient number of deputies support a bill before its passage.

The power of the Czech President is circumscribed; subject to election by the legislature, having limited executive authority and largely ceremonial duties, it bears little comparison in its executive power to that of its American counterpart. Under a law introduced in 1961 but altered in September 1997 the Czech President now has the same, but not greater, immunity from slander than any other Czech citizen. In sum, since 1993 in principle the power of the President has been reduced and in practice has become hostage to the ruling political party or coalition in Parliament.

THE PRESIDENT AS PERSONALITY

Despite the limited powers granted the President under the Constitution, a strong personality could enhance the powers of the post. The Czech Republic's first, and to date, only President was an individual both intent on and capable of doing so. He both wanted to increase the official powers and used his personal and moral authority to do so unofficially. He presented himself as disinclined towards politics and specifically towards becoming President. Yet he became Czechoslovakia's first post-communist President, serving until the dissolution of the Federation became likely in summer 1992. After being elected President of the Czech Republic by the new Parliament in

January 1993 Havel said he would stand for only one term but stood successfully for re-election in 1998.

He brought a personable, certainly dramatic, and perhaps unorthodox style to the presidency. He travelled the long corridors of the presidential palace on a child's scooter. He introduced colourful cars to the presidential motorcade so it would not resemble a funeral procession. He appointed various advisers, including rock stars, and made the unconventional American rock star Frank Zappa an honourary representative to the United States. Havel had the drab communist-era palace uniforms redesigned by the Czech costume makers for the film *Amadeus*, although detractors said the new apparel was more appropriate for doormen at downtown hotels.

Havel's delivery was similarly personable and dramatic. He made weekly radio broadcasts to the nation from the presidential retreat of Lány; his New Year's addresses have been routinely reproduced in literary publications such as *The New York Review of Books*. When, as the first post-communist leader to address a joint session of the US Congress, Havel forewent a teleprompter and read with his eyeglasses, he so impressed the assembly that one senator proclaimed: 'If I could speak like that I could run for God'.[11] Havel has been summarized as 'a leader who writes his own speeches; he is an iconoclast who rehearses'.[12]

Havel earned acclaim abroad; but his position at home was more ambiguous. To be sure, there was much public support, even admiration and adoration, especially in the earlier post-communist years.[13] He has consistently remained one of the country's most respected politicians but he has also been seen as aloof, living in an intellectual ghetto. This view was reinforced by his choice of Czechoslovakia's greatest artistic figures as a set of unofficial advisers and by policies, such as his amnesties, which were widely criticized as misguided idealism. It was suggested that Jan Stráský, prime minister after the June 1992 elections, would be a more suitable president than Havel because, while educated, he was more like the population than the exceptional Havel.[14] On NATO membership, for example, Western observers wrote that while Havel was 'virtually the only passionate proponent of NATO membership among Czech officials' he also 'had little impact on public opinion'.[15] His visits to local pubs did little to revive his reputation as an approachable figure. His restitution of family property on Wenceslas Square provoked a messy public squabble with his brother and sister-in-law and reminded the population of his wealthy background.

In the fledgling Czech Republic, Havel became a force of compromise and was supported by several parties, including the Czechoslovak Social Democratic Party, the Civic Democratic Party and Christian Democratic Party. He accepted the coalition's nomination for the Presidency on 18 January 1993 and was elected by Parliament on 26 January with a majority of 8 votes, being sworn in at Prague Castle on 2 February. But he was not universally popular, with Communist and Republican deputies boycotting the ceremony, charging that his election was illegitimate.

Amid the cabinet crisis of December 1997 (explained below), Havel accepted the support of the four main political parties on December 10 to stand for a second five-year term. Opposed by Communist Party representative Stanislav Fischer and right-wing Republican Miroslav Sládek, Havel failed to win an outright majority in the first, and secret, ballot in either the upper or lower house of Parliament, held 20 January 1998. With Sládek in temporary detention for contempt of court and unable to stand or vote for the presidency, Havel was the only candidate in the second round of voting. Still, he received 99 votes from 197 MPs present, giving him a majority of one; he did only slightly better in the Senate, winning 47 of 81 votes.

Havel's approach to the presidency has been to remain above party politics and, as he explained, to safeguard Czech national interests and democracy. Others have not seen him acting as such. He has been accused of overstepping his ceremonial post, and of being too political. For example, his New Year's Address in 1995 was interpreted as a criticism of the government, of siding with the opposition and of presenting absolutist views of 'a classical left-wing intellectual' nature.[16] He has been accused of engineering politics. Miroslav Macek, a senior politician from the ODS which lost out from the creation of a new government in 1998, charged that in appointing the interim Cabinet Havel sought to manipulate political parties and to govern in an 'elitist way'.[17] At crucial political junctures, Havel has also had to be restrained. For example, in negotiating a new government after the November 1997 downfall of Klaus' coalition he said that new elections were best for the country but that as President he 'could not fight for it'.[18] Havel was asked to reschedule a broadcast on TV Nova for the day before the June 1998 elections because the Central Election Committee thought he would not remain impartial and thus contravene the law against campaigning two days before the ballot. Indeed, as campaigning began, Havel warned voters against supporting extremist parties because they would 'sooner or later turn against those who voted for them'.[19] And in the talks to form a new government after the June 1998 elections Havel met with leaders of all major parties except the Communists.

Entering his second term as President of the Czech Republic, Havel described a new 'style' to his Presidency, to be 'less visible' but at the same time 'more energetic and more radical' and with 'an unwavering voice'. He pledged to be more active in domestic politics and to restrict his trips abroad. He also reduced his traditional weekly radio broadcasts from the presidential retreat at Lány to once a month,[20] although his deteriorating health likely contributed to the scaling-back of some activities.

For many years the most popular Czech politician, Havel has seen his popularity, perhaps inevitably, receding. In early 1998 he carried the support of 60 percent of Czechs, placing him fourth among the country's politicians, behind the interim Prime Minister Josef Tošovský and two members of the Czech Social Democratic Party.[21] Yet despite the development of a stable and functioning political system in the Czech Republic, as is illustrated below, Havel the individual is integral to the political system. Thus, his poor health has been worrisome. He had an operation to remove part of his right lung due to cancer and has been hospitalized several times with pneumonia.

He suffered the death of his wife Olga, who endured with him his communist-era persecution. Claiming that Olga would have wanted such, Havel remarried on 4 January 1997, within a year of her death. His new bride was the 43-year-old actress Dagmar Veškrnová, 17 years his junior. For some Czechs at least, Havel's relatively prompt remarriage, and to a woman perceived as having less stature than Olga, also cost the President some respect.

Constitutional restrictions, Havel's health and potential political opposition to his candidacy prevent him from standing for a third term, and therefore the question of his successor looms large in Czech politics. When the Czech hockey team won the gold medal at the Nagano Olympics, Havel phoned its goalie Dominik Hašek. With calls of 'Hašek for President' from the street, Havel offered him the post. Hašek declined, but the incident underscores the problem of an emerging power vacuum.[22]

PARLIAMENT

Legislative power in the Czech Republic is specifically invested by the Constitution in the country's bicameral Parliament. The lower house, called the Chamber of Deputies, predated the birth of the Czech Republic in having been the Czech National Council, established by the constitutional reforms of 1968. The Chamber of Deputies contains 200 Deputies, elected for four years. Candidates must be 21 or older. The Constitution stipulates that 'Parliament's agreement shall be required for treaties concerning human rights and fundamental freedoms, political treaties and economic treaties of a general nature, as well as those for the implementation of which a law is needed'.[23] Legislative bills can be introduced by a Deputy, a group of Deputies, the Senate, the government or the board of representatives of a territorial unit of the Republic. The Cabinet is only answerable to the Chamber of Deputies, which can employ votes of confidence and demand that members of the executive appear before it or its committees. The President can dissolve the Chamber of Deputies in cases where it fails to attain quorum or refuses to debate a bill presented by the Cabinet.

Parliament's upper house, the Senate, cannot be dissolved, although it was only in the Czech Republic's fifth year of existence that the Senate was first convened. On 19 December 1992 the Czech National Council rejected the option of filling the new Senate with Czech deputies from the former Federal Parliament. Klaus' political rival Dienstbier accused him of creating 'an authoritarian state' by stalling the creation of the Senate in late 1992, despite constitutional provisions to do so, as it would have diffused his parliamentary power.[24] At 174, the federal MPs posed a significant challenge to other bodies and the idea was abandoned. This left the Senate empty and defunct. By not activating this new body, the nascent Czech Republic not only deprived itself of a second legislature, but also made itself vulnerable to political crises that would demand use of the Senate. This came to the fore following the inconclusive Lower House elections in 1996. Functionally, the Senate seats 81 senators who, like their American counterparts, enjoy six-year terms. Again as in the US, one-third of Czech Senators stand for elections every two years. The minimum age of senatorial candidates is 40. On 27 September 1995, Parliament affirmed the formation of the Senate and elections were held in November 1996, with the Senate finally coming into operation in January 1997.

In post-communist Czechoslovakia there was tension between Parliament and the President, a feature that has also characterized the Czech Republic. One point of disagreement illustrates the operation of Parliament. Contradicting a presidential constitutional commission, the Czech parliament adopted a 'list system' by which parties made a list of their candidates in priority of their importance who then gained seats in parliament based on the percentage of votes won by the party.

The importance of Parliament to the whole of the democratization process in the Czech Republic cannot be over-emphasized, even though the authority of Parliament diminished in the course of the 1990s. With political power located in Parliament a system of political parties naturally emerged.

THE GOVERNMENT

Members of the Cabinet, who run the governmental ministries, tend to be sitting MPs from the governing party or parties, but they may also be from the Senate or entirely from outside the legislature. The Cabinet is headed by the Prime Minister who characteristically is the leader of the party with the most parliamentary seats. From the inception of the Czech Republic until November 1997 the Prime Minister was Václav Klaus. He was succeeded by an interim Prime Minister Josef Tošovský who stepped down to allow for the June 1998 elections which eventually saw Miloš Zeman assume the post.

The Cabinet has tended to have several Deputy Prime Ministers in order to distribute positions to the government coalition parties. A reward for loyalty to the government, these posts became channels for disagreement between coalition partners. Tension has also existed between the Cabinet and the President. Prime Minister Klaus in particular was accused of ignoring, or at least not responding, to Havel, as Havel himself charged in a March 1995 speech.[25]

The strength of the office of Prime Minister need not come only from the polity. Indeed, power in that office derives from sources outside it. As some have argued, 'Klaus was a strong prime minister because he built a potent political party around a broadly popular set of reform policies and not for any other constitutional reason'.[26] But the Cabinet is also the 'most common source' for policy initiative, 'in part because members of the coalition parties usually channel proposals through that forum, in part because proposals generated outside the government have less chance of success' and also because the Senate did not operate until January 1997.[27]

The Cabinet, then, is the fulcrum of the Czech political system but, as in other similar political systems, without a parliamentary majority, the functioning of the Cabinet, and then of the whole polity, becomes infirm. The success of Czech politics has been the ability of party leaders to maintain coalitions, a feature to which this chapter returns presently.

PRIME MINISTERS AS PERSONALITIES

The Czech Republic has had three Prime Ministers. The first was Václav Klaus, elected with a plurality of votes in the Czech Lands in June 1992, who governed from the outset of the Czech Republic to November 1997. He was succeeded by Josef Tošovský who was interim Prime Minister between January and June 1998, and then Miloš Zeman assumed the post following negotiations after the inconclusive elections of that year.

Born in 1941 in Prague, Klaus trained as an economist. He was sympathetic to the Prague Spring but was neither a Communist Party member nor a signatory of Charter 77. Instead, he has been seen as one of the 'grey' men of Czechoslovak political life, able to float in between the two political poles. He took advantage of liberalization to study at Cornell University in 1969. His career included work in the state bank and the Academy of Sciences as an economist, although he also worked with free-thinking economists in the 1980s and contributed to underground newspapers. The first post-communist Finance Minister, he became chairman of Civic Forum in October 1990. His emphasis on marketization contributed to the split of Civic Forum and he subsequently led the emerging right-wing faction that became the Civic Democratic Party. He led the party to win a plurality of seats in the Czech Lands in the June 1992 elections and as a result became Prime Minister of the Czech Republic within the federation in July 1992. Fluent in several European languages, he won international esteem for his economic reforms but such acclaim was not matched at home where many saw him as arrogant.

His successor, Josef Tošovský, was nine years younger and also worked in the Czechoslovak state bank in the mid-1980s and was posted to the London branch of the Živnostenská Banka in 1989. He became Governor of post-communist Czechoslovakia's Central Bank and then that of the Czech Republic, in which capacity he won numerous international awards including European Banker of the Year. Like Klaus, then, Tošovský enjoyed praise abroad but faced doubts at home as people questioned his role in a series of bank failures. His dedication to work and serious demeanour, in contrast to what had become the bombast of Klaus, made Tošovský an appealing choice as an interim premier during a time of economic and political uncertainty.

Miloš Zeman, the third premier, was born in 1944 in Kolín, east of Prague, and also had a background in economics, having studied in the late 1960s at the Prague School of Economics. He joined the Communist Party in 1968 during the Prague Spring but was expelled under normalization. He subsequently worked in fitness and sport organizations as well as in economic institutes including the Institute of Forecasting in the Academy of Sciences. He joined Civic Forum during the Velvet Revolution and was elected to parliament in 1990 as a Civic Forum MP. In 1992 he became a member and a successful parliamentary candidate of the Social Democratic Party. He was elected Party leader in 1993 and gained increasing political popularity through his sensationalist if unsubstantiated attacks on the government for corruption during privatization. Zeman may be much more the proverbial 'man of the people', a characteristic that has aided his popularity as Czechs tired of Klaus' perceived conceit. A heavy smoker and described as a 'shambling' individual, Zeman appears more like the electorate than the sleek, tennis-enthusiast Klaus. Zeman has claimed to be the only current serving party leader to have been protesting on the streets in November 1989; he has also refused to partake in voucher privatization.[28]

THE CONSTITUTIONAL COURT AND THE JUDICIARY

The division of powers sought in the Czech Republic between the Presidency, the Cabinet and Parliament is further achieved by an independent judiciary. A Constitutional Court, composed of 15 judges appointed for 10 years by the President but with the agreement of the Senate, was established to protect constitutional rights and affirm the constitutionality of legislation and its compatibility with international human rights agreements. It began operations in 1994. As matters can be brought before the Constitutional Court by the President, 41 MPs or 17 Senators, this organ risks being commandeered by the opposition when it wishes to stall legislation or for the government when it cannot secure parliamentary passage of bills. The usage of the Constitutional Court and its decisions suggests that 'it is becoming an effective organ whose possible participation in legislation must be taken into account by the parliament at the very time of adoption of laws'.[29] The downside of this view is that Court may become a political tool and upset the separation of powers desired by the framers of the new Czech political system. In addition to the Constitutional Court, the Supreme Court oversees legal issues from the judicial system. The Czech judicial system was criticized in the European Commission's July 1997 assessment of applicant countries, a view that would find sympathy among average Czechs who view the courts as generally inefficient and particularly incapable of prosecuting cases of financial mismanagement.

REGIONAL AND LOCAL GOVERNMENT

The Czech Republic is a centralized state. Communist-era regional and district levels of government were ended in 1991 but a successor form of decentralized local and regional authorities has been discussed but not achieved. The sensitivity of this issue was demonstrated by the electoral success in 1990 of the Society for Moravia and Silesia. This organization drew support from the 13.2 percent of the Czech Republic's population that described itself as Moravian rather than Czech in the 1991 census. Despite the objective described by its name, the group supported the Civic Forum-Public Against Violence government. But when the new Czech constitution was being debated at the end of 1992, Moravian representatives, backed by the Social Democrats, called for a division of the new country into Bohemia and Moravia-Silesia. The proposal was defeated, prompting several Moravian MPs to oppose the adoption of the new Constitution. After the breakup, representatives of the more fringe Moravian Initiative, such as Pavel Kos, even called for a Moravian army, because the 'Bohemian' army would not 'protect' Moravia.[30] Having just gone through one divorce, the Czech government after 1993 was not intent on laying the groundwork for another nationally-based fissure in the new country and resisted giving Moravia autonomy. Rather, the Klaus government acted to the contrary by seeking to undercut Moravia's potential political influence by proposing to subdivide it three ways as part of a wholesale reorganization of the country into eight regions. Finally, legislation adopted in 1997 provided for 14 regions, with four in Moravia, that would come into being on 1 January 2000. Regional elections are expected to be held by 2001.

While reorganization was adopted at the sub-national level, efforts to increase local representation followed the revolution. In 1990 the number of municipal governments increased from 4,000 to 5,700.[31] But here, too, decentralized administration and governance continued to be open-ended. The ODS had also proposed establishing stronger local administrations but this was sacrificed after the minority position it gained after the 1996 parliamentary elections. The Klaus government contended that local or regional governments had to be sizeable enough to be rational. But this view also ensured that decision-making would not be decentralized; indeed, major decisions on local affairs themselves remain the prerogative of the national level. Thus, while the philosophical creed of Czech politics has been to allow for local, grass roots initiatives, increasing representation and responsibility at the local or sub-national level has been stalled, or even thwarted by the central government.

MEDIA

While not a formal part of the constitutional arrangement of the country, the media play a consequential role in the democratization process and repluralization of political life. Immediately after the November revolution independent media proliferated and the new government undertook measures to end state control. By mid-January 1990 over 25 new major publications appeared. A modification to the press law of 1966 was brought before the post-communist parliament at the end of January 1990, terminating censorship and allowing the private individuals to establish newspapers.[32] A new law has been under discussion in the Czech Republic but remains to be implemented. In print media, after the revolution communist mouthpieces shed their party controls. Other newspapers, some with a dissident *samizdat* pedigree such as the daily *Lidové noviny* and the weekly *Respekt*, also began publishing regularly. By May 1990 Czechoslovak Television had also surrendered its monopoly and a new, independent Open Channel began broadcasting.[33] Liberalization did not necessarily correspond to quality. Havel said in August 1990 that foreign radio services such as the BBC, Voice of America and Radio Free Europe should continue their broadcasts to Czechoslovakia 'because in many ways they were more capable and qualified than the domestic media'.[34]

The number of media outlets suggests a thriving media community; at the end of 1998 the Czech Republic had nine major newspapers. To the indigenous print media are added English-language newspapers that cover Czech affairs such as the weekly *Prague Post*. But questions of quality and objectivity in all Czech media persist, in part because of the high level of foreign ownership and particularly because Czech journalists generally lack the initiative and resources to engage in investigative journalism. At other times, the news media concentrate on frivolous issues. This may be particularly true of commercially-run TV Nova,[35] which was launched in February 1994 and attracted 70 percent of Czech viewers in under two years.[36] Lapses in objective or comprehensive coverage by the media have become apparent in crucial junctures in Czech politics. One was the unsubstantiated charge against Prime Minister Klaus that he built a villa in Davos, Switzerland with ill-gotten funds from companies benefitting from large-scale privatization. The story persisted, in part because news groups lacked funds to investigate on-site. Another case was the daily revelation in early 1998 of financial scandals involving all major political parties except the Communist. The timing of the stories suggests that either information was leaked to journalists or that journalists were pressured to do so. In either case, it suggests that the investigative journalism integral to established democracies has not yet fully developed in the Czech Republic.

POLITICS IN PRACTICE: PARTIES AND PARTY POLITICS

Having described the arena in which Czech politics is played, it is time to consider the players. Personalities, as is often the case in politics, are important, but the parliamentary system also places substantial importance on political parties.

With the exception of the Communist Party, most of the nine major political parties that participated in the 1992 federal elections fought the elections within their respective republic rather than nation-wide. This meant that by June 1992 a separate party system had *de facto* been created in the Czech Republic.[37] In fact, while damaging to the federation, the nascent Czech Republic was said to have 'inherited a relatively stable system of major political parties'.[38] The five-percent threshold of votes that is required to allow a party to sit in Parliament necessarily discriminates against smaller parties. It also encourages party discipline. While some parties ruptured, as shall be seen in the leading party of Klaus, the party list system and electoral threshold have maintained a fair level of discipline within parties.

Of votes cast in the Czech Republic during the 1992 federal elections, eight parties received a sufficient percentage to sit in parliament. But that left 21 percent of votes unrepresented in the Chamber. Shifts in voting and especially the amalgamation or elimination of smaller parties meant that by the 1996 election 6 parties entered parliament and the amount of votes unrepresented fell to 10 percent.[39] Most interests were therefore represented in parliament. Included in this representation, until at least the June 1998 elections, were the extreme left Czech Communist Party and the far-right Republicans, who together carried as much as 20 percent of the vote.

A synopsis of the main parties is necessary before further examining the workings of Czech politics. At the far right of the Czech political spectrum is *Sdružení pro republiku-Republikánská strany Československa* (SPR-RSČ), or the Republican Party. Founded on 26 December 1989, the Republican Party has been openly racist, particularly towards Romanies, but also towards Germans. It is led by the demagogic Miroslav Sládek, who had worked for the communist censorship authority. He has been charged with inciting racism but whose parliamentary seat has prevented prosecution. The Party's success was limited in the June 1990 elections; combining with the right-wing All-People's Democratic Party, the Republicans gained just under 1 percent of the popular vote. Its platform of nationalism, including general xenophobia and calls for the reincorporation of Carpathia into Czechoslovakia, won it 6 percent of the votes in the June 1992 elections and 14 parliamentary seats. The party opposed the breakup of Czechoslovakia and condemned MPs who voted for dissolution as traitors. Republican deputies voted against the adoption of the Czech Constitution on 16 December 1992. Its platform thereafter became ardently pro-Czech and xenophobic, attacking the presence of guest workers in the Czech Republic (largely socialist-era Vietnamese and Cubans). Although differences emerged, the Party's relations with Czech neo-Nazi skinheads was 'open and celebrated' with the skinheads providing party security.[40] Republican rhetoric has been particularly vicious towards the Romany population, although the party has attempted to legitimate its racism by asserting that Czech Romanies run criminal organizations and bear responsibility for the country's increased crime.[41] The Republicans returned to Parliament after the 1996 elections with 18 seats in the Chamber of Deputies but polling under 4 percent in the 1998 elections it failed to qualify for any parliamentary seats. The drop in popularity may be due in part to television reports in advance of the elections showing the substantial Moravian home of Sládek's girlfriend: the insinuation was that it was purchased with Party funds.

Aside from that issue, Republican electoral support has declined as a result of the failure of some of its major policies, such as its opposition to the signing of the Czech-German Reconciliation and entry into NATO and its denunciation of the re-election of Havel as Czech president. Billboard portraits of Sládek, with his black, parted hair, were frequently augmented by the graffito of a Hitlerite black moustache. The influence of the Republicans should not be discounted especially as it represents a darker but enduring strain in Czech political culture.

Until the outcome of the 1998 elections centre-right parties constituted the Czech government. The leading party was *Občanská demokratická strana* (ODS) or the Civic Democratic Party. The ODS originated from the February 1991 split of Civic Forum, becoming the more right-wing, market-oriented flank of the apolitical umbrella organization. ODS was the most popular political party in the Czech Republic, winning 29 percent of the popular vote in the June 1992 elections, and led the coalition government from the June 1992 elections until 1997. Headed by Václav Klaus, it advertized itself as the party of both transition and stability. Its 1996 electoral platform was 'Freedom and Prosperity, Stability and Continuity and the Non-Revolutionary Solving of Problems' and it won 39 seats in the Chamber of Deputies and held 30 in the Senate.

For all the electoral success of the party, internal dissension was frequent. Klaus was seen as the party's 'guiding light', but his strict control of the party brewed resentment. The ODS fractured in late 1997 and early 1998, when other leading members left it to form the rival Freedom Union. Undeterred, Klaus was re-elected leader of the ODS and led it to second place in the June 1998 elections with 27.7 percent of the vote and 63 parliamentary seats.

Unie Svobody (US), or the Freedom Union, emerged after a split in the ODS. It was founded on 17 January 1998 at Litomysl when 30 of 70 parliamentary members of ODS switched to US. Former Interior Minister Jan Ruml, who challenged Klaus' running of ODS, was elected party chairman on 2 February 1998. Ruml has been criticized as an ineffectual politician but the US drained votes from the ODS in June 1998, winning just under 9 percent and 19 seats.

The next main centre-right party is the *Křest'ansko-demokratická unie-Československá strana lidová* (KDU-ČSL) or the Christian Democratic Union-Czechoslovak People's Party. It is an heir to the interwar centre-left Catholic People's Party (ČSL) and one of the four parties in the Communist-era fictional 'coalition' government. The party has been moderately right-wing and Christian-democrat. It has also drawn much of its electoral support from southern Moravia and eastern Bohemia. In June 1992 it carried just over 6 percent of the vote and 15 parliamentary seats; in the next elections it won 18 seats in the lower house and 13 Senate seats. Its performance gained its members four cabinet posts. Its party leader since March 1992, Josef Lux, was skilled at avoiding open conflict within his party and at preserving its independence in the three-way governing coalition between 1992 and 1997. But after the 1998 elections, when it carried 9 percent of votes in the 1998 elections and received 20 seats, Lux jockeyed unsuccessfully to form a coalition government and was forced into opposition. Lux stepped down as party leader in the fall of 1998 due to leukaemia. His resignation left the party rudderless; a new leader is expected to be elected in 1999 but the party has become increasingly divided between those willing to govern with the ČSSD and those who would see that as a breach of the party's distinctiveness.

Křest'anská demokratická strana (KDS) or the Christian Democratic Party was originally headed by Christian dissident Václav Benda, and was considered rare among right-wing parties in having a positive view of trade unions, seeing them as integral to society.[42] The KDS contested the June 1992 elections jointly with ODS and entered the governing coalition thereafter. A Party leadership contest in early 1994 was won by the 30-year-old Ivan Pilip. While Benda thought little of his successor, calling him a (political) 'dwarf', Pilip demonstrated political acumen and his career soared. He avoided the perceived trap of becoming Environment Minister, a post for which he was relatively unprepared, instead replacing the ill Petr Pit'ha as Education Minister in April 1994. He was also expected to bolster the position of the KDS, which was risking its political existence, especially after its poor performance in the 1994 municipal elections.[43] But the party then merged with the ODS in 1995, an act which served Pilip well. He was seen as Klaus' lieutenant in the party and after the monetary crisis of summer 1997 he ascended to Finance Minister. Several members of ODS who broke away to form the US in later 1997 and early 1998 were originally in the KDS.

Občanská demokratická aliance (ODA) or Civic Democratic Alliance, was the third and smallest party of the coalition that governed the Czech Republic until 1997. Like ODS, ODA emerged from Civic Forum and was often considered the party of intellectuals. ODA was largely areligious but supported market reforms. While it won 13 seats in the Chamber of Deputies and 7 in the Senate, and was rewarded disproportionately well with 4 cabinet posts, its share of the popular vote subsequently slipped below the five percent threshold.

Leadership disputes and accusations of corruption weakened the party's electoral chances. Its leader Jiří Skalický said he wanted to sue businessman Kamil Kolek for charging that he was blackmailed into contributing to the ODA. Skalický later resigned as party chairman—the only one in the Czech Republic to do so—due to financial scandals, although he was not personally implicated and the donations were alleged to have been made before he became party chairman. Michal Žantovský became party leader in March 1997. His previous posts, including ambassador to Washington and Havel's press secretary, suggested that he might be effective but he was soon criticized by his own lieutenants, who by September 1997 had produced a report critical of the party leadership and the party's public performance. Divisions within the Party deepened over adherence to its original right-wing views. Senior ODA members resigned, including Justice Minister Vlasta Parkanová and Party spokesman Mojmír Hampl, the latter declaring in March 1998 that the ODA 'has nothing to tell the voters' and is 'paralyzed by personal disputes and personal hatred'.[44] The ODA failed to win any seats in the 1998 elections.

Between 1991 and 1997 the composition of the centre-right spectrum was largely consistent while the left was substantially in flux. The two ends swapped fortunes in 1997 and 1998, with two left-wing parties emerging as clear, well-defined contenders. Earlier, however, leftist parties' fortunes fluctuated as they experimented with electoral groupings and alliances. For the 1992 elections a 'Left Bloc' was created of leftist parties, including the Communist Party of Bohemia and Moravia, but excluding the Social Democrats. The Left Bloc gained 14 percent of the vote and 35 seats. But this left-wing alliance did not endure, splitting into the Communist Party, the Party of the Democratic Left (SDL) and another faction, registering itself as a political party in August 1993 under the name Left Bloc. In 1996, the left-wing parties fought the election independently. Neither the Left Bloc nor the Party of the Democratic Left won enough votes for the threshold, winning 1.4 and 0.13 percent, respectively. By 1996, the outlines of the left were clear. The key centre-left party was that of the Social Democrats, while the far-left was Communist.

Česká strana sociálně demokratická (ČSSD) or the Czech Social Democratic Party, derives from a party founded in 1878 but which was absorbed into the Communist Party after the 1948 communist takeover. Following its interwar traditions, the party advocates a strong presence of the state in the economy and the provision of social safety measures such as a guaranteed level of income. Its leader, Miloš Zeman, conceded that because Social Democracy was suspended in Czechoslovakia it was slow in catching up to West European political culture as communism.[45] Nevertheless, the party seems to be modernizing its tenets and can be considered generally centrist.

Indeed, both the Social Democrats and Zeman were able, by 1995, to overcome popular views that they were too much associated with the far left. The ČSSD has enjoyed exponential political growth, gaining six percent of the popular vote in 1992, climbing to 26 percent in 1996, translating into 61 seats in the Chamber of Deputies and 25 seats in the Senate. It also received defections of MPs from the Communist Party. The ČSSD won a plurality of votes in the 1998 elections, forming the government after much negotiation and the tolerance of the ODS. The ČSSD enjoys the support of West European Social Democratic parties and is notable for its political success among non-communist leftwing parties in the region.

Komunistická strana Čech a Moravy (KSČM) or the Communist Party of Bohemia and Moravia was established within the federal Communist Party in 1990 and has generally ranked at least fourth highest in the popular vote. KSČM is at best partially 'reconstructed', continuing to celebrate its era of rule and the achievements of communism. It is the only communist party in the region not to have shed its name and which continues to defend its historical record. This position was not universally endorsed by its members. But attempts by its party leader, former film director Jiří Svoboda, to modernize and deradicalize it were blocked, and following the KSČM's third party congress in June 1993 he and his supporters left the party to create the Party of the Democratic Left. The KSČM continues to be the party of the far left, winning 24 seats in the Chamber of Deputies in 1996 and 22 in 1998 as well as a pair of seats in the Senate.

Czechoslovakia and then the Czech Republic never suffered the multiplicity of parties of Poland but it has had a variety of small parties which have been unable to gain, or retain, sufficient votes to sit in parliament. While new parties have been created, mergers or coalitions of smaller parties and absorptions by larger have occurred. The Liberal Social Union, for example, was created specifically for the elections of 1992. A centrist grouping, it consisted of the Agricultural Party, the Greens and the Czechoslovak Socialist Party. The latter became the Liberal Social National Party a year later. The small parties of the Free Democrats and Liberal Social National Party merged, the latter led by Czechoslovakia's post-communist Foreign Minister Jiří Dienstbier. Despite his personal popularity and his attractive platform of a balanced budget with continued social welfare, he and his party failed to win a parliamentary seat after 1992.

Special-interest parties have existed, and at times have secured some balance of parliamentary power. The Movement for Self-Managing Democracy-Society for Moravia and Silesia sat in the federal parliament; fearing an inability to retain support in its geographic base, it renamed itself the Bohemian-Moravian Union of the Centre. Other staple-issue parties have included the Movement for Retired People for Social Security, which became the Pensioners for Social Security.[46] But despite encouraging polls, the party won no seats in 1996 or 1998. Czech politics revolves around political parties with larger agendas and platforms.

Czech politics is a vibrant arena because of the centrality of a multi-party system. The electoral threshold places practical limits on the number of parties. Klaus called the eventual reduction of parties to five major ones a 'large step forward'.[47] But the number of parties, and their occasional merger and fragmentation, ensure that the Czech political stage will continue to have some fluidity. Remarkably, Czech politics has also been very stable; even with the end of Klaus' coalition government in November 1997, the country had one of the longest serving governments in Europe. How such stability and fluidity can be reconciled constitutes one of the critical issues of the drama of Czech politics.

THE CABINET AND COALITION POLITICS

In 1995, Klaus proclaimed the Czech transformation to have been completed. It was shortly after this proclamation—one which should have bolstered Klaus' popularity—that his government and ultimately his own premiership would come under severe attack. The implications were also far-reaching: with the collapse of one of the longest-serving governments in the whole post-Soviet space, many feared that hopes of post-communist stability in general were threatened, and some foresaw a return of communism.

Nevertheless, it is very important to observe the deep consensus underlying major issues of the reform agenda. It underlines how, even in the face of immense challenges, the Czech political system remained fundamentally secure (although the Czech public generally felt otherwise). Indeed, the collapse of one government, the installation of a caretaker cabinet, and elections that produced a minority government do not represent political turmoil but political evolution: they underscore the maturity, rather than the immaturity, of the young Czech political system. But this is not an orthodox view. Writing in 1995, Sharon L. Wolchik commented on the 'difficulty that Czech ... leaders have experienced in creating a stable party system' and attributed it to communist-era one-party rule. Comparing interwar coalitions to postcommunist Czechoslovakia, she concludes that the latter 'have generally been fleeting'.[48] And certainly many Czechs interpreted the governmental changeovers not as the usual, if protracted political horsetrading of democracy, but as full-scale crises that fell outside normal politics.

The cabinet and coalition difficulties of November 1997, or indeed in early 1998 or summer 1998, should not be seen as a crisis. By late 1997, the lifespan of Czech cabinets had exceeded the average life of a cabinet in the region and indeed also that of Western Europe.[49] Interwar Czechoslovakia's political system, deemed so successful, was maintained by frequent cabinet reshuffles and intensive coalition negotiations. Czech politicians and the public would have benefitted from reflecting on the 'energy that [was] needed to be invested in coalition maintenance'.[50] But Klaus' government continued to endure. This next section considers how the seeming political stability of the Klaus coalition came unravelled.

THE FALL OF THE KLAUS GOVERNMENT

The business of governing started auspiciously for the new Czech Prime Minister in January 1993. As the Czech National Council became the parliament of the new Czech Republic in late 1992, its political memberships transferred as well. Thus the results of the June 1992 federal elections in the Czech Republic returned a coalition of the ODS, KDU-ČSL and the ODA, led by Klaus. At 105 of 200 parliamentary seats, its majority was just comfortable. As in the coalition government of post-communist Czechoslovakia, government posts were spread among the parties and party leaders also made Deputy Prime Ministers.

This coalition was expected to win the next parliamentary elections, set for June 1996. Risks to its electoral prospects that had emerged in mid-1995 from a preliminary economic downturn and labour dissatis-faction had seemed to dissipate by the end of that year. Indeed, November 1995 polls suggested that the coalition would win a major-ity of 120 of 200 parliamentary seats.

The results of the election of 31 May and 1 June 1996, however, generated different results.

As shown in Table 2.1, the three-party coalition was re-elected; it carried over two percent more of the popular vote than in 1992 but received six less seats, giving it a minority of 99 of 200 seats. The ČSSD won 26 percent of the popular vote, four times its 1992 returns. The surge in ballots for the Social Democrats was not simply a reflection of their popularity but also the redirection of left-wing votes that were previously 'wasted' on small parties. This outcome, then, was also indicative of the consolidation of a political party system. As Czech sociologists Petr Matějů and Blanka Řeháková write, the shift to the left in 1996 'could not have happened without a maturation of the political stage in the Czech Republic between the two elections and, in particular, without a further crystallization of the left-right political spectrum'.[52]

The ideology of most of the remaining parties preempted coopera-tion with the coalition parties. The notion of a coalition with the mod-erately left-wing Social Democrats, the third largest party, soon proved unworkable particularly because the ODS defined itself antithetically to the ČSSD, the former following Klaus' right-wing market and the latter supporting substantial 'state intervention'. In any case, the ČSSD ruled out a four-way coalition. President Havel formally asked Klaus to form a government, but Klaus remained vulnerable to the demands of his coalition partners. A tangible result of this pressure was the 26 June 1996 agreement reducing the total number of ministerial posts to 16 and limiting those held by ODS to eight. Klaus' party nevertheless retained the key ministries of Finance, the Interior and Foreign Affairs.

TABLE 2.1 1996 ELECTION RESULTS[51]

PARTY	% VOTE	SEATS
Civic Democratic Party (ODS)	29.6	68
Christian Democratic Union (KDU-ČSL)	8.1	18
Civic Democratic Alliance (ODA)	6.4	13
Social Democratic Party (ČSSD)	26.4	61
Communist Party (KSČM)	10.3	22
Republican Party (SPR-RSČ)	8.0	18

More significantly, Klaus was also exposed to the demands of the ČSSD; his coalition passed the initial vote of confidence because the ČSSD agreed to be absent. A means to sustain the minority government in office was achieved on 27 June 1996, when ČSSD Chairman Miloš Zeman was elected chairman of the parliament; and six days later, the Social Democrats won chairmanship of five of 12 parliamentary committees.

Klaus' position was also assisted by a legalist feature: until the Senate was elected, the Chamber of Deputies retained the Senate's privilege of being undissolvable. Klaus did not have to face new parliamentary elections because they could not be held until the Senate was filled, and that would not be until elections in November 1996. The Senate elections eased Klaus' position only moderately, and less than was expected. The very terms of the Senate elections provoked disputes, with Havel and Klaus challenging each other on the timing of the elections. By the 16 October deadline 569 candidates had registered for the 81 Senate seats. The election was two-staged, with a first round on 15–16 November and the second one week later. To win a seat outright candidates were required to secure a simple majority in the first round of voting; as feasible as this seemed, only four candidates were successful. The second ballot prompted party leaders to eliminate competition or persuade likely unsuccessful candidates to endorse their own candidates. The Chairmen of the KDU-ČSL and ODA, Josef Lux and Jan Kalvoda, objected to Klaus' attempts to secure endorsements for the ODS from candidates of theirs who had failed to pass the first round. While Klaus' party was leading, and would have won 76 of the 81 seats in a plurality-vote system, it only won 32.[53] In the final elections to the Senate, Klaus' ODS won 31 of 81 seats, less than was expected. Nevertheless, candidates for the Coalition won a majority of 52 of the 81 seats.

Whatever security Klaus could draw from the different interests and balancing factors in Czech politics, he would continue in a minority position in parliament and would also therefore remain susceptible to pressures from within the coalition and especially from the opposition Social Democrats. It was also following the June elections, in September 1996, that the ČSSD first surpassed the ODS in public opinion polls.[54]

The 1996 elections also had broad implications for Czech politics. For some, the results indicated that Czech voters were exasperated by the tension between Havel and Klaus and had sought to add new players to the political scene. Certainly voter turnout was down. From the post-revolutionary turnout of 97 percent in 1990, the first round of Senatorial elections registered a 35 percent turnout and the second round fell to 30 percent.

While the elections of 1996 minimized the influence of smaller parties, they did not eliminate them and did not threaten the existence of the party political system. No extreme parties did particularly well but both the Republican and Communist Parties remained on the political landscape, together polling about 20 percent. But to say that results generated deadlock is inaccurate. A certain amount of impasse emerged, but rather than stagnation, the exertion of interests and mobilization of political tactics by competing groups may offer evidence of a healthy political party system. Given that Klaus' government had since 1992 operated on the basis of a multiparty coalition, it was well-acquainted with compromise. To be sure there had been earlier problems. The ODA's Kalvoda charged in January 1995 that the secret service was spying on his party. Nevertheless, the parliamentary logrolling would test the ability of the parties, particularly of the ODS, to compromise even further.

The results of the Senate race had already indicated to Klaus' ODS that the party had to tackle social demands; capitalizing on these issues, some of the ODS' coalition partners came to support the Social Democrats in the second round of the Senate. In response to the growing success of the ČSSD, the ODS platform emulated Social Democrat proposals, including those on social issues and measures to combat corruption.

Rhetoric aside, Klaus' position seemed more secure when MP Tomáš Teplík joined the ODS in March 1997, giving Klaus' coalition a majority of one seat in parliament. Teplík was one of two ČSSD MPs expelled from the party in December 1996 for voting in favour of Klaus' 1997 budget. As one study of Klaus' government observed, it was 'unified on all the key votes and is expected to survive until the next general election in 2000'.[55]

But after the monetary crisis that began in May 1997 (discussed in Chapter 3), the era of Klaus seemed over. Indeed, the influential Czech weekly *Respekt* featured a full front-page caricature of Klaus as an old dejected man, sitting alone on a parkbench. Public opinion at the end of May 1997 indicated that 40 percent of Czechs would permit Klaus to stay on but on condition that Ministers were fired; an equal number wanted Klaus removed.[56] Some of the most favoured Czech politicians were sacrificed, including Industry and Trade Minister Vladimír Dlouhý of the ODA. A deteriorating economic predicament, made all the more notable by the forced devaluation of the Czech Crown, sank the Klaus government's popularity further. By July one major survey found only 19 percent of citizens satisfied with the cabinet's work; 81 percent, however, were decidedly dissatisfied.

Despite this record public discontent, both Klaus and his coalition government endured additional challenges, particularly over the economy. Even though the sharp increase of interest rates abated some-what, economic problems exacerbated the government's unpopularity. For example, Finance Minister Ivan Pilip announced in August that a balanced state budget in 1997 would be impossible, with the deficit expected at an unprecedented 20 billion crowns. Shortly thereafter Pilip warned that public sector workers could expect a wage freeze. Increases in unemployment were expected across the economy. Once the lowest in Europe, Czech unemployment crawled up to 4 percent at the beginning of 1997, even though it dipped to 3.8 percent in April. After the messy railway workers strike (Czech Railways being the country's largest employer), the government announced plans to fire 17,000 of its personnel. Social unrest was a growing issue among publicly-paid employees. Tens of thousands had gone on strike in 1994 and 1995, including doctors.

Other aspects of the economy were faltering. The Crown suffered historic lows against the Dollar and Deutschmark. It was in this situation that Klaus' government counted on two prominent recent successes of its foreign policy—tangible progress on EU and NATO membership—to bolster its popularity. But that was not the case: through Klaus' pre-sumptuous rhetoric, Czechs expected the former and were ambivalent about the latter. The coalition showed signs of weakening. It was noisily split on the sale of tanks to Algeria and then witnessed the coalition-member Christian Democratic Union siding with the opposition Social Democrats in fighting the privatization of the IPB bank, and jointly attacking the sale as 'nontransparent'. Christian Democratic Chair Josef Lux, presumably believing that the coalition parties could and should have buried any political ambitions of their own, charged that govern-ment decisions had become politically motivated. Party priorities were dictating national politics.

But Klaus and his coalition still soldiered on. This political durability rested not so much on public opinion as the dynamics of politics among the main Czech political parties. Despite internal disagreements, the coalition partners needed each other. Klaus' Civic Democratic Party remained the leading political organization, and it retained much support outside Prague, but it could not govern alone. By contrast, the smallest coalition partner, the ODA, risked losing seats in Parliament and was therefore likely to support coalition policies to stay in power. It was also in danger of implosion. Following the December 1996 resignation of Jan Kalvoda, Michal Žantovský was elected party leader in March 1997. He had been Havel's spokesman earlier in the decade and then became Czech ambassador to Washington. There was division within the ODA between those who wanted the party to retain its right-wing economic principles and others, dubbed the 'pragmatists', who concentrated on promoting Dlouhý. While Dlouhý was seen as a suitable successor to Kalvoda, not least because of his immense personal popularity, he opted not to run. Ironically, his Communist Party membership (which he only renounced in January 1990), became more of hindrance well into the 1990s than before, even though he professed a pro-market ideology. Žantovský espoused neither position and was attractive in part as a compromise figure capable of healing the party. He was not to prove entirely successful.

Lux's Christian Democrats remained the real challenge to the coalition. Lux was increasing his own prominence and garnering popular support by differentiating his position from the coalition's right-wing views on labour disputes, social spending and rent controls. But Lux rejected overtures from the opposition Social Democrats. This was taken as further evidence of Lux's political acumen, not committing while maintaining all possibilities. Indeed, Lux would have been imprudent to commit his party to the ČSSD. The Social Democrats led the ODS by 10 percent in opinion polls, but this still only gave them less than a third of the vote and it made clear that, after an election, they would need to form a coalition. A KDU-ČSL deal with the ČSSD would still have resulted in a coalition with insufficient seats to form a government and which would be unlikely to be able to do so in future.

At the same time, having the bicameral system in operation permitted greater flexibility. The Lower House can be dissolved, allowing for elections. Had the Senate been sitting at the time of the deadlocked June elections, the ODS could have countered its minority position by calling early elections. Instead, Klaus' government met with attacks from the ČSSD which moved for the resignation of Dlouhý and Finance Minister Ivan Kočárník. This motion only failed because the Communists, seeking not just piecemeal dismissals but the removal of the entire government, voted against it.

Klaus instituted two packages of economic measures in April and May 1997 which sought to curb government spending, restrict certain imports to aid the country's deteriorating balance of payments, and pledges of improved financial governance. But it was with the devaluation of the Crown thereafter that Klaus at last admitted that the economy was facing serious difficulties. In June 1997, Klaus' coalition government was subjected to a vote of confidence, which it survived by 101 to 99. With that hurdle barely passed, Klaus' government faced parliamentary acceptance of its budget. In return for the support of independent MP Josef Wagner, the second ČSSD member expelled in December 1996, Klaus backtracked and consented to new privatization plans being subject to review by Parliament.

The most serious challenges to Klaus' rule came not from inside or even outside the coalition, but from inside his own party. Dissension over Klaus' leadership style—particularly his 'autocratic', nonconsultative practices—had been brewing for some years. By 1996 Deputy Party Chairman and Foreign Minister Josef Zieleniec, nicknamed the party 'godfather', was already touted as a possible successor to Klaus as party chairman. In August 1996 Zieleniec urged more open party debate. Differences between the two men resurfaced less than a year later when Zieleniec charged Klaus with not conferring with the Cabinet and Party. A specific issue of contention within the party arose when it was revealed that Klaus did not advise ODS members of a warning he had received from the IMF of looming economic problems. But again 'peace' was made between Klaus and Zieleniec on 5 June 1997. The ODS then pledged in a party statement to augment communications within the party and the coalition.[57] Still dissatisfied, Zieleniec resigned his party and government posts on 24 October to protest Klaus' leadership. For an unassuming character, Zieleniec made his exit as bombastic as possible to draw attention to failings in Klaus' leadership style. Zeman responded by stating that he expected Zieleniec to return to politics and that he would make a suitable Prime Minister. Zieleniec's resignation, however, only removed some of the ODS opposition to Klaus' leadership; a subtler, and ultimately successful attack came from Ivan Pilip and Jan Ruml. It is hardly surprising, therefore, that Deputy Chairman Miroslav Macek's internal party report noted a 'crisis of confidence' in the organization.

Outside the ODS itself pressures mounted on the government. Cabinet ministers were sacrificed, including Dlouhý. President Havel swore in three new cabinet ministers on 9 November 1997. The appointees were people largely seen as having served the country reliably and, if not politically unaffiliated, at least not as career politicians. Thus, Karel Kühnl, Prague's ambassador to the United Kingdom, became Minister for Trade and Industry, and former dissident historian Jaroslav Šedivý, who served earlier in the 1990s in diplomatic posts, succeeded Zieleniec as Foreign Minister. As if symbolizing the infirmity of Czech politics, Havel became ill during the inauguration ceremonies and had to be hospitalized.

Again it seemed that Klaus might continue to endure as Prime Minister. But continuing disclosures of ODS profiteering from suspicious privatization deals further discredited Klaus' position within the party. These included revelations of an ODS bank account in Switzerland to which anonymous large contributions were made and the maintenance of parallel party financial records in order to mislead both party members and the public about ODS finances. ODS members became increasingly dismayed at this duplicitous management, feelings that were heightened by the announcement by former tennis star Milan Šrejber that he made an anonymous 7.5 million crown donation to the ODS in return for what he claimed was preferential treatment in acquiring a major steel refinery. Not only was tension building within the ODS but Lux then withdrew from the coalition, ensuring its downfall. Now lacking the parliamentary numbers to sustain his premiership, Klaus resigned on 30 November 1997. No longer Prime Minister, Klaus nevertheless ran for and was re-elected as ODS chairman. *Lidové noviny*, to which Klaus had contributed during its communist-era underground existence, wrote that if his reelection resulted in the Czech right being marginalised then he was acting 'selfishly' rather than demonstrating 'basic political responsibility'. Other media charged that his 'political blindness' could further destabilize the country.[58]

Havel asked Lux to form a new government but with the stipulation that Lux would not necessarily lead it. Havel explained that the government head could be from another party or be unaffiliated. Klaus rejected a compromise government as 'a hybrid cat-dog'.[59] Again, a non-partisan and respected personality was needed, and this was found in the person of Czech National Bank Governor Josef Tošovský who was sworn in on 2 January 1998. Klaus derided Tošovský's Cabinet for being composed of the ODA and KDU-ČSL which, he said, together won only 14 percent in the previous election. ODS Deputy Chairman Jiří Payne called the Cabinet the 'Coup-Lux-Clan', while Tošovský's other detractors promptly declared that he was elected by no one. While these comments represented political positions, they also indicate an important objective point: new elections had not been called and, for all its defensive rhetoric, the Tošovský government did not have a popular mandate.

Tošovský seemed to think that Klaus was deliberately impeding the establishment of the interim Cabinet. Tošovský explained that he had asked parties to submit nominations for candidates for his Cabinet, but only received them from ODA and KDU-ČSL. Tošovský received none from Klaus, even after encouraging him to do so. Tošovský concluded that he could not allow internal problems of the ODS to influence the functioning of his government and then nominated people from the ODS himself.[60]

Klaus refused to support Tošovský's government unless Ivan Pilip resigned from the post of Finance Minister. Because Pilip had been Klaus' lieutenant in the ODS as well as a senior member of his Cabinet, it seemed from the public viewpoint inconceivable that Pilip had no knowledge of the Party's financial dealings and was therefore called simply 'power-hungry'.[61] Pilip aside, Klaus refused to support Tošovský's government unless defectors from the ODS left their posts in the new Cabinet and he proclaimed that his party 'could never put up with such a government'.[62]

Despite Klaus' suggestion that the Cabinet was merely a continuation of the KDU-ČSL and ODA, it also contained many of those who attacked Klaus within ODS and then left it. As well as Pilip, who continued as Finance Minister, these personalities included Michal Lobkowicz who ramained as Defence Minister. KDU-ČSL holdovers included its party leader Lux, who also retained the Environment portfolio, while survivors from the ODA's share of the Cabinet included Justice Minister Parkanová.

In addition to being generally perceived as politically neutral, it was hoped that Tošovský's international accolades as Governor of the Central Bank would help to restore domestic and foreign confidence in the management of Czech economic and political affairs. This was an ironic calculation considering that for many, both within and outside the country, Tošovský bore at least some responsibility for bank failures and frauds. In addition, his government lacked the legitimacy of an electoral mandate. But in spite of these difficulties, Tošovský insisted that his cabinet was not a 'caretaker' government and proposed a substantial agenda. He promised a popular, if also necessary, programme of making government transparent and of implementing domestic reforms and continuing foreign policy initiatives. His role was perhaps comparable to the 'interim caretaker government of "nonpartisan experts"'.[63] that ran the First Republic when the *pětka* tottered. Nevertheless, the Czech economy continued to wither, with the Czech Crown dropping to new lows and polls indicating that 51 percent of Czechs believed that their income declined in 1997 and 64 percent believing their income was lower than under communism.[64]

Under the Czech Constitution, new elections can be held only after the failure of three successive confidence votes in the lower house against the government. The best way to bring about new elections, Havel said, was in fact to support the new government. The ČSSD gave its backing to Tošovský's government in return for a promise of early elections, which most major parties wanted regardless, and agreement to present its privatization plan within eight weeks. On 28 January 1998, with the support of the ČSSD, US, KDU-ČSL, and ODA, the Tošovský government secured 123 votes to 71 in a confidence vote. But the Tošovský government then deliberately made itself short-lived by attaching a confidence vote to legislation on the privatization of state-owned property. The government would be defeated if the legislation was not passed outright, or if the law was not considered by Parliament within 90 days the President would have the right to dissolve the House.

While the Tošovský government planned its own demise, the ODS tended increasingly towards fragmentation. Former Interior Minister Jindřich Vodička said he planned to leave ODS by not paying his party subscription, due in March, and that he would join a new party called Right Alternative. Klaus continued his attack on Pilip, calling him a 'liability' and declaring that it was 'only to the benefit' of ODS if such people quit it.[65]

The ODS schism was codified after an extraordinary congress at Litomyšl on 17 January 1998. The breakaway ODS members formed a new political party called the Freedom Union (US). The new organization saw itself as largely representing small and medium business and hoped to gain at least 10 percent of the popular vote in the next election.[66] At a US nationwide meeting shortly thereafter former dissident and post-communist Interior Minister Jan Ruml was elected chairman. The US then decided it was necessary to cooperate with all centre-right parties. The progammes of the US and ODS did not differ substantially, lending credence to the attack by ČSSD spokesman Stanislav Gross when he said that the ODS-US split was a ruse by ODS to increase indirectly its share of the popular votes.[67] While this was to some degree rhetorical, the ODS still sought a *modus vivendi* with its fellow centre-right parties by specifically asking them not to preclude post-election cooperation by attacking each other during the election.[68] Such tactics did not prevent additional defections of figures such as Lobkowicz from the ODS to the US.

The ODS was not alone in suffering internal disintegration. The ODA was rapidly losing members, partly due to the party's sagging credibility after the emergence of illegal party donations. As the election campaign geared up, nine ODA MPs or Cabinet Ministers had defected, including party co-founder Pavel Bratinka, Deputy Chairman of the Chamber of Deputies Karel Ledvinka and Parkanová, Dlouhý and Kühnl.

As the internal stability of several political parties floundered a cascade of revelations regarding financial impropriety shook their public credibility. Deputy Prime Minister and Environment Minister Jiří Skalický resigned over financial scandals involving the ODA. He refused to divulge the names of the donor companies, but asserted they were not connected to privatization. He also said that his party would donate any illegitimate contributions to charity. Havel thereafter asked him to answer the charges which he did in a three-page letter which upheld the legality of the party's actions. Havel said the response disproved some of the charges against the ODA but did not exonerate it entirely. It emerged that the ODA received party donations through a dummy company in the Virgin Islands. Dlouhý, who was questioned by police, tried to explain the situation by stating that corporate donors, including major foreign firms such as Philip Morris and domestic ones like Vítkovice, were 'mediators' for the actual donors. The explanation only provoked more confusion and suspicion. By February 1998 the party had slipped in opinion polls to below the 5 percent threshold.[69]

Financial scandal also affected the ČSSD after KSČM Chairman Miroslav Grebeníček said that his party gave the Social Democrats 10 million Crowns, although this is likely to have dated back to late 1989.[70] Havel responded to further allegations against the ČSSD by pledging that the BIS, the state secret police, would investigate.[71]

The ODS could do little to remove the financial tarnishes. Within a month of having been elected a Deputy Chairman of ODS, Bohdan Dvořak resigned. He said that he could not defend the image of the

Party in the wake of its financial scandals. Even when the ODS announced that the financial consultants Deloitte and Touche would conduct a 'forensic' audit the Party's accounts, the Party said it would not release the final report. In addition, the allegations circulated of a further 7.5 million crowns of unknown origin donated to the ODS.[72] Corruption seemed to spread widely, with former ODS Deputy Chairman Libor Novak spending 41 days in jail while being investigated for his role in financial impropriety.[73] Klaus was personally also accused of building a private villa in Davos, Switzerland. This was later disproven and TV Nova, which aired the original charges, was forced to apologize.

Some semblance of routine was reintroduced into Czech politics when Havel announced that he would stand for a second term as Czech President. But concomitant uncertainty was generated by his making the announcement from his hospital bed. Initially Havel's candidacy seemed uncontested. Even two days before the parliamentary vote Havel said 'I can imagine someone else being president and I even regret not having opponents with greater political support than those running against me'.[74] His previous rival, Republican leader Sládek was originally expected not to be able to stand because he was in police detention for defamatory remarks. In the end, however, he stood, as did the Moscow-educated astrophysicist Communist candidate Stanislav Fischer. To punish Havel for his part in terminating Klaus' government and in replacing it with the 'hybrid' Tošovský government the ODS withdrew support for Havel's presidency. Havel's regret at the lack of competition for the posts must have dissipated; instead of being unchallenged, he was re-elected by a majority of a solitary vote. And this Havel achieved only by the growing split in the ODS which resulted in 30 of its 69 MPs defying Party orders by voting for him.

The larger political picture was itself unencouraging. Ironically, as the June 1998 elections approached, satisfaction with Tošovský's government increased by 10 percent to about 60 percent. But this was clearly a government meant to be temporary and Czech dismay with the economy was vocal. Almost 29 percent of Czechs said that they favoured communism over the present government, an increase of over 10 percent from November 1997.[75] Only 5 percent of Czechs reported satisfaction with the economic transformation.[76]

Now out of office the ODS' support kept slipping. At 10 percent, it received its lowest backing ever in early February 1998, while ČSSD carried 29 percent.[77] A poll in early March gave the ČSSD 25 percent of votes, while the US received 13 percent and the ODS continued at 10 percent. The KDU-ČSL and KSČM each received 8 percent, the Republicans 5 percent and the ODA dropped to 1 percent.[78]

Zeman seemed keen to slant the political system to his advantage. Before campaigning began, he proposed increasing the five percent threshold and suggested changes to the allocation of votes to avoid parliamentary stalemate. The KDU-ČSL rejected forming a coalition with the ČSSD—largely over differences on the Czech-German Declaration and Zeman's proposed economic strategy—but said that it would allow the Social Democrats to form a minority government.[79]

While the US' Ruml said that he would consent to a ČSSD minority government, Zeman also rejected forming a coalition with US, ODS or ODA although he said a coalition with the Christian Democrats remained a possibility. The ČSSD announced a five-point electoral programme, a key feature of which was their 'clean hands' campaign against corruption in politics. Zeman also announced that he planned to rescind the phone monopoly awarded by Klaus' government to SPT Telecom until 2000. By contrast, the ODS' campaign centred on transparent property ownership and economically efficient government. In other words, the ODS was offering, with somewhat different rhetoric, the same policies that had lost it public confidence.

With the ČSSD still retaining a substantial lead in the polls, Havel said that the person who became Prime Minister should lead a coalition and also that he need not be leader of the largest party. Unsurprisingly, Zeman, to whom the comments were indirectly addressed, discounted them. To hasten the holding of the election, Havel signed a constitutional amendment on 25 March 1998, approved by both Houses of Parliament, which halved the term of sitting MPs and thereby allowed early elections.

The ČSSD seemed to making an assault on some of the key features of the Klaus government. The Party discussed moves to dismiss the entire board of directors of the National Property Fund which is responsible for overseeing privatization. At the same time, it dropped its insistence on a referendum on NATO membership. This was not so much a measure to align the Party with public opinion (and, as mentioned in Chapter 4, Czechs were generally apathetic about or even opposed to membership), as acceptance of the reality that the Party's efforts in parliament to force the referendum would not succeed. Even though the Social Democrats dropped their insistence on a referendum, Zeman said the matter should not be resolved by Tošovský's parliament but the next, namely his.

Rumors circulated in late March 1998 that Zeman had informed Havel that he would leave politics due to the 'Bamberg Affair' when Czech-born Swiss entrepreneur Jan Vízek charged that in the early post-communist era Zeman had promised him governmental appointments in return for donations to the ČSSD. Fearing retaliations from Zeman, Vízek released his version of the details of this deal, which Vízek alleged included giving ČSSD 8 million crowns.[80] Far from stepping down, Zeman launched his election campaign by making light of the affair. He christened his campaign bus, nicknamed after him as 'Zemák', with a bottle of Bamberg champagne.

As the elections neared, the ČSSD enjoyed the benefits of confusion and infighting among the centre-right. The US was unprepared to wage an election and was particularly lacking in firm leadership; despite founding the party, Ruml announced that he would not be a candidate in the elections. The US thus was unsure who should lead it or run for leadership, and at times even contemplated approaching Tošovský to be a candidate. This uncertainty gave Klaus the opportunity to consolidate his grip on the remainder of the ODS. The US programme was also vague and to the extent that it was seen advocating one, it was accused of being 'hardly different' from that of ODS.[81] In personal relations, however, a clear gulf existed between Klaus and Ruml. At a meeting of former prisoners in Jáchymov the two politicians turned their backs on each other, did not shake hands and also refused to share a television studio.[82] Intra-party strife obscured the central question for the elections: economic well-being. General dissatisfaction, but especially of those on fixed incomes, explained the rise of the Party of the Pensioners for a Secure Life which had climbed to third place in the pre-election polls. The Party failed to win seats, however. Its leader, retired communist-era army officer Eduard Kremlička (who was likely receiving an above-average pension), fulfilled his pre-election pledge that if his party did not pass the threshold he would eat a beetle. (An earlier search at the Prague zoo failed to find a particular breed so he ate one that happened to crawl across his plate at a restaurant.) The defeat of such a staple-issue party was not representative of the larger outcome.

The three centre-right parties together received 45 percent of the vote, as indicated in Table 2.2. The ODA did poorly, which may reflect that its emphasis on the market did not chime with popular experience. A large share of the population was still supportive of

TABLE 2.2   1998 ELECTIONS RESULTS[83]

PARTY	% VOTE	SEATS
Social Democratic Party (ČSSD)	2.2	74
Civic Democratic Party (ODS)	27.7	63
Christian Democratic Union (KDU-ČSC)	9.0	20
Freedom Union (US)	8.6	19
Communist Party (KSČM)	11.0	24
Republican Party (SPR-RSČ)	3.9	0
Pensioners for a Secure Life (DŽJ)	3.1	0

market reforms, but virtually an equal share voted for the centre-left or far left. The Social Democrats won the most of any party, polling 32 percent, buoyed by Zeman's pledge to investigate corrupt privatization. This plurality of votes, however, meant that Zeman commanded only 74 of 200 parliamentary seats. The Communist Party slipped from 24 to 22 seats but still won about 10 percent of the popular vote. The Republicans, by contrast, polled under 4 percent and were unable to sit in Parliament.

This diffusion of votes presented difficulties for the formation of a government. The ODS-US split ruled out cooperation, and even with the Christian Democrats, they could not form an outright majority. Aware of their position as a potential power broker, the Christian Democrats nevertheless ruled out entering a coalition with the Social Democrats alone, insisting that they would only do so with the Freedom Union. This three-way coalition of the Freedom Union, the Christians Democrats and the Social Democrats was apparently preferred by Havel, the first two ideally tempering Zeman's left-wing inclinations, particularly on increased public spending and hindering privatization.

After a month of convoluted negotiating, an unlikely deal was struck between Zeman and Klaus; the negotiations excluded Havel. Under what became known as the 'opposition agreement' Klaus allowed Zeman's Social Democrats to form the government, making it the first left-wing government in the Czech Republic since the end of communism. This arrangement had some parallels to the outcome of the June 1996 elections, when Klaus made a working arrangement with Zeman that allowed the Social Democratic leader to be parliamentary speaker; after the 1998 elections, Klaus held that position while Zeman formed the government. This outcome served Klaus even more favourably than it did Zeman two years before. Not only had Klaus gained a position of prominence free of responsibility, but also, crucially, the Social

Democrats would be accountable for what would be almost certain continuing economic difficulties, some of which were the result of the delayed painful side effects of Klaus' economic transformation. Klaus would be in the enviable position to reap political benefits from having a Social Democratic government face popular distress from his own reforms. Commented Havel's chief political adviser Jiří Pehe: 'Mr Klaus will have the CSSD under control' whilst the Social Democrats 'will be swimming in the sea of problems he created. He can bring it down and ride back on a white horse'.[84]

The opposition agreement came into operation on 19 August when Zeman's new government was confirmed with a parliamentary vote of confidence of 73 votes to 39. This outcome was only possible because, as under the agreement, ODS MPs left the Chamber in order not to vote. Perhaps the Zeman-Klaus understanding is encouraging for Czech politics because it suggests that, if not coalitions then at least working agreements can be achieved of diverse, arguably incompatible, personalities and philosophies. And therein the view of the Czechs as rational and pragmatic could be restored, and some confidence in Czech politics retrieved after the tarnishing events of the years leading to the July 1998 elections.

At the same time, however, Klaus' compromise with Zeman further discredited the ODS. The Party's standing and integrity might have been resuscitated somewhat by simply entering into opposition rather than appearing intent on acquiring some political leverage at any cost. This tactic could also prove a counterproductive arrangement as Zeman's government may not last its full term. Zeman referred to his Cabinet during its inauguration as a 'suicide government', and explained the absence of female members with a remark that women should not have to be obliged to kill themselves.

When Klaus resigned he said he would go into 'constructive opposition'. What might be more helpful for Czech politics is the construction of opposition. The very durability of a Klaus' coalition government may have been disadvantageous for the development of Czech politics as a whole. Said Pehe in another context:

> The absence of a strong opposition had devastating effects. Most importantly, the Klaus-led coalition lacked any realistic feedback with the result that many communist-style habits quickly returned to the political area. With the opposition so weak, why should the government consult with anyone? Anyway should it communicate with other political forces, or even with the people? With a political culture based on a lack of dialogue, the notion of 'we know it all' prevailed.[85]

In as much as 'establishment politicians' can be said to have been created in the short space of the post-communist era, many of these have already left political life. Czech political life would benefit greatly from the entry of new, young political talent and from existing parties refamiliarizing themselves with popular needs and sentiments. This is unlikely to happen, and in these circumstances it is all the more likely that, loved or hated, Klaus will remain pivotal to Czech politics. The striking feature of Czech politics should not be that Klaus fell but that he endured so well. He may seek to replace Havel as president, who, if not stopped early by health problems, is nevertheless constitutionally limited to two terms. But Klaus need not aim for that post. In the later months of 1998 Klaus opportunistically shifted his stated political values by criticizing the ČSSD for its lack of attention towards social welfare. If the economy continues to slide, Klaus may maneuver himself into position to be Prime Minister again. Zeman's suggestion in September 1998 that he would leave politics by 2002[86]—presuming his government can endure until then—only makes Klaus' potential return even easier.

That governments can change is a decidedly positive feature of the Czech political system. The definitive transition to democracy occurs with the transfer of power from a 'group of people to a set of rules'.[87] The nature of deals made across the political spectrum, but necessarily excluding the extremes, is indicative of both a consensual approach to politics and an acceptance of the rules of the game. The velvet transformation of politics has occurred; the same cannot be said so clearly of the economy.

1. Timothy Garton Ash, *We the People: The Revolutions of 1989* (London: Granta, 1990), p. 124.
2. Radiozurnal, 2 February 1993, in Foreign Broadcast Information Service, *Daily Report: East Europe* (hereafter cited as FBIS), 3 February 1993, p. 10.
3. See, for example, Václav Havel and Václav Klaus with commentary by Petr Pithart, 'Rival Visions', *Journal of Democracy* (Vol. 7, No. 1, January 1996), pp. 12–22. For a discussion, see also Timothy Garton Ash, 'Prague: Intellectuals and Politicians', *The New York Review of Books* (12 January 1995), pp. 34–41.
4. See, for example, Václav Klaus and Tomáš Ježek, 'Social Criticism, False Liberalism, and Recent Changes in Czechoslovakia', *East European Politics and Societies* (Vol. 5, No. 1, Winter 1991), p. 40.
5. See Jiri Pehe, 'The Controversy over Communist Managers', *Report on Eastern Europe* (7 September 1990), pp. 6–10.
6. See the collection of articles regarding Kavan in http://blisty.internet.cz/x2; and Lawrence Weschler, *Calamities of Exile: Three Nonfiction Novellas* (Chicago: University of Chicago Press, 1998).
7. Právo, 30 March 1998.
8. ČTK, 18 November 1998.
9. See Chapter 1.

10. Jana Reschová and Jinriška Syllová, 'The Legislature of the Czech Republic', in David M. Olson and Philip Norton (eds), *The New Parliaments of Central and Eastern European* (London & Portland, OR: Frank Cass, 1996), p. 85.

11. Quoted by US Democratic Representative Robert J. Mrazek, *International Herald Tribune*, 23 February 1990.

12. Michael Simmons, *The Reluctant President* (London: Methuen, 1991), p. xvi.

13. A book was even published of children's letters and drawings to Havel: *Mylí pane Prezidente!* (Prague: Státní pedagogické nakladatelství, 1992).

14. *Mladá fronta Dnes*, 26 January 1995.

15. Jane Perlez, 'Despite Havel, It's Check, If Not Mate, on NATO', *International Herald Tribune*, 24–25 December 1997.

16. *Denní telegraf*, 3 January 1995.

17. *Právo*, 3 January 1998

18. ČTK, 8 December 1998.

19. RFE/RL Newsline, 1 June 1998.

20. *Mladá fronta Dnes* and *Lidové noviny*, 2 February 1998.

21. *Mladá fronta Dnes*, 17 February 1998.

22. *Mladá fronta Dnes*, 23 February 1998.

23. Article 49 (2) of the Czech Constitution.

24. Jane Perlez, 'The Fist in the Velvet Glove', *The New York Times Magazine*, 16 July 1995.

25. See, for example, Jiří Leschtina's commentary in *Lidové noviny*, 16 March 1995.

26. Mitchell Orenstein, 'Václav Klaus: Revolutionary and Parliamentarian', *East European Constitutional Review* (Vol. 7, No. 1, Winter 1998), p. 47.

27. Andrew T. Green and Carol Skalnik Leff, 'The Quality of Democracy: Mass-Elite Linkages in the Czech Republic', *Democratization* (Vol. 4, No. 4, Winter 1997), p. 76.

28. Vincent Boland, 'Penchant for witty allusions', *The Financial Times*, 22 November 1995.

29. Reschová and Syllová, 'The Legislature', p. 87.

30. *Český deník*, 23 January 1993.

31. Aleš Kroupa and Tomáš Kostelecký, 'Party Organization and Structure at National and Local Level in the Czech Republic Since 1989', in Paul G. Lewis (ed.), *Party Structure and Organization in East-Central Europe* (Edward Elgar, 1996), pp. 102–3.

32. Jiri Pehe, 'An Overview of the Democratic Revolution', RFE, *Report on Eastern Europe* (9 March 1990).

33. See Kevin Devlin, 'Postrevolutionary Ferment in East European Media', RFE, *Report on Eastern Europe* (13 July 1990), pp. 47–53.

34. RFE interview with Havel in, *Report on Eastern Europe* (1 August 1990).

35. In particular, see the transcription of and commentary on a TV Nova news broadcast presented in Jan Čulík, 'Media in the Czech Republic: The Current State of Affairs', presented at BASEES, Cambridge University, 4 April 1998; available at http://blisty.internet.cz/9803/ 19980330k.html#10.

36. Kevin Done, 'A jewel in the crown', *The Financial Times*, 22 November 1995.

37. Gordon Wightman, 'The Development of the Party System and the Break-up of Czechoslovakia' in Gordon Wightman (ed.), *Party Formation in East-Central Europe* (Cheltenham: Edward Elgar, 1995), esp. pp. 60–61.

38. Kroupa and Kostelecký, 'Party Organization', p. 89.

39. Petr Matějů and Blanka Řeháková, 'Turning Left or Class Realignment? Analysis of the Changing Relationship Between Class and Party in the Czech Republic, 1992–96', *East European Politics and Societies* (Vol. 11, No. 3, Fall 1997), p. 520.

40. Stanislav Penc and Jan Urban, 'Extremist Acts Galvanize Roma Population', *Transitions*, (Vol. 5, No. 7, July 1998), p. 39.

41. *Political Extremism and the Threat to Democracy in Europe* (London: Institute of Jewish Affairs for CERA, 1994), p. 18.

42. See Kroupa and Kostelecký, 'Party Organization', p. 94.

43. *Mladá fronta Dnes*, 28 April 1994.

44. REF/RL Newsline, Vol. 2. No. 36, 23 March 1998.

45. *Lidové noviny*, 4 March 1994.
46. Český deník, 12 April 1994.
47. *Lidové noviny*, 17 February 1995.
48. Sharon L. Wolchik, 'The Czech Republic and Slovakia', in Zoltan Barany and Ivan Volgyes (eds), *The Legacies of Communism in Eastern Europe* (Baltimore, MD and London: The Johns Hopkins University Press, 1995), p. 167.
49. Green and Leff, 'Quality', p. 64.
50. Leff, *National Conflict*, pp. 59–60.
51. See Karen Henderson, 'Did the Right Win the Czech Election?', *Contemporary Politics* (Vol. 2, No. 3, Autumn, 1996), pp. 127–38.
52. Petr Matějů and Blanka Řeháková, 'Turning Left or Class Realignment? Analysis of the Changing Relationship Between Class and Party in the Czech Republic, 1992–96', *East European Politics and Societies* (Vol. 11, No. 3, Fall 1997), p. 520.
53. Green and Leff, 'Quality', p. 81.
54. STEM poll, in *Právo*, 20 September 1996.
55. EIU, *Country Report: The Czech Republic* (2nd Quarter, 1997), p. 6.
56. *Mladá fronta Dnes*, 21 May 1997.
57. *Právo*, 6 June 1997.
58. *Lidové noviny* and *Hospodářské noviny*, 5 December 1997.
59. ČTK, 9 December 1997.
60. *Mladá fronta Dnes*, 2 January 1998.
61. *Mladá fronta Dnes*, 9 January 1998.
62. *Mladá fronta Dnes*, 16 January 1998.
63. Carol Skalnik Leff, *National Conflict in Czechoslovakia: The Making and Remaking of a State, 1918–1987* (Princeton: Princeton University Press, 1988), p. 62.
64. RFE/RL Newsline (No. 190, 7 January 1998).
65. *Právo* and *Lidové noviny*, 8 January 1998.
66. *Mladá fronta Dnes*, 19 January 1998.
67. *Lidové noviny*, 9 March 1998.
68. *Mladá fronta* dnes, 16 February 98.
69. RFE/RL Newsline Vol. 2, No. 38, 25 February 1998.
70. *Respekt*, 9 February 1998.
71. *Mladá fronta Dnes*, 27 March 1998.
72. *Mladá fronta Dnes* and *Hospodářské noviny*, 22 January 1998.
73. *Mladá fronta Dnes*, 27 March 1998.
74. Reuters, 18 January 1998.
75. *Mladá fronta Dnes*, 25 February 1998.
76. *Lidové noviny*, 5 March 1998.
77. *Mladá fronta Dnes*, 12 February 1998.
78. *Mladá fronta Dnes*, 11 March 1998.
79. See *Mladá fronta Dnes*, 10 and 25 February 1998
80. *Mladá fronta Dnes*, 30 March 1998.
81. *Lidové noviny*, 9 January 1998.
82. Právo, 1 June 1998.
83. Karen Henderson, 'Social Democracy Comes to Power: the 1998 Czech Elections', *Labour Focus on Eastern Europe* (No. 60, Summer 1998), p. 7.
84. Quoted in Robert Anderson and Kevin Done, 'Surprise left-right deal by Czech parties', *The Financial Times*, 9 July 1998.
85. Jiri Pehe, 'The Disappointments of Democracy', *Transitions* (Vol. 5, No. 5, May 1998), p. 39.
86. *Právo*, 7 September 1998.
87. Adam Przeworski, *Democracy and the Market* (Cambridge: Cambridge University Press, 1991), esp. p. 14.

Chapter 3

PATCHWORK VELVET: THE BURST BUBBLE OF THE CZECH ECONOMIC TRANSFORMATION

The transformation of the Czech economy may be the most striking feature of the new country. Not only was the Czech Republic seen as the forerunner of economic transformation in the post-socialist bloc, but this transformation was also fundamental to the development of new Czech values. To the Czech contributions to the world vocabulary of 'Velvet Revolution' and 'Velvet Divorce' was added the 'Velvet Recovery'. Yet as in political life so too in economic: the Czech velvet shows signs of fading.

Czechoslovakia was applauded as the leader of post-communist economic reform. It introduced ground-breaking privatization and boasted macroeconomic indicators to impress even successful market economies. So triumphant was the economic transition that Klaus declared that the Czech Republic would not apply for EU member-ship, hungrily coveted by other post-communist countries, but instead would wait to be invited to join. Klaus even rejected reference to the Czech Republic as an 'emerging market', a 'transition economy' or a 'post-communist state'; by the mid-1990s, he claimed, the Czech Republic already had a fully functioning market economy and was a 'normal' country. Klaus was not alone in this view; both the Czech public and foreign observers came to believe in the Czech 'economic miracle'.

Klaus' bold and brash assertions about the Czech economy are not the only reasons to study it, although his claims provide a helpful, and legitimate, measuring stick against which to test the transformation. The economic reforms were also fundamental in making a new society and a new, or renewed, Czech person. It is here that the extent and quality of that transition bears the most significance for the long-term nature of the Czechs and their society. And just as Klaus put the emphasis on economic reform for the reconstruction of Czech politics and society, so the economy would be his undoing.

In addition to being a fundamental task of the Czech Republic the economic transformation represents the vindication of the Velvet Divorce and therefore must succeed. It also represents an effort to return to the values, if somewhat glorified retrospectively, associated with interwar Czechoslovakia. Then, with only twelve million inhabitants, Czechoslovakia was one of the richest and most productive economies in the world. In addition to restoring national pride (and perhaps also proving that Czechoslovak economic success could be repeated without its large historical German minority), the post-communist government wanted to ensure a successful transformation in its own right.

The Czech post-communist economic transition is also of intrinsic interest. Klaus joins voices with economists worldwide in noting that Central and East Europe has undertaken a unique and unprecedented project: making a transition from left to right. As the Polish economic reforms began in 1990 it was said that communism had turned fish into fish soup, but never in history had fish soup been reconstituted into an aquarium. Klaus was not only intent on reconstituting the Czech aquarium, but on making it superlative.

While sharing characteristics with the whole transformation process, the Czech Republic is also unique, possessing unparalleled circumstances and prompting singular questions. Features particular to the Czech transformation are many. First, it is distinctive for the radical nature of the transition. Second, the Czechoslovak economy was the most centralized of the communist economies. Third, it had been a leading industrialized and market-oriented economy in the interwar period and, therefore, prompts tests of the full extent of transition and how well a previous market economy can reestablish its standards. And fourth, from a more strictly economic point of view, the Czech economy was atypical of transition economies by performing well in some indicators but poorly in others.

While these characteristics of the Czech transition elevate the importance of the country in circles of economic theory and international finance, it is the rise and demise of the Czech economic miracle, and its wider implications, that bear special relevance. Once called by international observers 'the most successful free-market economy of the post-communist countries',[1] by 1997, the Czech Republic was cited as an example of 'financial anarchy' in the post-communist world.[2] The striking changes in the fortunes of the Czech economy are also unusual in the overall post-communist transformation process. The largely unanticipated downturn in the Czech economy brought with it two further features: the political costs to the post-communist world's most stable and enduring government, and the implications of the economic transition, and its weaknesses, for the nature of Czech society. For, as we shall see, it is also in this realm that historical legacies are influential, both as myth and in reality, and in which the policies of the post-communist federation feature most prevalently. It is also in the economic realm that contradictory aspects of the new Czech identity emerge.

This chapter reviews the making and breaking of the Czech 'economic miracle'. Because the changes introduced in post-communist Czechoslovakia between 1990 and 1992 are fundamental to an understanding of the economy of the Czech Republic, this chapter considers thematically the transformation since 1990, examining macro- and microeconomic requirements for change and the extent to which they have been achieved. These include: privatization; industrial restructuring; the restructuring of the workforce, unemployment and labour productivity; price liberalization; currency reform and convertibility; the creation and reform of financial institutions and banking; and foreign trade and investment. Social issues connected to the economic transformation are then assessed, leading to an overview of the bursting of the Czech economic bubble. A final section assesses the quality and character of the Czech economy and offers a prognosis. First, however, brief consideration of the origins of the thinking behind the transformation provides background to the process in practice.

PRE-TRANSFORMATION: CONDITIONS AND THINKING

Czechoslovakia emerged from communist rule with economic conditions that invited rapid economic transformation. It had had low inflation, modest monetary overhang, a small budget deficit, a slightly positive hard currency trade balance and one of the smallest hard currency debts of the post-communist world. Poland and Hungary, by contrast, were hindered by foreign debts accumulated in the 1980s. Possessing an extremely centralized, tightly controlled command economy proved a blessing to the Czechoslovak transformation as the reformers were in a better position to enact a radical transformation than in Poland or Hungary, where economic experimentation and political decentralization had allowed vested interests to take hold within the planning and production system, such as those of unions and plants managers who could hinder change. Not only were such constraints relatively limited in Czechoslovakia, but the centralized system also meant that economic reforms could be driven more easily from the top, once the management itself was replaced.

The new Czechoslovak political management that assumed control in December 1989 had contemplated the types of change it desired, even though objective structural features of the post-communist Czechoslovak economy reinforced the adoption of shock therapy.[3] These structural features were enhanced by psychological and subjective considerations. The technical level of Czech education and training was considered high by the OECD, and Czech economists deemed the country's skilled workforce to be its primary comparative advantage,[4] although technology and infrastructure were no longer competitive. The Czechs were also considered more psychologically prepared for the economic transition—while they shared some history with the Poles and Hungarians with theoretical economic experimentation, they did not have the legacies of the practical failures endured by them. In addition, the Czechs were buoyed by the historical knowledge of their economic success in the interwar period. As some Czech analysts contend 'perhaps the most salient factor' in the success of the transition is the 'advanced economic position of the Republic in the 1930s. The Czech people are acutely aware of this legacy and they resent the relative decline of their country's economic position after the 1948 Communist takeover. Combined with the historical identification of the country with Western civilization, the legacy provides a strong force driving the Czechs to focus on regaining the status of an advanced economy'. Partly because of this historical and psychological legacy, the Czech leadership enjoyed 'unparalleled population acceptance of the radical transition policies and their tough outcomes'.[5]

But not all features of the economy dictated the application of shock therapy. Czechoslovakia would find it difficult to adjust to world markets. While the country had not incurred foreign debts comparable to those of Poland and Hungary, it also lacked these countries' experience of the world market. Significantly, Czechoslovakia was deeply integrated into the Council for Mutual Economic Assistance (CMEA) and would suffer from the collapse of that market. 60 percent of socialist Czechoslovakia's trade was with CMEA members and roughly one-third of Czechoslovakia's post-communist economic contraction was attributable to the disbandment of the CMEA.[6]

Whatever headstart Czechoslovakia may have had in its economic transformation, it still remained a phenomenal challenge and the process would have a profound impact on the nature of Czech society. As committed and confident as they were, the Czech economic reformers both contemplated their reforms carefully and implemented them cautiously. While Poland began shock therapy on 1 January 1990, which included forcing the population to cope with prices that soared exponentially while wages lagged behind, the Czechoslovaks waited a full year to implement a moderate programme. In addition to the presence of a core of market reformers, the Czechoslovak leadership was also more successful in conveying its vision to the population. Parallels are drawn between Poland and Czechoslovakia; in Poland, 'it might be argued that one of the ingredients of the political problems which eventually faced the first Polish reform government was that it did not devote enough time to communicating with the electorate'. In contrast, Klaus' victorious party in 1992 'had made a considerable and sustained effort to communicate with the citizenry'.[7] Differences of opinion certainly existed regarding economic reform. Valtr Komárek, a leading Czech proponent of gradual reform, still favoured the market; even so, by 1991 his political importance was decreasing. Most notably, differences on economic reform split Civic Forum, creating Klaus' pro-market ODS and Dienstbier's welfare-minded OH; the latter would be defeated in the June 1992 elections. But these differences were differences of degree: both views advocated the centrality of the market. It is relevant now briefly to consider the intellectual origins and content of the Czech economic reforms.

KLAUS' ECONOMIC REFORMS: THE INTELLECTUAL ORIGINS AND THEORY

To call what the Czechoslovaks, followed by the Czechs, undertook in their economy an 'experiment' is to misrepresent the preeminent thinking in the country. Much thinking about economic reform occurred in Czechoslovakia before the November 1989 revolution and economic departments and institutes, particularly the Institute for Prognosis which was re-established within the Academy of Sciences in 1988, became places of quiet but energetic discussion. The leaders of the post-communist economic transformation knew each other and worked together. And despite political repression in the country, economists were generally allowed the freedom for their theoretical discussions, some of which were published in the West.[8] It is perhaps significant to recall from the previous chapter that all three of the Czech Republic's Prime Ministers, as well as many other senior Cabinet Ministers, were economists and many had taken part in these debates before the Velvet Revolution. In the revised introduction to an article written by Klaus and Ježek in September 1989, the authors explained that they were not subject to self-censorship, that the intellectual climate in the Institute was 'quite liberal' and that for them, the Revolution 'brought no important change in this respect'.[9]

Despite their image as market-reformers, the Czech economic reformers were aware of the limitations of theory. In the same article the authors argue that neither they, nor their detractors, have a strategy or blueprint for reform.[10] While an economic theorist, Klaus derided abstract thinkers—referring to them as outside observers on Mars or in an ivory tower—who would expect the changes to proceed more quickly and less painfully, and emphasized that the economic transformation was occurring in a social context.[11]

While Klaus had such caveats, he also utterly rejected alternatives to the market, and confidently pronounced that the third way leads to the Third World. Klaus seemingly assigned an ambiguous role to the state. He clearly intended to use the state to democratize the economy, particularly through privatization. Even an unmitigated free-marketeer must agree that in Czechoslovak circumstances, the state would logically and necessarily have to be employed to create a market. But Klaus would also discreetly use the state to limit the social consequences of change, to avoid large-scale industrial restructuring and concomitant unemployment: as much as creating a full market was his aim so too was it to preserve social peace during the transition. His thinking, however, was to avoid a social backlash and the resulting profound irony that 'economic liberalization could, perversely, lead on to the re-empowerment of the state'.[12] Klaus rejected Karl Popper's call for an 'open society and piecemeal reform' in favour of Friedrich von Hayek's belief that the millions of divergent views contained within society could be reconciled through the market and would create traditions and conventions. Klaus thus believed that the market would provide the personal empowerment that Havel, conversely, contended had to come from non-official organizations of 'civil society' and which could not come simply and organically from the market. The seemingly contradictory aim of the Klausite liberals was to employ 'precisely the constructivist devices so loathed in much liberal theory, in the belief that they will deliver the country to a purported condition of spontaneous, undirected order'.[13]

Specifically, the reformist programme can be summarized as the replacement of the irrationality of the command economy with the mechanisms of the market. This was to be achieved through maintaining macroeconomic stability, and, at least initially, tight controls

on wages and a fixed exchange rate (although this was not so important as importing still generally required governmental permission). At
the same time prices and trade were to be liberalized and property
privatized, allowing for the creation of labour and capital markets.

It is now helpful to review how the economic reformers reconstructed the economy and how far they implemented their goals. This
will be done by considering major areas and sectors of the economic
transformation: privatization; industrial restructuring; unemployment
and labour productivity; price liberalization; currency reform, namely,
the gradual reduction of governmental control of the outflow of
foreign currency; and new trade patterns and economic integration.
The chapter will then assess the nature of the new Czech economy,
including how it has changed society, before considering how the
Velvet economic miracle imploded and offering a prognosis.

IMPLEMENTING THE ECONOMIC TRANSFORMATION

Privatization

Through privatization post-communist Czechoslovakia transformed
itself and led the world in some of its innovations. The challenge of
privatization was all the greater in Czechoslovakia because it had the
most profound nationalization in Eastern Europe: virtually the entire
economy, both production and employment, had been controlled by
the state. The magnitude of Czechoslovakia's post-communist
privatization can be summarized, anecdotally at least, by Klaus' quip
that had he privatized Czechoslovakia at a rate comparable to that
of Britain's Prime Minister Margaret Thatcher, he would require
600 years. Instead, 80 percent of Czech assets had been privatized by
1994, the fastest and most thorough privatization undertaken by any
post-communist state.[14]

Privatization was conducted as a highly centralized process; it was
the most centralized of Central European and probably of all post-
communist privatization programmes. Free-marketeering Klaus used
state power to jump-start the liberal economy. But Klaus' privatization
had an important democratic element: people were deliberately to be
included in the process. Privatization, therefore, was not merely an act
of economic transformation, but was also political and psychological.
The reformers were intent on recreating an entrepreneurial middle
class, one that could continue the economic reforms and would have
an enduring stake in their success.

Czechoslovak privatization consisted predominantly of two processes: 'small privatization' and 'large privatization'. The process of 'restitution', historical and moral correction, also intentionally hastened privatization. Restitution has also been called 'reprivatization' and was estimated as accounting for as much as 30 percent of state-owned real property,[15] and unofficially also affecting 30 percent of the population. It is here that a consideration of privatization must begin.

Restitution

Restitution involved the return of property to those from whom it was confiscated by the Communist regime. While the economic reformers were dedicated to building a market economy, they had other motivations in the restoration of property: 'contrary to dominant theories of property rights, a particular notion of corrective justice not only legitimates new Czech property rights, but inspires their creation as well'.[16]

Restituting property on grounds even partially informed by morals, rather than strictly by economics, posed several practical problems. The Surveyor in Ivan Klíma's *My Golden Trades* illustrates the problem of restitution when the communists seized his family's property: 'Our building was confiscated by our own people and they were worse than the foreigners, and on top of that there was no one to drive them out'.[17] In short, the Czechs did this to themselves. An entire entrepreneurial and owning middle class, as well as small- and medium-sized farm owners, were dispossessed, their property redistributed, amalgamated with formerly private or state property, sometimes improved, often throughly neglected for forty years, and also destroyed.

The reformers approached restitution pragmatically. They feared the complications and delays in privatization that restitution could entail. Once restitution was adopted, in part due to public pressure, it generally went on the basis of restituting the property rather than compensating the owners monetarily. This decision, adopted less frequently elsewhere in the former Soviet world, meant that privatization was not seriously delayed by the need to establish the value of such properties. Occasionally, restitution delayed privatization because, in some cases, only parts of an enterprise could be auctioned. For instance, the land or a building housing an enterprise might be subject to restitution while the business itself was eligible for sale.

The greatest complication to restitution came not from establishing value but from history. The date by which property had to have been confiscated in order to be eligible for restitution was critical. Originally to include property nationalized after 1955, the date was amended to 25 February 1948, coinciding with the Communist takeover. This date ignored German property seized after the war, which was only a limited political issue within post-communist Czechoslovakia (although a highly contentious one among the Bavaria-based Sudeten German lobby, as discussed in Chapter 4) and seemed to be justified as part of the whole expulsion. The 1948 date also allowed the Czechoslovak government to reject a claim by Liechtenstein for 1600 sq kms of land the principality owned within the borders of the new state but that were seized in 1918. Another issue, however, was that of Jewish property confiscated under the German occupation which was not returned to its Czechoslovak owners. Jewish property claims were partly addressed by legislative amendments passed in 1994. Wary of German expellee claims, Klaus rejected a newspaper charge of retreating from his original position of no further restitution by responding that the confiscation of Jewish property was 'exceptional' and therefore not precedent-making. He added that the amendment allowing Jewish restitution moved his party to accelerate the end of all restitution.[18] Historical redress had economic pragmatism that could be transmuted into political and economic expediency.

Another reason for selecting the date of 25 February 1948 was that it affirmed the vast nationalization that had already occurred before that date under the post-war coalition government, thereby reducing the number and size of restitutions resulting from con-fiscations made thereafter. Some contested cases of restitution of property seized before February 1948, however, still remain in the courts.

In addition to the date of the seizure determining restitution, those receiving restituted property were required to be Czechoslovak citi-zens residing in the country. Émigrés were thus legally disqualified, which obviously dismayed some, but others circumvented this require-ment by regaining citizenship and establishing a Czechoslovak address even if they did not take up *de jure* residency.

The reformers circumvented such problems by allowing former property owners six months to file for restitution. From an economic viewpoint, restitution was important because it made available property that would house many new retail and services outlets, rein-vigorating the consumer market so lacking under communism.

Overall, with restitution completed, the path was clear for the first round of 'small privatization'.

Small Privatization

On 25 October 1990 the federal parliament enacted the small privatization law for small industry and the retail and service sectors. This put small, particularly retail properties, up for auction. The auction was open to all Czechoslovak citizens, despite initial insistence from shop employees that they be given preferential rights to buy the premises. The unrestricted sale of property in Czechoslovakia was another important distinction from other privatization schemes in Eastern Europe. This form of privatization was done to reform people as well as the economy, to make them into shopkeepers and small entrepreneurs.

Ironically, however, those eligible to participate in the first round were restricted to 'qualified persons', which meant the same types of people eligible for restitution, namely resident Czechoslovak citizens. Unsold enterprises were reauctioned in a second round in which foreigners could participate. Potential buyers were required to deposit either 10,000 Crowns or 10 percent of the property's value and pay an entry charge in each auction of 1,000 Crowns. The auctions began in January 1991, with some suspicion that Czechoslovak citizens were used as fronts for purchases by foreign money. In view of Havel's reference in the 'Power of the Powerless' to one, it is perhaps ironic that the first property sold through auction was a greengrocer's.

Because of the neglect of the consumer sector by the communist regime, the items of interest in small privatization was overwhelmingly the property itself rather than stock. An administrative oversight did not account for the possibility of stock being in shops going on auction, and such goods were eventually excluded from the auction price. As the privatization of the retail sector was achievable through a decentralized system and drew upon many small entrepreneurs requiring only modest start-up cash, 'the privatization of most trade and service establishments could deliver a nearly immediate improvement in the satisfaction of the basic needs of the large masses of East European consumers'.[19]

Such problems notwithstanding, a major study of Central European privatization concluded that 'the Czech Privatization Program seems to have been remarkably successful in avoiding major scandals that could have slowed down the whole process, and to have been extremely efficient in reallocating control over a large number of shop premises in a short period of time'.[20] As successful as small privatization was, it still left much of the economy to be privatized.

Large Privatization

The Transformation Act of 26 February 1991 was directed towards 'large privatization', namely entities that were too large to be purchased by a single individual. This category of property included banks and heavy industry, other aspects of the service sector such as hotels, and large retail outlets like departments stores and wholesale trade stores. Again Czechoslovakia became a post-communist transformation leader, becoming the first country to enact large privatization (although Russia did so about the same time, but with resounding accusations of insider takeovers).

Each enterprise had to assess its financial standing and to prepare a privatization plan. Property to be privatized was deposited with three National Property Funds, one federal and one in each of the two republics. The foremost form of sales was through vouchers, giving rise to the term 'voucher privatization'. Each booklet of vouchers equated to one thousand points which represented a share of companies offered for privatization. In the first wave of voucher privatization, the booklets were available from October 1991 to February 1992. Each Czechoslovak citizen wishing to partake was required to pay 1,000 Crowns, but this was clearly presented as an administrative fee rather than a sales charge. Citizens were to have access to and ownership of the property to which they contributed through taxation and confiscation under communism. Klaus' commitment to privatization was symbolized by his signature on the cover of every voucher book.

Interest in voucher privatization was initially limited, with only 30 percent of the population participating, until 28-year-old Viktor Kožený launched Harvard Capital and Consulting in 1991. The name, appropriated without the University's knowledge, was chosen by Kožený because he had studied for an MBA at Harvard athough he studied only for one of two years and was not awarded the degree. That economy of the truth did not preclude his fund from promising a ten-fold return on investment within a year and his entry into the voucher scheme 'did ensure broad public participation'. Nearly 9 million Czechoslovaks, 80 percent of the adult population, participated in the voucher privatization scheme, of which one-tenth allocated them to Koženy.[21] Individual ownership of privatized companies was not to become a significant feature of the Czech transition because 72 percent of the population put their shares into 436 private investment funds. The most important of these investment funds were founded by state-owned banks which then led to the situation whereby shares intended for private ownership were repurchased, if indirectly, by the state. The nickname given to this was 'incest privatization'. The government, in turn, had to place limitations on the economic prowess of these new funds by limiting their purchase of companies to 20 percent of their shares.

When the split of the Czechoslovak federation became inevitable the two republics planned to continue the privatization but thereafter went their separate ways. Czech voucher privatization resumed in May 1993. 10 percent of Slovaks placed their vouchers with Czech investment funds, while only 1 percent of Czechs gave them to Slovak funds.[22] A second wave of voucher privatization in the Czech Republic was completed in late 1994. Although on a smaller scale than the first round it generated almost the same response from investors.

PRIVATIZATION AS AN ECONOMIC AND SOCIAL PROCESS

In another triumphalist statement typical of the Czech economic reformers, Economy Minister Karel Dyba, a communist-era officemate of Klaus at the Economics Institute, announced on 14 November 1994 that 'as of now, there is nothing left to privatize in the Czech Republic'.[23] A Polish analyst concluded that Czechoslovakia's privatization plan, despite some problems, was 'original', implemented 'systemically', and was the furthest and most effective among post-communist states in dealing with state property.[24] A Western economist has written: 'The Czech experience provides an exemplary model of how to implement a system of voucher privatization and demonstrates that it can quickly create a shareholder culture where none has existed before'.[25]

But while the Czechs may have led the region and perhaps the world in privatization, substantial economic, social and political questions arise from its efficacy. Beginning with the economic, some question the principle of voucher privatization. The noted Hungarian economist János Kornai calls the process the replacement of 'impersonal state ownership with an equally impersonal private ownership'.[26]

Part of the aim of Czech reformers through privatization was to set contours determining who could own denationalized property. With large-scale privatization, the reformers sought to avoid what material-ized throughout post-communist Eastern Europe, namely the sale of nationalized assets only to those endowed with the money to purchase them. This concern applied both to the select few at home, namely connected communists, and foreign prospectors. Even Havel, who had more muted views on the economy than Klaus, argued in August 1990 that the communist-era structures had not been thoroughly broken by the November Revolution. He called for a 'second revolution' which would include rapid privatization to restructure ownership. To a large degree Czech privatization limited the extent of 'crony capitalism' or 'nomenklatura privatization' that became common in other parts of the post-communist world. Two camps could be discerned on the nature and especially the pace of privatization. The first were those still in power in various ministries and enterprises. These generally preferred slow privatization or even just leasing, so as to 'maintain control over their valuable empires'. The other group, consisting of new reformers and particularly clustered around the Ministry of Privatization, pushed for swift and largely unqualified privatization. The latter group prevailed, and in so doing, helped 'to break the monopoly of the *nomenklatura* and create a new class of small-scale entrepreneurs who would therefore support the reform program and the new government'.[27]

The privatization process prompts a large economic question raised by Western economists as to whether privatization in itself was insufficient to restructure these economies.[28] The political and social aims of privatization, especially by voucher, was not entirely based on economic sense. In a measure atypical of post-communist privatiz-ation, anyone could submit proposals to buy state property being tendered for privatization. But this did not mean that the most suitable candidates were making bids. It also meant that, with restrictions on foreign participation, voucher privatization starved the Czech economy of foreign capital. And, generally, Czech companies under total or majority foreign-ownership have outperformed indigenously-owned firms both domestically and internationally. Examples are found in truck and bus production, with Karosa and Avia prospering after the acceptance of eventual majority foreign-ownership, while Liaz and Tatra relied on Czech investment and faced escalating debts and layoffs.[29]

In statistical terms, privatization was a success; by the end of 1994, 80 percent of the economy was privately owned.[30] The Privatization

Ministry was formally closed in 1996. Even with privatization of some major industries still to be undertaken, the contribution of state-owned enterprises to the Czech economy became less than that of Italy or France.[31] But this masks features of the economic transformation that remain a problem, including industrial restructuring and the redistribution of the work force.

While the socioeconomic and class restructuring of Czech society is considered presently, some concluded that the privatization process did not result in new management and owners. From the outset, some economists concluded generally that in Eastern Europe, the 'transition is being directed and driven by those same people who had misdirected and defended the politico-economic status quo before 1989'.[32] In the Czech Republic by 1996 privatization 'left a very scattered share ownership' and continued privatization promised that 'participants' motives will be regarded with the greatest suspicion by both workers and management',[33] thereby further undermining the economic success of the process. But takeovers of firms by their communist-era managers are relatively few in the Czech Republic compared to almost anywhere else in the post-communist world.[34]

The professionalism, reliability and general utility of investment funds have also often been questioned. As Czech economists have noted, legislative control was lacking on the 500 funds in the country and 'the rules for their establishment were sketchy and their founders were not required to give proof of competence'. In addition, 'few appeared to have any staff qualified to make decisions or, with any experience in the financial sector'.[35]

Privatization also meant that ownership was left murky and the development of corporate governance undeveloped. Even economists otherwise approving of Czech privatization warn 'the Czech system is not yet a model for corporate governance in transitional economies, because it is not yet clear how the Czech system will evolve'.[36] Privatization also gave rise to corruption, including the conviction of Jaroslav Lizner, Director of the voucher privatization agency, for accepting bribes of 8 million Crowns in the second wave of privatization. Kožen also claimed that he had extensive details on official corruption, but it is important to note that Czech privatization has generally been considered more legal and proper than elsewhere in Eastern Europe.

In other areas of ground-breaking market developments there are serious economic, social and political consequences. TV Nova's February 1994 launch signalled the start of the first private national, and commercial, television station in the post-socialist bloc. It overcame Klaus' hesitation about journalists by granting him a free weekly 5-minute broadcast, the calculated value of which is $38,000. Klaus' combined airtime vastly outflanked that offered to his political rival Zeman. TV Nova's general practice led the Czech Republic's broadcasting board to fear, as one observer commented, 'that a country that once had a state television monopoly now has commercial monopoly'.[37]

But many timebombs from privatization would remain. Economically, large segments of heavy industry continued either directly or indirectly under state control, as did the banks. Indeed, the issue of major ownership was complicated because state-run banks tend still to have controlling interests in precisely the enterprises that have not yet been subject to full market forces. *The Economist* magazine declared voucher privatization 'has failed dismally in the Czech Republic' even though similar forms have worked in the Baltic.[38] In view of the pioneering nature and successes of Czech voucher privatization, this may be unduly harsh; the achievements of privatization in the Czech Republic are neither myth nor miracle but include elements of both.

INDUSTRIAL RESTRUCTURING

A subsidiary feature of privatization was industrial restructuring, which had implications not only for the amount of the economy produced by the private sector but also its competitive nature and the distribution of the workforce throughout the economy.[39] The command economy supported selected industries, particularly heavy industry at the expense of consumer and light goods. This was profoundly so in Czechoslovakia because much of its industrial plant predates communism and is therefore even more outdated than that of its socialist-era neighbours.

With competition came the defeat of outdated and uncompetitive industries. GDP contracted in the Czech Lands by 21 percent between 1990 and 1992, while industrial production fell by 33 percent in the same period. While the decline in GDP effectively ceased in 1993 and generated limited expansion in 1994, industrial production fell again in 1993 and had only a slight increase in 1994.[40]

Nevertheless, relatively few companies went bankrupt, indeed not enough, and less than in the rest of Central Europe. The Czech Republic continues to have a bloated, inefficient economy. Different measures, internal and external, direct and indirect, continue to be taken to restructure the economy. The international economic community has applied explicit pressure for the Czech government to privatize larger industry. For example, the International Finance Corporation, jointly with other leading institutions, issued a US$ 250 million loan to the large Nová Huta steel mill. A condition, however, was that the state reduce its share to a minority position.[41]

Major industry remains owned by large banks, themselves state-owned. This relationship is an unintended parallel with interwar Czechoslovakia in which industry was inexorably connected to the banks. Privatization of either large industrial enterprises or of the major banks is unlikely to occur without privatization of the other: this interdependence will complicate and impede the privatization of both important sectors. While the Czech state-owned banks often control unprivatized large industry it may also be that, because of the banks' own financial problems, they will be less likely to finance uncertain or unviable industries. Tošovský explained after resuming his post of Central Banker late in 1998 that Czech banks were unlikely to save troubled companies because, still being predominantly state-owned, they were conservative in their lending.

One of the key overall changes that Klaus and Ježek prescribed was the liquidation of economic activities. They noted that new economic activity would only come with the death of the old and stipulated that the '*Exit* [from the market] has more significance than entry'. It is perhaps the close of that sentence which is most revealing: Exit 'is more difficult to administer'.[42] The country experiences a psychological resistance to making people unemployed. As one manager of a privatized brewery confided, 'Firing people is not something that we do here'.

Czechoslovak, and its successor Czech privatization, was a great experiment. It succeeded in privatizing much of the Czech economy and exposing people to the practices of the market. But in economic terms, it is still deemed not to have gone far enough. Even in 1998 the International Monetary Fund (IMF) recommended to the Czech government that it accelerate privatization.[43] Industrial restructuring must continue, and with that, the nature and distribution of the Czech work force.

RESTRUCTURING THE WORKFORCE, UNEMPLOYMENT AND LABOUR PRODUCTIVITY

The Czech transformation was striking for its absence of unemployment. For several years post-communist Czechoslovakia and the Czech

Republic led all of Europe in having the lowest unemployment, which stood below 3 percent. Prague was said to have 'negative unemployment' because jobs could not be filled, particularly in services relating to its booming tourist trade.

Under communism no real labour market existed; until about 1960 workers were generally assigned to companies. And while there was some labour mobility thereafter, centrally-fixed wages were an impediment to worker commitment and innovation. The lack of competition in the socialist economy meant that inefficient firms sold uncompetitive or even utterly undesired goods and employed unmotivated but complacent staff. The expectation of a full-scale transformation, as launched in the Czech Republic, would mean, in principle, wholesale unemployment as inefficacious firms and workers were pushed out of the market.

But, in practice, mass unemployment did not materialize; it would only be in the later 1990s that unemployment would become statistically significant. But this record was double-edged. It hid both in rhetoric and reality the fact that full restructuring had not occurred and that more of the workforce would face layoffs. Part of Klaus' success was a 'tripartite' management of the economy by which government, trade unions and business met and agreed major aspects of the transition, particularly on wages and social security. These arrangements were set out in lengthy written documents entitled 'the General Agreement of the Czech Republic'.[44] Called, tellingly, the Council for Social and Economic Accord, this forum particularly attempted to avoid, or at least settle, social disputes. It sought not only to build consensus but also to ease in effect the pressures of industrial restructuring on the workforce. The free-market Klaus government also undertook numerous measures to reduce the count of the unemployed and the actual measures that would render people unemployed. On the official calculation of low unemployment one Czech economist comments: 'part of the explanation ... [was] the sizeable reduction in labor force participation of both women and older workers in the first two years of transition in the Czech Republic'.[45]

Unemployment was also kept down by making people seek work. Differentiating itself from some countries in the region, the Czech Republic operated 'very tight conditions' for people to receive unemployment assistance. This was also for limited periods a regime which compelled the unemployed to seek work.[46] Not only has the redistribution of the workforce not been completed but the quality and productivity of its labour has not been adequately improved. As a Czech economist notes, 'By 1994 the Czech economy had gone through a slower and less complete labor adjustment than the Polish and Hungarian economies, where labor productivity started approaching the pre-transition levels'.[47]

Trade and Industry Minister Vladimír Dlouhý encouraged foreign investment particularly by arguing that the Czech Republic had a skilled work force, generally cost only one-fifteenth of the price of comparable work in neighbouring Germany. While such logic holds, and the OECD among others lauded the ability of Czech workers, Czech labour productivity was considered to be only one-third of the EU average.[48] Even Dlouhý came to recognize that Czech labour productivity was unacceptably low.

To some extent, the communist-era work ethic remained: as one Czech social scientist observed, 'For the majority, jobs continue to be "socialist": easily available and poorly rewarded. Only for a limited but still increasing number of workers are jobs—especially the genuine "service class" jobs—becoming "capitalist" in that the requirements and salaries are high'.[49]

Even with governmental measures, low unemployment would not last. Previously under 3 percent, the unemployment figure crawled up to 4 percent at the beginning of 1997, even though it dipped to 3.8 percent in April.[50] By January 1999, however, unemployment officially stood at 7.48 percent.[51]

The rise in unemployment is a necessary feature of transition; in the Czech Republic it was simply one that, especially for political expediency, was massaged oratorically and delayed practically. The increase in unemployment in the later 1990s demonstrates all the more the need to build social safety nets alongside the new labour market. The political salience of social security contributed greatly to the 1997 defeat of the centre-right government and to the 1998 electoral successes of the centre-left.

PRICE LIBERALIZATION

Privatization was by itself insufficient to recreate market mechanisms in the transition process. In command economies money lacked the role of its capitalist counterparts: a rational allocator of value. Money had to be made into a recognized representation of value. Both goods and labour in the socialist economy had values arbitrarily assigned by central planners. Not only was value distorted in the domestic economy but it also made international trade meaningless. Prices, therefore, had to have meaning and currency had to become a rational allocator of value within the country and a means of facilitating exchange with the outside world.

In addition to being arbitrarily set, prices were low because the actual cost of production (regardless of whether the production was efficient or not) was subsidized by the socialist system. Part of the subsidization came from the price of consumer durables being set arbitrarily high in order to subsidize the cost of non-durables, particularly food. Post-communist Czech reformers needed prices to reflect the real value of commodities and to reduce and eventually eliminate subsidies. To achieve these ends, prices were liberalized on 1 January 1991, following Poland, as mentioned, by precisely one year. While both countries were committed to forms of shock therapy, the Czechoslovaks benefitted from going second. They observed the experience in their reforming northern neighbour and could prepare the population, at least verbally, for such price increases. Prices generally rose by 75 percent in a single increment, with a further increase in 1992. Between the end of communism and the June 1992 elections, prices for meat increased 166 percent, dairy products 275 percent, and textiles and shoes 158 and 221 percent.[52] While these figures may seem, and to the Czech consumer were, in fact large increases and more than those endured in gradualist-reform Hungary, they were not generally as severe as those in Poland.

Consumers in the Czech Republic also faced the imposition of a new consumers' tax which coincided with the birth of the new state. The tax had the effect of raising food prices by an average of 8 percent.[53] By 1994 the remainder of price controls were removed throughout the economy, save for rent and energy, which became politically sensitive issues. Klaus' ODS tended to support the abolition of price controls, albeit gradually, while the left-wing ČSSD opposed them. Energy price increases and the removal of rent controls also became delicate issues during the collapse of Klaus' government in 1997 and the creation of its temporary successor under Tošovský. But that government approved energy and rental price hikes on 11 March 1998, to come into effect in July. The price of electricity and gas was expected to increase by 24 percent and 27 percent respectively, while rent, including that of many tenants in privately-owned accommodation, would also climb by 27 percent. A 7.5 percent increase in pensions was announced at the same time.[54]

Because virtually all prices were set under communism, inflation was also a function of central planning. The price rises that occurred following the removal of central pricing and production subsidies brought inflation. Seeing that some 1990 prices may have been set as long ago as the 1950s, the increase would be substantial, causing considerable inflation. Inflation was 1.4 percent in 1989 and jumped to 10 percent in 1990. With price liberalization on 1 January 1991 inflation jumped, understandably, by 58 percent, and settled down in 1992 to 11 percent, climbing to 21 percent in 1993 and back to 10 percent in 1994.[55] The effects of inflation were limited because the Czech Central Bank pursued a tight monetary policy; this may have aided consumers, but it incurred the criticism of Klaus and Dlouhý who argued that the policy may have also limited economic growth.

The implementation of the last stages of price liberalization were hindered by politics, the plans of the Klaus government to increase rent and fuel prices incurring popular resistance. The Tošovský government also planned to continue these changes. In 1997 and 1998 the Social Democrats capitalized on the effects of these increases on lower or fixed income earners, contributing to their electoral success. But Czech prices are now overwhelmingly determined by the market.

CURRENCY REFORM AND CONVERTIBILITY

As with prices, so currency denotes value. The Czechoslovak Crown under communism was meaningless as an instrument of domestic or international exchange. But the post-communist Czechoslovak reformers were in a favourable position regarding currency reform. They inherited some foreign exchange reserves and a small foreign debt. They devalued the currency and established a fixed exchange rate but allowed for limited convertibility within the country. Czechoslovaks were allowed initially to exchange up to 2,000 Crowns, then 5,000 Crowns, the fact of the transaction recorded in their passports. Internal convertibility undercut the blackmarket trade in currency.

Klaus was cautious about making the Crown fully convertible. Admitting that there are advantages to introducing full convertibility, he argued for gradual convertibility for three reasons. First, he contended, the Czech economic transformation and the economy as a whole needed to be, and had been secured by a firm nominal exchange rate. The second reason was that full convertibility would end the state's ability to have an autonomous monetary and financial or macroeconomic policy, allowing the economy to be conditioned by outside forces, a feature Klaus thought inappropriate to his country which had a purposeful and rational policy already and was not in need of disciplining. The third reason maintained that full convertibility would unduly expose the Czech economy to the instability caused by the brisk movement of capital searching for better interest rates. He therefore considered full convertibility to be a medium- or even long-term aim.[56]

On the regional level, Klaus sought to extricate Czechoslovakia from communist economic structures. The CMEA was presented as a regional economic forum, even an Eastern European equivalent to Western Europe's common market, when in reality it served as a larger, Moscow-driven planning agency for the socialist bloc. While Czechoslovakia's initial political foreign policy did not lobby for the dismantling of the Warsaw Pact,[57] its economic foreign policy unambiguously pressed for the termination of the CMEA. This was achieved in 1991. Part of the rationale was to avoid artificial distortions to Czechoslovak trade but also to remove communist influence on the international convertibility of its currency.

The post-communist reform of currency required an added dimension following the Velvet Divorce. On 8 February 1993, the two republics split the Czechoslovak currency, imposing limitations on withdrawals from bank accounts to facilitate the introduction of two separate national currencies. Much as independent Czechoslovakia had sought to distance itself from Austria-Hungary in 1918 with the prompt introduction of a new national currency, the government of the new Czech Republic was keen to launch a new currency. Initially, just as 'Czechoslovakia' was stamped on old Austro-Hungarian notes after 1918, 'Czech' was stamped on defunkt Czechoslovak 1000- and 500-Crown notes. Czech National Bank Vice Governor Miroslav Keroušsaid this was done not out of tradition but 'technicality'.[58]

The Czech Crown was tied to a currency basket made first of five foreign currencies in which the Deutschmark and US Dollar were the most important, and then one composed of a 65 percent D-Mark weighting and 35 percent US Dollar. The exchange rate remained fixed between 1991 and 1997. Its convertibility was also gradually introduced so it was freely convertible even for current account transactions and partly for capital account transactions by 1 October 1995. The management of the Czech Crown seemed successful. The overall prosperity of the Czech economy, particularly the influx of foreign capital, initially resulted in calls for a *re*valuation of the currency. But this scenario ended as the strong currency contributed to an increasing Czech trade; the currency was allowed to float freely on 26 May 1997 after a major attack by speculative investors, and during the monetary crisis of summer 1997 the Crown suffered historic lows against the Dollar and Deutschmark. The Crown was devalued during the economic crisis that followed but, even at the time of the June 1998 elections several leading investment houses considered it as much as 15 percent overvalued.

Currency will continue to be a problem for the Czechs and devaluation is not a panacea. It was anticipated to aid some sectors, particularly steel, which are capable of increasing their production rapidly. But the benefits are outweighed and it is not a long-term solution.[59] Finance Minister Pilip was unhappy with the Crown's strengthening in early 1998, warning that it could lead to economic 'instability'.[60]

FINANCIAL INSTITUTIONS AND BANKING

Central to the post-communist economic transition is the creation of financial markets. Under communism, capital for investment was centrally allocated. It was therefore imperative, as with consumer goods and labour, to create mechanisms to allow for their supply and exchange. The Prague Stock Exchange was established following voucher privatization; it initially opened only for a half-day each week, requiring over a year before functioning full-time. Once operational, the Czech Republic's financial institutions took long to accommodate to Western standards. Two foreign observers wrote in 1994:

> the capital markets are still lacking in much of the infrastructure necessary to attract issuers and investors. Basic informational documents such as annual reports and quarterly financial statements, essential to informed investment decision making, are not widely available. Most companies do not yet have the expertise of records with which to produce them. The legal and regulatory framework to ensure transparency in the capital markets is also rudimentary. While basic security laws exist or are being drafted, they are often ambiguous and ridden with loopholes. Even where laws exist, there are no credible enforcement mechanisms owing to a lack of trained lawyers and judges.[61]

The lack of legal and bureaucratic provision for the establishment of financial markets has blighted the Czech transition. The Czech Republic is especially lacking in laws to combat money laundering.[62] Its insufficient copyright laws earned the country criticism, being cited as a major producer of pirated CDs.[63] The lack of legal controls in the financial sector was a result of the laisser-faire attitude of the Klaus government. These liberals 'considered laws that would protect the privatization process from abuse as an unnecessary hindrance. First, they argued, you need to create a market, and its "invisible hand" will take care of the rest'.[64] Havel has criticised the lack of bureaucratic reform arguing that it has done 'a great deal of damage' to the country'.[65] More Czech small businesses were concerned with difficult bureaucratic procedures than their counterparts in post-communist Europe,[66] while the European Bank for Reconstruction and Development's 1998 *Transition Report* found that, of Central and East European states, only Poland and Hungary had engaged in significant institutional reform.

Even more damaging than the lack of legal provisions is the charge against the Czech Republic of being a prime example of 'financial anarchy' in the post-communist world.[67] Its banks have been the soft underbelly of the entire transition, weakening the economy in practice and the country's economic reputation abroad. This must come as a surprising development, not least because the Czech Republic was the first Central European country to privatize a bank. And Klaus, as the birth of the Czech Republic approached, told EBRD President Jacques Attali that that the Czech Government would not provide state guarantees for the EBRD's Czech operation, instead encouraging direct cooperation with private sector banks without state involvement.

In reality, virtually none of the banking sector has been privatized, remaining substantially in direct state control or run by the National Property Fund. A comparative study of Central European small privatization found Czech banks accounted for disproportionately little financing investment.[68]

More significantly, in 1995 banks began collapsing, with 12 bankrupt in the next two years, prompting the first financial disaster for the Czech Republic and denting both domestic and international confidence in the Czech economic miracle. Due to bad loans and insufficient funds to cover for private deposits banks were unable to provide cash for customers' withdrawals. But because of a general lack of information on the status of banks (a problem in itself) the population was unaware of the situation. The manifestations of the Czech banking crisis were distinct from the classic situation of clients queuing for withdrawals (with the exception of Banka Bohemia). The Czech government also repaid much of the lost savings. Nevertheless, the crisis had made public the unaccountable ownership of banks and the lack of transparency that allowed those with inside knowledge to make corrupt deals and to clean out—to tunnel, as the expression became—the holdings of the banks. Other scandals came to public knowledge in April and May 1997. One concerned Kreditní Banka which had collapsed due to loans to relatives of the management. Even though the government knew of the Bank's operations since 1993 no investigation was undertaken until considerable opposition pressure was placed on Klaus' minority coalition after the June 1996 elections. In another case, two senior managers of IPB, the Czech Republic's third largest bank, were charged with embezzlement and misuse of internal information. They were arrested to prevent them from prejudicing witnesses.

General responsibility was pointed at the Klaus government for allowing such banking fraud to develop through its failure to reform this sector, particularly its 'nonchalant approach' to closing legal loop-holes.[69] But the few arrests and the government's pledge in 1996 to 'clean-up' banking did not reassure the public. And regardless of responsibility, financial costs were incurred universally: public money equivalent to 8 percent of the Czech Republic's 1995 GDP went to repaying savings lost in Czech banks.[70] By early 1998, at least 163 billion Crowns of public money went to shore up Czech banks, most of which was unrecoverable.[71]

While economists both within and outside the Czech Republic called for bank privatization, the real outcome was political wrangling that delayed bank privatization further. Unsurprisingly, the opposition ČSSD capitalized on the embarrassment for the Klaus government. Even the government-coalition partner KDU-ČSL joined with the ČSSD in opposing the privatization of the IPB bank, calling the sale 'nontransparent', and demanding that future purchases of banks require Cabinet approval.

The collapse of Klaus' government was sparked in part by the banking crisis. This also left bank privatization in limbo. Klaus' government had approved the sale of controlling shares of Československá Obchodní Banka and minority shares of Komerční and Česká Spořitelna. Shortly before the coalition collapsed, Finance Minister Pilip announced that the four largest banks would be privatized before the close of 1997. In March 1998 he said that the terms for the privatization of these three main state-owned banks would be made during the Tošovský government. Meanwhile, bank shares lost value (Komerční lost 7 percent on 3 February 1998), and Tošovský pledged to accelerate bank privatization. Zeman, however, gained popularity by calling for tighter reviews of bank privatization and pledging to halt it until at least 2000.[72] The cost of bailing out state-owned banks, and Western calls for bank privatization will, however, likely move the Social Democrat government to proceed nevertheless with bank privatization before then.

Economic issues compound the political issues pertaining to Czech banks, particularly regarding loans. For example, the Komerční, the largest bank in the Czech Republic and indeed in Central Europe, had received neither interest nor principal payment on a fifth of its loans. As one report concluded: 'These cases make a mockery of claims from Czech bankers that their loan books are not as bad as they look. Their reports show that nearly a third of all outstanding provisions and collateral are woefully insufficient'.[73]

The Czech Republic's three largest banks remain on the privatization bloc, a process which may be aided by expressions of interest of minority shares by the EBRD and International Finance Corporation. But Czech banking, with its unclear practices, state-involvement and extensive cross-ownership, remains a sector of the Czech economy in need of further transformation.

FOREIGN TRADE AND INVESTMENT

Domestic liberalization has been dovetailed by international liberalization. Trade is key to the overall buoyancy and success of the Czech economy. Even before absorption into the Habsburg Monarchy, Bohemia had diversified trade, particularly with Western Europe. Trade was crucial to the economy of interwar Czechoslovakia, being one of the greatest trading nations of the age, and remains so now for the Czech Republic. The ethos of trade for the Czechs may be demonstrated in the annual Brno industrial trade show. Run for nearly four decades, it is among the largest in the world and operated without state subsidy. Major Czech industries also indicate the nation's proclivity to trade, including its historical and international reputation in such industries as vehicles, glass, optics, electronics and arms.

The Czech Republic wants to be a trading nation, deeply integrated into the European and world economy. Post-communist Czechoslovakia took strides in reintegrating the country into world financial institutions and the global market. Reintegration and improving Czechoslovakia's balance of payments was a particular challenge as the communist

No

regime had run a negative balance of trade. Ironically, the only area of Czechoslovak foreign trade which was positive was that dealing with developing countries, particularly Ba'athist regimes in the Middle East, and notably Iraq. Much of this trade was financed by Czechoslovak credits, which was a risky practice regardless, but one exacerbated when Prague joined the US-led alliance against Iraq in the second Gulf War in 1990–91. Post-communist Czechoslovakia's change in politics and foreign policy also meant that it jeopardized many of these trading relations. Havel's support for the Dalai Lama threatened, although ultimately did not sever, Czech trade ties with China, although links with Cuba and North Korea virtually collapsed over his pursuit of human rights issues.

Prague moved towards economic reintegration. In 1990 it regained IMF membership and secured most-favoured nation status from the US. Thereafter, the Czech Republic took at least some measures to make itself accessible and attractive to foreign investors. For example, its levels of protection were deemed considerably lower than the OECD average.[74] From a bureaucratic point of view, 100 multinational corporations working in the region found the Czech Republic had the most straightforward customs procedures.[75] Noting in particular the consequences of the May 1997 devaluation of the Crown, Klaus also wanted the Czech Republic to have balanced trade.

Achieving new trading practices and patterns meant a wholesale change in trading patterns. The redirection of post-communist Czech trade from its former socialist partners to Western, capitalist markets ranks high as one of the major aims and achievements of the reforms. This was both an economic and political imperative; trading with viable economies would not only force Czech industry to be more efficient and competitive but also would symbolically denote the nation's extraction from the East and its rightful return to the West. But so successful did Czechoslovakia's economic reorientation seem that it led to fears of 'foreign domination'. This section first considers the creation and preservation of trading relations with Slovakia and changed trade with Russia before considering the impact of the influx of German foreign capital and the process of integrating the Czech Republic into the European Union.

The greatest economic challenge to the newborn Czech Republic was expected to come from the separation from Slovakia. Slovakia was the Czech Republic's largest trading partner and the Czech National Bank estimated in 1993 that exports to Slovakia could decline by 30 percent, a situation compounded by the inability of many Slovak firms to pay invoices.[76] But Prague managed the issue successfully, even creating benefits from necessity. The Czech Republic shed financial responsibility for some Slovak projects, including the Gabčikovo-Nagymaros dam, military conversion and some nuclear power plants (although the Czech Republic faced problems of its own). In other areas, political agreements streamlined the economic fallout. The November 1992 law on the separation of the federation agreed that fixed assets located in one republic would become its property. Otherwise, in accordance with the ratio of Czechs to Slovaks in the population, federal property was generally to be divided 2:1, from military hardware to the national debt.

Trade was to be managed by the Council of the Customs Union, as agreed on 18 January 1993, to be chaired by Vladimír Dlouhý and based in Bratislava. The establishment of new economic relations was not always smooth; Slovakia frequently broke the customs union and challenged the division of some federal property, including 4 tons of gold, ownership of the national airline and specific government buildings in Prague. Slovak banks had also incurred debts to the Czech Republic. In order to force an agreement on the division of outstanding federal property, on 17 March 1993 Klaus announced the suspension of the transfer of shares from the first wave of voucher privatization to Slovak citizens.

Economic legacies also meant that the two countries would duplicate each other's production and compete counterproductively. For example, Czechoslovakia was licensed to produce the Soviet T-72 main battle tank. Slovakia produced a new version of the T-72 with the assistance of four West European arms companies only to have the Czech Republic undertake another remake of the tank with a French company. Ultimately, the Czech Republic has recovered economically from the split. Indeed, Klaus' disbelief in the co-existence of two economies in one country—although this was as much a political point as an economic principle—has been confirmed by the entry of the Czech Republic into EU accession talks ahead of Slovakia.

The successful reorientation of the Czech economy from the socialist world is evident in statistics; over 60 percent of communist Czechoslovakia's trade was with fellow socialist states. This dropped to 50 percent in 1990, and continued to fall to 40 percent in 1991 and by 1992 was only 20 percent of Czechoslovak trade.[77]

The Czech Republic did not reject trade agreements which were rational. The Soviet successor states have provided a market for Czech products from beer to locomotives and electrical train components.[78] The expectation was that contracts with Russia would ease the financial problems of several major Czech enterprises and prospective Czech-Russian joint ventures could eventually increase Czech output.[79]

While forging new trade links, energy dependency remains for the Czech Republic, a legacy of Czechoslovakia's asymmetrical relationship to the Soviet Union. The Czech government has been intent on diversifying its energy sources, signing deals with new oil suppliers such as Norway, and participating in the construction of a new gas pipeline from Germany. Nevertheless, structural limitations remain. For example, Russia is the sole producer of nuclear fuel for the types of reactors used at the Czech Dukovaný power plant. Ironically, it was the Czech Republic which had problems because the Russian supplier halted supplies of the fuel due to non-payment of debts.[80] Russia only accounts for 5 percent of Czech exports; the Russian crisis of 1998 therefore had a manageable impact on the Czech Republic. The Czech Republic now has a good economic arrangement with the Russian Federation.

The Czech Republic has been keen to be involved in trade and foreign investment. Opening the Czech economy to such opportunities has, however, provoked political and cultural problems, in particular in its relations with Germany. Britain and France were interwar Czechoslovakia's primary trading partners; after 1989 Germany and Austria assumed those positions. Germany also led very substantially in foreign investment, and the two countries accounted for 90 percent of all foreign investment in post-communist Czechoslovakia. While American investment increased in 1993 and thereafter, many Czechs were worried about possible Germanization. The Czechoslovak Ambassador to Washington summarized this feeling in February 1990 by declaring:

> The German-speaking parts of Europe, including Austria, will succeed where the Hapsburgs, Hitler and Bismarck were unsuccessful—in Germanizing Central and Eastern Europe by purely peaceful and laudable methods of market economic development.[81]

Czech newspapers feature cartoons of German Chancellor Helmut Kohl driving a Mercedes through Czechoslovakia or roadsigns, shaped like the country, declaring 'Tschechoslowakei: Zimmer Frei'. Fears mounted that German economic influence would translate into political leverage.[82] The first Czech Minister for Economic Cooperation, Stanislav Bělehrádek, noted in February 1993 that 47 Czech newspapers were now under German ownership, some sold by local officials under 'suspicious circumstances'. He added that these takeovers could influence the 1994 local elections.[83] German acquisition of Czech print media has continued and includes major dailies like *Mladá front Dnes* and *Lidové noviny*. Czech politicians have responded to Czech fears of foreign, especially German, economic influence, by proclaiming that capital is not national or political but simply international and economically-motivated. But newspapers in 1998 still asked why more American investment has not been forthcoming.

Part of the answer may be that the Czech Republic does not do enough to attract foreign investment. As mentioned, Dlouhý stressed the low costs of Czech labour, but even his CzechInvest Agency, dedicated to securing foreign investment and advocating the elimination of trade restrictions, was stymied by the Ministry of Finance. CzechInvest claimed that it could document lost investment worth $1 billion. Indirectly, the Klaus government also sought to curb the strength of labour unions. Otherwise, however, the Klaus government differentiated itself from Western governments by generally not offering concessions to potential foreign investors. Indeed, while Klaus was pleased when Japan's Nomura showed interest in Investiční a Poštovní Banka, the Czech Republic's third largest bank, he had previously opposed foreign ownership of such institutions. The Klaus government's view effectively said: 'the Czech Republic should be an attractive enough investment location without the need for additional incentives'.[84]

Often, the Cabinet demanded guarantees (as it is entitled to do) from foreign investors. When, for example, after much competition from British Aerospace, a combined offer by Boeing and Czech Airlines ČSA to purchase a 34 percent stake in Aero Vodochody was accepted by the Cabinet on 30 March 1998, the buyers had to put forward nearly a billion dollars of guaranteed credits and are obliged to remain investors in the company until the credits expire at the end of 2008.

The Czech government was intent—with certain caveats discussed in the next chapter notwithstanding—on integrating the country into the European Union. To this end, Czechoslovakia signed an Association Agreement with the EC in December 1991, along with, although separately from, Poland and Hungary. The Czechoslovak Association Agreement had to be renegotiated after the split, the Czech successor agreement being signed on 1 February 1995. The Republic applied for EU membership on 17 January 1996. It was one of five post-communist countries, along with Cyprus, that were judged by the EU to have made sufficient economic and political progress in their transformations in order to commence accession talks with Brussels. The EU's assessment was made on the basis of three broad criteria: democratic credentials, the quality of market reforms and the expected capacity to compete within the EU's internal market; and the ability to meet convergence criteria. The European Commission announced on 15 July 1997 that it would begin accession talks, but that the process would take at least four years.

Talks with the EU have not always been straightforward. The EU, for its part, faulted the Czech Republic for its failure to reform its arms sales industry and banking sector. Classed before the end of the Cold War as the world's fifth largest arms exporter in absolute terms—and the largest in per capita terms—the Czech Republic remained attracted to arms sales, provoking a particular crisis over arms sales to Algeria. While military sales have slumped in all East European countries after communism, it was specifically the Czech Republic (and perhaps Bulgaria) that was considered capable by outside observers of salvaging its arms industry.[85]

The Czech Republic was deemed overall to have a functioning market economy. However, it was faulted for inadequate oversight of banks and the capital markets. Also, it applied unilateral import quotas on apples from the EU, which led to the EU's imposition of a 100 percent import tariff on Czech pork, poultry and cider. Prague rescinded its April 1997 import quotas five months later, after Agenda 2000. Further problems with agricultural relations can be expected. Klaus particularly has been known for his ambiguous, even hostile and arrogant stance towards the EU (see Chapter 4).

Despite these difficulties, the Czechs are keen to show that they are doing more than is necessary to meet the criteria for accession. According to Jan Amos Havelka of CzechInvest: 'The massive drop in our farming subsidies is just one instance in which the Czech government is actively preparing for entry to the European Union prior to accession negotiations'.[86] For the most part, Czech preparation for EU membership must now concentrate on enacting domestic reforms, including legal and bureaucratic practice.

While trade has been successfully reoriented westward, development within the country, both societally and geographically, has been inconsistent. This section offers an overview of changes in the Czech Republic where the economic transformation has bisected social life. These include unemployment and social inequalities, the environment and pollution, and the provision of healthcare.

First, however, the unevenness of economic change is evident in the metamorphosis of Prague relative to the rest of the country. On the surface, most towns have enjoyed some economic development. At a minimum, town squares have been refurbished. Often, however, these are cosmetic changes, and ones that do not extend far or widely into small towns or rural areas. Instead, Prague has been the main recipient of foreign investment and of tourism. Already the consideration of changing distributions of employment highlighted the capital city's unique paucity of available labour. The Czech Statistical Office's own quantitative maps illustrate the economic divergence in the country. Prague and its immediate area are featured as bright red, showing the most economic growth, while lighter shades of red and pink extend outwards, marking much more limited development.

Prague has benefitted immensely from tourism. But tourism is an underdeveloped and a fluctuating industry. Komárek identified such economic possibilities immediately after the Velvet Revolution by observing that his country only gained one-fiftieth of the US$10 billion generated by tourism annually in Austria.[87] In the early 1990s Prague became 'the' European city to visit for foreigners, boosting the country's hard currency earnings. And while the Czech Association of Travel Agencies calculated foreign currency earnings of US$3.75 billion in 1997,[88] the Ministry of Regional Development registered a 10.5 percent decline in foreign currency earnings from tourism in that year over 1996. Substantial in its own right, this was also the first decline in tourist revenues in the history of the Czech Republic,[89] and suggests that it cannot be relied on as an economic pillar.

Prague's economy is also derived from industries resulting from foreign interest and domestic need, such as construction. While construction went into recession in 1997, due especially to cuts in government orders, the construction of houses and flats expanded. But these increases were localized around Prague.[90] Generally, construction company profits declined by 56 percent in 1997, although increases early in 1998 suggested an upturn.[91] Recognition of the capital's economic standing is seen in the government's rent increases, which were 14 percent higher in Prague than in the rest of the country.[92]

Just as there is a sense of growing geographic inequality, so too is there increased social stratification. We have already seen how economic reform aimed to be a democratizer—democratic in the sense of involving and enriching as many citizens as possible. Unlike elsewhere, even in Poland and Hungary, the lack of communist-era political reform in Czechoslovakia meant that vested interests were relatively few. To recount but one external assessment, 'The Czech government was able to enact a privatization program that was not designed to appeal to the special interests of sectoral insiders, but rather relied on the support of wide masses of the population for a very open and competitive privatization process'.[93]

The Czech transformation, especially privatization, must be among the most fair and honest of all the post-communist world. As mentioned earlier, unlike in many other transition societies, large-scale crony capitalism has been very uncommon in the Czech Republic. But popular perceptions suggest otherwise. In an article suitably translated as 'From unjust equality to just inequality?', Czech sociologists Petr Matějů and Blanka Řeháková found that 93 percent of Czechs and Slovaks believed inequality had grown and found it objectionable.[94] Czechs still believe that 'it remains clear that on average it is mostly former Communists who still enjoy significantly better positions than people who never were Communist Party members'. The most likely explanation for this derives from deploying their communist-era assets and connections to the capitalist environment.[95] A particular case arose, albeit in the very early stages of transition, in the southern Moravian town on Hodonín where the local office of Civic Forum published a list of communist managers who were using their economic power to thwart democratic reformers.[96]

Nevertheless, if there was a pronounced 'mafia' in post-communist Czechoslovakia it was probably felt, ironically, to be one of dissidents and intellectuals[97] rather than nomenklatura. The average Czech's view stems partly from an ingrained sense—whether true or mythical—of egalitarianism as a characteristic of Czech society. This is a notion to which we will return briefly in the final chapter.

The practical significance of this view is tangible, taking the form of electoral support for left-wing parties and echoes earlier sentiments in Czech political history. Socialist parties garnered 47.6 percent of the vote in the 1920 elections. This trend seems particularly relevant in explaining the electoral success of the Social Democrats in 1996 when industrial workers clearly began to associate their socioeconomic interests with that party.[98]

These views are all the more surprising because quantitative sociological studies find Czech society to have the least conflict between rich and poor among Central European countries. The Czech Republic achieved the lowest poverty rate in the entire post-communist world.[99] In some ways, this was probably reinforced by the communist legacy which reinterpreted rights as economic rights, and thus guaranteed health care, housing and work. In addition, Czechs are inclined to believe that success is determined foremost by 'hard work' rather than family background, connections and social attributes like ethnicity or religion.[100]

Some enterprise managers thought that mass privatization would generate 'a large number of small shareholders unable to exercise effective governance'.[101] Provision by the government of bids competing against those of insiders minimized this scenario. The concentration of voucher shares in investment funds, while suggesting that Czechs forfeited being active shareholders, nevertheless also helped to build corporate governance. Czech managers also did not make that many bids for their own companies and were not routinely successful when they did.

Regardless of the truth of perceptions of social stratification, the economic transformation in the Czech Republic, as elsewhere in post-communist Europe, has adversely affected those on fixed incomes. This is true not only of pensioners but also of government employees and even the medical profession. Often these people undertook additional work to supplement their incomes. Recognizing the need for a professional and committed administration, the Czech government introduced a 25 percent wage increase in 1992 for those who forewent work on the side.

More broadly, the Czech Republic has witnessed numerous labour disputes. There were significant strikes by teachers and health workers in 1995, 1996 and 1997 and by public-sector employees generally in June 1998. Threatened strikes by medical workers in October 1995 even led to the resignation of Health Minister Luděk Rubaš. The government later had a messy labour dispute with the Czech Railway Union, the largest body of workers in the country. By the close of August 1997 the government dismissed 17,000 Czech Railway employees.[102] Labour unions threatened further strike action on

26 March 1998 if Government plans to privatize brown coal enterprises before the June elections went ahead.[103] Similarly, the Czech Railway Union threatened strikes if the government privatized part of the Eastern Bohemia railway (an idea which the government denied planning).[104]

The railways dispute is symptomatic of a wider deficit in the transport sector. It was expected that the government would discontinue over a third of Czech Railways trainlines (although the government planned continued state-control of main lines). In addition, the electricity to the main offices of Czech Railways was cut off at the end of August 1997 because of non-payment of bills.[105]

In July 1997 Klaus consented that a meeting of the Council for Social and Economic Accord had fulfilled many labour demands, including a higher minimum wage, potential improvements to collective bargaining and abandonment of the strike bill, but he still rejected a union offer to support social harmony if the government lifted its austerity programme for six months.[106] While Klaus disagreed in principle with the corporatist system, it and various social welfare schemes anaesthetized social opposition to his reforms. It also won him international praise. As a World Bank study wrote in 1994, 'Like Sweden, but probably more successfully than other countries in Central and Eastern Europe, the Czech Republic has a centralized wage bargaining system in which trade unions are involved both in setting wage norms and enforcing policy. Wage moderation may have helped to maintain employment in state and private enterprises, thus easing the tasks of labor market policy'.[107]

At times, the government's relationships with businesses and unions have been good. Large-scale miners' strikes were threatened throughout northern Bohemia in March 1998 when brown coal companies were slated for privatization. But unions applauded the government when it asked the miners not to strike and offered to negotiate.[108]

Ecological damage and energy consumption, however, remain difficult policy arenas. As the world's former most inefficient energy consumer, the Czech Republic has a tremendous legacy to overcome. Indeed, environmental degradation has been called 'the most serious physical legacy' of communist rule.[109] The Klaus government has been criticized for ignoring this issue, although Klaus was, unsurprisingly, adamant that he had done enough to redress environmental degradation. Those who make this issue a central or especially the solitary concern of their political being would never be satisfied with government initiative. But even in Havel's harsh attack of Klaus' government on 9 December 1997 the President acknowledged the efforts of the government in the environment. Havel said that it would be unreasonable to accuse of it of financially neglecting the environment and he acknowledged improvements in pollution levels. But, he added, it was insufficient to address industrial pollution; instead, clean industries have to be built. External observers called the ČSFR one of the 'most active' post-communist states in initiating environmental legislation. These laws remained in effect in the new Czech state and required compliance with EU standards earlier than stipulated by Brussels.[110]

Satisfying ecological needs is particularly difficult for the transition economies. They are attempting to retain economic performance built on inefficient enterprises with little, if any outside assistance in achieving conversion. Nuclear energy has been another area of attempted reform. Environmentalists hoped that the replacement of Jiří Skalický in 1997, who resigned because of party financial scandals, with Martin Bursík would halt the building of the Temelín nuclear power plant. But the project proceeded, and despite popular environmental concerns, 69 percent of the population support the construction of Temelín.[111] When an American loan for the completion of the Temelín plant was postponed due to Austrian intervention in Washington, Klaus retorted: 'This Austrian reaction is really impossible for me. The completion of Temelín is absolutely necessary for us, and all reasonable Austrians within and outside the government know that. Nevertheless, they are playing this card for the election campaign'. Klaus also declared that the ecological 'catastrophe' in the Czech Republic was not in southern Bohemia with nuclear power plants but in northern Bohemia due to coal power plants.[112]

Overall, ecological damage has assumed relatively low political importance. Post-communist Czechoslovakia passed 9 and 8 laws on environmental regulation in 1991 and 1992 respectively. The Czech Republic thereafter had a much thinner record. The position of Klaus' ODS was that the Party had done a sufficient amount for the environment; its philosophical position, supported by centre-right ODA, was that the environment was a 'good' to be treated within the broader economic transformation and thus largely left to market forces. In the 1996 elections all major political parties except the ODS included taxation of environmentally-inefficient or offending companies.[113]

The 9 percent difference in the Czech Republic's health status with that of neighbouring Austria is attributable to air pollution.[114]

Environmental issues thus add to the burden faced by the country's healthcare system which requires a massive financial injection. The post-communist Czechoslovak government, as the Klaus coalition thereafter, tried to redistribute the costs of healthcare through new health insurance funds. But the initial annual budget was already depleted within six months of its start in 1992 and spending in the first half of 1993 already approached that for all of 1992.[115] Klaus also aimed to relieve public health spending with private insurance plans to which all Czechs were obliged to belong. Many of these private insurers proved unable to meet their financial commitments particularly for the payment of prescriptions. The government then absorbed the losses making what was colloquially called a 'donation'. Quite apart from the budgetary implications, the medical insurance program generally caused 'panic' because 'people knew they had to register but did not know how or where'.[116]

The government also tried to ease medical costs to itself by decentralizing the programme to local government and by introducing a system of partial additional fees for medical treatment in 1992. This was done without the requisite regulatory system, which caused 'an entirely predictable cost explosion'.[117] Hospital staff believed the health system to be in such chronic declined that they mounted the Czech Republic's largest strike on 1 November 1995. Quite apart from the deteriorating state of healthcare, doctors' pay remained an issue. The Cabinet was forced to rule in March 1998 that doctors should receive a 4 percent pay increase after doctors and insurance companies failed to reach an agreement.[118]

The opposition defeated a motion by Tošovský's government to introduce charges for hospital stays or doctor consultations. Tensions between health management and medical insurers increased so much in early 1998 that the Association of Czech and Moravian Hospitals threatened to reduce services to critical cases if the deadlock was not broken.[119] Doctors and nurses remain poorly paid. The Czech government proposals to charge 80 Crowns per day for hospital stays and charges for Emergency Room use of 50 Crowns per day and 100 Crowns during evenings and weekends.[120] In the leadup to the June 1998 elections Zeman said he might increase medical insurance rates temporarily by half a percent if it alleviated the crisis in health care.[121]

While there are rough edges to the Czech velvet economic transformation, it must be remembered that this transition is among the best of the region. It was the high expectations and the unabashed self-confidence that Klaus portrayed in his own rhetoric before 1997 that made the puncturing of the Czech economic miracle all the more notable.

THE EXPLODED MIRACLE AND THE FUTURE OF THE CZECH ECONOMY

In some senses, the end of the Czech miracle should not have been unexpected. A consideration of developments in the Czech economy before 1997 suggests that all was not well. The government's efforts to manage social peace during the transformation gave way to numerous strikes. Economic pressures, including some inflation, rising unemployment, the imposition of new consumer taxes and plans to end rent control added to the feelings of considerable segments of the population that they were economically disenfranchised while others enriched themselves. Evidence that crony capitalism was not widespread apparently did little to assuage these views. The collapse of some banks and the corruption of others lent credence to this idea and suggested that, if not corrupt itself, the Klaus government was at least irresponsible in not having enacted procedures and legislation to impede such activities.

Even domestic economic indicators suggested a downturn. 1996 showed a decline in foreign investment, to $1.4 billion from the 1995 figure of $2.5 billion. Industrial production, which had increased considerably in 1995, fell sharply in 1996, and continued declining in the first two months of 1997. With such economic indicators worsening, the government announced its 'Correction of economic policy and other transformation measures' on 16 April 1997. This cut public expenditure by 20 billion Crowns. It also emerged that the IMF had warned Klaus of impending economic difficulties in March 1997, a report he kept even from his own party and which fuelled ODS Deputy Chairman Zieleniec's subsequent attack on him. From having criticized the inefficiencies of the EU, Klaus now had begrudgingly to accept economic recommendations from external bodies. The government presented these economic policy changes as necessary measures to fulfil the transformation, rather than mistakes in their own right. Nevertheless, a population imbibed on Klaus' positive rhetoric was now told to tighten its belt. The velvet economic transformation was becoming frayed.

To be sure, this was still a smoother and fairer transition than in many other post-communist countries, and these issues in themselves did not break the economy. In fact, as suggested in the preceding chapter, what is remarkable is not that Klaus finally resigned in November 1997 but how well his minority coalition government managed to retain power in 1996 and 1997. The Czech velvet transformation and the Klaus government ended not because of these socio-economic pressures but due to a structural fault in the economy.

The specific cause is to be found in trade and foreign investment. Because of the Czech economic successes in 1994 and 1995 expectations, especially by foreign investors, were of sustained growth; this led to what were called 'excessive' capital inflows in 1995 and 1996 (even though, ironically, foreign investment decreased in 1996). While foreign capital was certainly wanted, its influx adversely affected the country's currency and trade balance, particularly with the EU. The Klaus government tried to counteract these developments with the Export Guarantee and Insurance Company which insured some of the country's exports. But, as with other emerging economic problems, Klaus rationalized the trade deficit by saying that it arose from Czech imports of industrial equipment which would then bolster the Czech economy. But the imbalance continued to worsen and could not be explained away. The trade deficit in 1994, which had actually improved slightly on that of 1993, was US$ 900 million; in 1995 the deficit increased to US$ 3.7 billion, and in 1996 reach almost $6 billion.[122] The Central Bank undertook to defend the Crown, spending US$3 billion of its reserves, but decided to float it on 27 May, resulting in it losing over 10 percent of its value the same day.

The devaluation put greater pressure on Klaus' state budget. The Klaus government had planned in mid-1997 for a budget surplus. But government plans to decrease corporate taxes signalled that government spending would have to be reduced in the area of social welfare. Instead, while the Klaus government entered 1996 with a budget surplus of 1.7 billion Crowns, it had a budget deficit of 8.5 billion Crowns by the first quarter of 1997.[123] The government was also forced to cap public employee salaries as part of its second austerity budget, announced the day after the devaluation. The government's situation was exacerbated by the costs of repairing the damage caused by floods that affected much of Central Europe. Total flood damages in the Czech Republic were estimated at 60 billion Crowns. Some of the costs were offset by monetary assistance from external bodies such as the EU and EBRD, and flood bonds were also issued and the private sector was expected to absorb some cost as well. But the government was nevertheless faced with unanticipated expenditure at the most inauspicious time.

Klaus' statements of reassurance about the vitality of the Czech economy, already diminished by the fact of his April and May budgets, were further undermined by a series of foreign evaluations of its performance. In the comparative study of 115 countries on their economic freedom, the Czech Republic placed behind Estonia and Lithuania, and just above Hungary.[124] Once much richer than Slovenia, the Czech Republic was overtaken by Slovenia in 1997 in terms of per capita GDP. And the Czech government received indicators that annual growth had fallen in 1997 to 1.0 percent of GDP, down from the 3.9 percent growth registered in 1996.[125] It was also in July 1997 that Agenda 2000 was issued; while it found the Czech Republic fit for accession negotiations, the report was by no means the resounding endorsement of the Czech transformation that Klaus' early confident proclamations would have led his population to expect.

A combination of a structural development in the economy and the shattering of popular perceptions led to an economic and psychological implosion. This sentiment was perhaps summarized after Klaus' resignation when Havel charged him with creating a mire that allowed 'the most immoral people' in the Czech Republic to avail themselves of the transition. This would be a helpful juncture at which to offer an overview of the Czech velvet economic transformation.

CONCLUSIONS: THE ECONOMY AND ITS PROSPECTS

According to the economic indicators used to measure the transformation of post-communist countries, the Czech Republic overwhelmingly has a market economy. To the extent that it is a fully-functioning, Western market-economy, it must also be measured in those terms. This is also a criterion on which Czech economic reformers insisted. Some economists suggest that no Western forms of capitalism have yet emerged in former Eastern Europe.[126] Such detractors notwithstanding, many indicators confirm the success of the Czech economy, both in terms of other post-communist countries and in its own right. For example, the important US credit rating agency Standard & Poor accorded a substantially higher rate to the Czech Republic than to EU member Greece or to any other post-Communist country.[127]

Other indicators suggest otherwise. As Table 3.1 shows, growth has been mixed. GDP grew in 1995 by 6.4 percent, a notable increase on the already significant 3.2 percent achieved in 1994. Nevertheless, estimates such as those of the EIU were of 4.7 percent GDP growth in 1996 and 5.3 percent in 1997.[128] Instead of growth of 1.0 percent was

KEY ECONOMIC DATA FOR THE CZECH REPUBLIC, 1990–1998
(figures in US$); na = not available; f = forecast

Czech Rep	1990	1991	1992	1993	1994	1995	1996	1997	1998
Nominal GDP (US$bln)	32.3	25.4	29.9	34.3	39.7	50.3	56.6	52.9	56.8
GDP per capita	9526	8721	8951	9273	9794	10531	11211	11566	na
GDP (% change)	−1.2	−11.5	−3.3	0.6	3.2	6.4	3.9	1.0	−2.7
Industrial production (% change)	−3.3	−22.3	−7.9	−5.3	2.1	8.7	1.8	4.5	1.7(f)
Budget balance (% of GDP)	na	−1.9	−3.1	0.5	−1.2	−1.8	−1.2	−1.0	−1.6
Unemployment (% of workforce)	0.8	4.1	2.6	3.5	3.2	2.9	3.5	5.2	7.5
Average monthly wage	182.6	128.5	164.3	199.6	239.5	307.8	356.4	333.4	na
Inflation (%)	9.7	56.6	11.1	20.8	10.0	9.1	8.8	8.5	10.7
Exports ($bn)	5.9	8.3	8.4	13.0	14.0	21.5	21.7	22.8	26.4
Imports ($bn)	6.5	8.8	10.4	13.3	14.9	25.1	27.6	27.2	28.9
Trade Balance ($bn)	−0.7	−0.5	−1.9	−0.3	−0.9	−3.7	−5.9	−4.4	−2.5

Source: *Business Central Europe* database

achieved in 1997, and negative growth followed in 1998, even though on 8 January 1998, the European Commission anticipated 1.2 percent GDP growth for the Czech Republic. This forecast, it said, was the first favourable results of the Klaus' government's economic measures.[129] The EBRD expected Czech GDP to fall by 1 percent in 1999 and calculated that the Czech economy had not regained GDP output of 1989.[130] It can, however, be argued that the drop accounts for the removal from production of shoddy goods that should not have been produced.

Other indicators showed downturns in the economy. Real wages fell in early 1998 for the first time in the life of the Czech Republic.[131] By 1998, the Tošovský government warned that if the economy did not pick up, unemployment could rise to 6 percent, [132] but also suggested that even 7 percent unemployment was manageable in the Czech Republic.[133] By January 1999 the figure had exceeded that, climbing to 7.5 percent.

Economic indicators, then, show various potential problems in the Czech economy. But longer-term risk may be found in areas less visible or measurable, especially in financial laws and regulation. The Czech Republic is considered to have a 'weak banking system', to lack appropriate bankruptcy procedures and an inadequate capital market which has inhibited efficient corporate governance.[134]

Such problems need not detract from the Czech economy being deemed a market economy, but much of the population is doubly-dissatisfied with the transition. On the one hand, the Czech economic ethos is towards consumer choice, the market and wealth, but they are not each benefiting enough from it. Czechs are not satisfied with the transition. According to a STEM poll in February 1998, just over half the Czech population believed the present economic situation to be better than before 1989 while 45 percent were either doubtful or disapproving.[135] A poll conducted at about the same time registered only 5 percent of Czechs satisfied with the economic transformation.[136] On the other hand, Czechs want wealth on a democratic basis; the new market environment renews the historic Czech trend towards egalitarianism. While they want wealth, they generally reject the social stratification that comes with it.

The Czech dichotomy between wealth and economic democracy may prove to be the impetus for a national solution: a hybrid of market economy with social security. Even from an economic viewpoint, as some Czech analysts observe, 'it is evident that *the existence of the welfare state in Czechoslovakia ... becomes the crucial condition for the success of all initiated changes*'.[137] This was a point never lost on the unbridled free-marketeer Klaus: to his credit, while the Czech Republic was seen as a leader in post-communist economic reform, the social safety net was also quietly if tentatively being constructed. It is not simply a function of being in opposition that by late 1998 Klaus was also calling for social reforms.

Just as the Prague Spring's 'socialism with a human face' captivated the West European left as a viable alternative, albeit in theory of course, to harsh Western capitalism and unreconstructed Soviet socialism, so too may Czechs today have the possibility of constructing the middle ground that so many Western societies elect governments to implement. After all, Czech production and employment in the private sector exceeds that of many West European states, while Czech society retained a strong imperative towards ensuring a distribution of wealth and opportunity.

It is Havel who has the colourful, even pastoral image of the Czech economy—that of the (privately-owned) bakeries and pubs.[138] But he also has the more realistic picture. He says that 'we will never reach paradise' but adds that routine problems conceal that the country is generally doing well and that the goals set by society after communism are being met with remarkable success.[139] The non-economist Havel probably has a fairer, more accurate assessment of the situation, than the economists who engineered the Czech economic miracle. They were almost bombastic in their declarations. In 1994, Czech Economics Minister Dyba had already discounted the Czech Republic's inclusion among 'emerging markets' by proclaiming triumphantly: 'Forget it ... we have already emerged'.[140] The official Czech news service pronounced in January 1993 that it had learned that the EBRD viewed the Czech Republic 'as the most attractive country in east and central Europe for its operations, particularly for ... its stability and the convenient structure of its economy'.[141]

To be certain, the Czech Republic had an auspicious economic beginning and has achieved much since. It began its existence with expectations of positive, even unprecedented, economic development. At the outset of the Czech Republic Dyba projected GDP to increase by as much as 4.5 percent.[142] From being the most nationalized economy in former Eastern Europe, the Czech Republic now has a massive market economy. It has developed some advanced services and consumer goods, particularly cars, to supply its population and has restored to private ownership all but the largest industries, banks and infrastructure. Testament to the transformation in pure economic terms is that 80 percent of production is derived from the private sector, higher than in many officially capitalist societies, and over 2.3 million people, accounting for 63.8 percent of all employees, now work in the service sector.[143] And some sectors and companies are experiencing remarkable success. The Czech telephone network SPT Telecom (the privatization of which was suspected of earning the ODS and ODA a sizeable kickback) reported net profits of over 6 billion Crowns in 1997, a 23 percent increase. Standard & Poor's gave it an impressive 'A corporate rating' and SPT announced that it would launch Eurobonds.[144]

One can agree that the transformation, at least technically, was completed early along. But such a narrow view of what constitutes transformation generates an incorrect assessment and helps to explain the raised but unfulfilled public expectations that contributed to the fall of the Klaus government in November 1997.

On a practical level, the short-term outlook for Czech political-economy will be higher public spending. The Czech Republic has always had public debts, even though they were sometimes masked by financing from sources outside the government budget. In early 1998 the Tošovský government anticipated having to increase social expenditure by 11.6 percent for 1999, an increase that would exceed expected governmental income.[145] This trend would become even more pronounced with the Social Democrats. Even before he was elected, Zeman said he was willing to tolerate budget deficits as high as 3 percent of GDP.[146] The ČSSD budget approved on 19 January 1999, with the necessary support of the Communist Party, was the first budget in history of the Czech Republic to have passed with a deficit.

The Velvet economic transformation was path-breaking; but its results are uneven. Some aspects and sectors of the economic have been developed to a high degree; others have been neglected almost entirely. The Czech economic transformation is a patchwork of velvet.

1 Kristian Palda, 'Czech Privatization and Corporate Governance', *Communist and Post-Communist Studies* (Vol. 30, No. 1, 1997), p. 83.

2 'Business in Eastern Europe', *The Economist*, 22 November 1997, p. 7.

3 As this chapter will demonstrate, post-communist Czech economic reformers neither intended nor implemented full shock therapy. The term as used here is meant only as an expression of radical reform.

4 T. Boeri and M. Keese, *Labour Markets and the Transition ni Central and Eastern European* (Paris: OECD, 1992); and Marie Bohatá, Petr Hanel and Michal Fischer, 'Performance of Manufacturing', in Jan Svejnar (ed.), *The Czech Republic and Economic Transition in Eastern European* (San Diego: Academic Press, 1995), p. 256.

5 Svejnar, 'Introduction and Overview', in *ibid.*, pp. 2–3.

6 Karel Dyba and Jan Svejnar, 'A Comparative View of Economic Developments in the Czech Republic', p. 42; and Ivan Šujan and Milota Šujanová, 'The Macroeconomic Situation in the Czech Republic,' in *ibid.*, p. 123.

7 Nicholas Barr, Stanislaw Gomulka and Igor Tomeš, 'Constraints on Change', in Nicholas Barr (ed.), *Labor Markets and Social Policy in Central and Eastern Europe: The Transition and Beyond* (New York: Oxford University Press, 1994), p. 101.

8 For early indications of post-communist studies, see for example, Karel Dyba and Karel Kouba, 'Czechoslovak Attempts at Systemic Changes', *Communist Economies* (Vol. 1, No. 3, 1989), pp. 313–25; see, also, the following reference.

9 Václav Klaus and Tomáš Ježek, 'Social Criticism, False Liberalism, and Recent Changes in Czechoslovakia', *East European Politics and Societies* (Vol. 5, No. 1, Winter 1991), p. 26.

10 *Ibid.*, pp. 37–8.

11 *Ekonom*, 1–6 January 1993.

12 Christopher G. A. Bryant, 'Economic Utopianism and Sociological Realism', in Christopher G. A. Bryant and Edmund Mokrzycki (eds), *The New Great Transformation: Change and Continuity in East-Central Europe* (London and New York: Routledge, 1994), p. 59.

13 Kieran Williams, 'National Myths in the New Czech Liberalism', in Geoffrey Hosking and George Schöpflin (eds), *Myths and Nationhood*, (London: Hurst & Company, 1997), p. 132.

14 East Germany had comparable privatization but, with the exceptional nature of German reunification, the Geman government and private investment in the East German economy, must be considered as a unique case.

15 'Statement on the Investment Climate in the Czech Republic', (Unpublished Document at American Embassy, Economic Section, Prague, February 1993), quoted in Hilary Appel, 'Justice and the Reformulation of Property Rights in the Czech Republic', *East European Politics and Societies*, (Vol. 9, No. 1, Winter 1995), p. 31.

16 *Ibid.*, p. 22.

17 Ivan Klíma's *My Golden Trades* (New York: Charles Schreibner's Sons, 1992), p. 226.

18 *Denní telegraf*, 7 May 1993.
19 John S. Earle, Roman Frydman, Andrzej Rapaczynski and Joel Turkewitz, *Small Privatization: The Transformation of Retail Trade and Consumer Services in the Czech Republic, Hungary and Poland* (Budapest: Central European University Press, 1994), p. xix.
20 *Ibid.*, p. 74.
21 Carol Skalnik Leff, *The Czech and Slovak Nations* (Boulder: Westview Press, 1995), p. 192.
22 Vic Dukes and Keith Grime, 'Privatization in East-Central Europe: Similarities and Contrasts in its Application', in Bryant and Mokrzycki, p. 165.
23 Vladan Sir, 'Coupon Privatization Over, But Much Remains To Be Sold', *Prognosis*, 11 January 1995.
24 Andrzej Jagodziń, 'Privatization in Czechoslovakia', *Uncaptive Minds* (Vol l. V, No. 1, Spring 1992), p. 86.
25 John C. Coffee, Jr., 'Institutional Investors in Transitional Economies: Lessons from the Czech Experience', in Roman Frydman, Cheryl W. Gray and Andrzej Rapaczynski (eds), *Corporate Governance in Central Europe and Russia* Vol. 1 (Budapest: Central European University Press, 1996), p. 183.
26 János Kornai, *The Road to a Free Economy* (New York: Norton, 1990), p. 91.
27 Earle, *et al.*, *Small Privatization*, p. 47.
28 Olivier Jean Blanchard, Kenneth A. Froot and Jeffrey D. Sachs (eds), *The Transition in Eastern Europe* (Chicago: University of Chicago Press, 1994), Vol.1.
29 EIU, *Country Report: The Czech Republic* (2nd Quarter 1997), pp. 20–1.
30 *The Economist*, 22 October 1994.
31 Palda, 'Czech Privatization', p. 83.
32 Ed Clark and Anna Soulsby, 'The Re-formation of the Managerial Élite in the Czech Republic', *Europe-Asia Studies*, (Vol. 48, No. 2, March 1996), p. 285.
33 EIU, *Country Report: The Czech Republic* (1st Quarter 1996), p. 6.
34 See, for example, Roman Frydman, Kenneth Murphy and Andrzej Rapaczynski *Capitalism with a Comrade's Face* (Budapest: Central European University Press, 1996), pp. 43–4.
35 Jaroslav Jirasek and Ilja Mracek, 'Footwear: Tipa', in Saul Estrin, Josef C. Brada, Alan Gelb and Inderjit Singh (eds), *Restructuring and Privatization in Central and Eastern European* (Armonk, NY: M. E. Sharpe, 1995), p. 106.
36 Coffee, 'Institutional Investors', in Frydman *et al.*, p. 183.
37 Normandy Madden, 'In the Czech Republic, All Eyes are on TV Nova', *Transition* (Vol. 2, No. 8, 19 April 1996), pp. 14–15.
38 'Business in Eastern Europe', *The Economist*, 22 November 1997, p. 7.
39 Sharon L. Wolchik, 'Czechoslovakia in the Twentieth Century', in Joseph Held (ed.), *The Columbia History of Eastern Europe in the Twentieth Century* (New York: Columbia University Press, 1991), p. 152.
40 Svejnar, 'Introduction,' in Svejnar (ed.), p. 7.
41 *The Wall Street Journal*, 1 July 1997.
42 Klaus and Ježek, p. 38.
43 *Hospodářské noviny*, 9 March 1998.
44 See the Agreement for 1993 in *Hospodářské noviny*, 12 March 1993.
45 Svejnar, 'Introduction,' in Svejnar (ed.), p. 11.
46 David Fretwell and Richard Jackman, 'Labor Markets: Unemployment', in Barr (ed.), p. 171.
47 Svejnar, 'Introduction,' in Svejnar (ed.), p. 7.
48 EIU, *Country Report: The Czech Republic* (3rd Quarter 1997), p. 8.
49 Jiří Večerník, *Markets and People: The Czech Reform Experience in Comparative Perspective* (Aldershot: Avebury, 1996), p. 30.
50 *Mlada fronta Dnes*, 13 May 1997.
51 Český statistický úřad, at http://www/czso/cz/cz/aktual/rei/rei98.htm.
52 Petr Mareš, Libor Musil and Ladislav Rabušic, 'Values and the welfare state in Czechoslovakia', in Bryant and Mokrzycki (eds), p. 80.
53 CTK, 18 January 1993, in Foreign Broadcast Information Service, *Daily Report: East Europe* (hereafter cited as FBIS), 21 January 1993, p. 22.

54 *Hospodářské noviny*, 12 March 1998.

55 Karel Dyba and Jan Svejnar, 'A Comparative view of Economic Developments in the Czech Republic', in Svejnar, *Czech Republic*, p. 23.

56 *Lidové noviny*, 4 February 1994.

57 See chapter 4.

58 *Mladá fronta Dnes* 7 January 1993.

59 EIU, *Country Report: The Czech Republic* (3rd Quarter, 1997), p. 7

60 *Hospodářské noviny*, 11 March 1988.

61 Karla Brom and Mitchell Orenstein, 'The Privatised Sector in the Czech Republic: Government and Bank Control in a Transitional Economy, *Europe-Asia Studies* (Vol. 46, No. 6, 1994), p. 917.

62 For a discussion and examples of legislation, see Petr Liška, *Praní Špinavých peněz v České republice* (Prague: RADIX, 1997).

63 The country is estimated to produce 5 million per year, although Bulgaria is believed to manufacture 12 million. Stuart Millar, 'Alarm as music piracy reaches record level', *The Guardian* (8 March 1997).

64 Jiri Pehe, 'Czech Fall From Their Ivory Tower', *Transitions* (Vol. 4. No. 3, August 1997), p. 23.

65 Havel's Address to Parliament, 9 December 1997.

66 Earle, *et al.*, *Small Privatization*, p. 282.

67 'Business in Eastern Europe, *The Economist*, 22 November 1997, p. 7.

68 Earle, *et al.*, *Small Privatization*, p. 276.

69 Jiri Pehe, 'Czechs Fall from Their Ivory Tower', *Transitions* (Vol. 4, No. 3, August 1997), p. 24.

70 *The Economist*, 26 October 1997, p. 131.

71 *Lidové noviny*, 10 February 1998.

72 *Mladá fronta Dnes*, 4 February 1998.

73 *The Economist*, 17 January 1998, p. 88.

74 EIU, *Country Report: The Czech Republic* (2nd Quarter, 1997), p. 8.

75 DHL Customs Report for Central and European Europe cited in *New Markets Monthly*, October/November 1998, pp. 20–1.

76 EIU, *Country Report: The Czech Republic* (2nd Quarter, 1993), p. 7.

77 Dyba and Svejnar, 'A Comparative View of Economic Developments in the Czech Republic', p. 42.

78 *Mladá fronta Dnes*, 31 March 1998.

79 EIU, *Country Report: The Czech Republic* (1st Quarter, 1996), p. 6.

80 *Hospodářské noviny*, 10 May 1994

81 Cited in Gene Kramer, 'US Urged to Help Czechoslovakia Avoid "Germanization"', *Associated Press*, 20 February 1990.

82 Rick Fawn, 'Central Europe since the Revolutions of 1989: States, Economies and Culture in a Time of Flux', in John Macmillan and Andrew Linklater (eds), *Boundaries in Question: New Directions in International Relations* (London: Pinter, 1995), pp. 69–86.

83 CTK, 11 February 1993. in FBIS, 16 February 1993, p. 15.

84 EIU, *Country Report: The Czech Republic* (4th Quarter, 1997), pp. 25–6.

85 *The Economist*, 22 October 1994, p. 102

86 *The Economist*, 12 July 1997.

87 *Christian Science Monitor*, 12–18 January 1990.

88 *Lidové noviny*, 18 February 1998.

89 *Mladá fronta Dnes*, 24 March 1998.

90 Report by Deutsche Morgan Grenfell, in 'Czech construction: down but not out', *New Markets Monthly*, June/July 1998, p. 4.

91 *Hospodářské noviny*, 13 and 24 March 1998.

92 *Hospodářské noviny*, 25 February 1998.

93 Earle, *et al.*, *Small Privatization*, p. xxiv.

94 Petr Matějů and Blanka Řeháková, 'Od nespravedlivé rovnosti ke spravedlivé nerovnosti? Percepe sociálních nerovnostíca sociální spravedlinosti v současném Československu', *Sociologický časopis* (No. 3, 1992).

95 Petr Matějků and Blanka Řeháková, 'Revolution for Whom? Analysis of Selected Patterns of Intergenerational Mobility in the Czech Republic', *Czech Sociological Review* (Vol. I, 1993); and Jaroslav Krejčí and Pavel Machonin, *Czechoslovakia, 1918–1992: Laboratory for Social Change* (London: Macmillan, 1995), p. 231.

96 See Jiri Pehe, 'The Controversy over Communist Managers', *Report on Eastern Europe* (7 September 1990), pp. 6–10.

97 Sharon L. Wolchik, 'The Czech Republic and Slovakia', in Zoltan Barany and Ivan Volgyes (eds), *The Legacies of Communism in Eastern Europe* (Baltimore, MD and London: The Johns Hopkins University Press, 1995), p. 170.

98 Petr Matějů and Blanka Řeháková, 'Turning Left or Class Realignment? Analysis of the Changing Relationship Between Class and Party in the Czech Republic, 1992–96', *East European Politics and Societies* (Vol. 11, No. 3, Fall 1997), p. 501–42.

99 Večerník, *Markets*.

100 *Ibid.*, pp. 40–1.

101 Earle, *et al.*, *Small Privatization*, p. 50.

102 *Právo*, 28 August 1997.

103 *Mladá front Dnes*, 27 March 1998.

104 *Hospodářské noviny*, 28 May 1998.

105 *Právo* and *Mlada fronta Dnes*, 28 August 1997.

106 ČTK, 24 July 1997.

107 David Fretwell and Richard Jackman, 'Labor Markets: Unemployment', in Barr (ed), p. 171.

108 *Hospodářské noviny*, 30 March 1998; and *Lidové noviny*, 31 March 1998.

109 Barbara Jancar Webster, 'The Environmental Legacies of Communism', in Barany and Volgyes (eds), p. 84.

110 Brian Slocock, 'Interest Groups and the Post-Communist Policy Process: Industry and the Implementation of the Czech Clean Air Act', in Iain Hampsher-Monk and Jeffrey Stanyer (eds), *Contemporary Political Studies, 1996, Volume 1* (Exeter: Political Studies Association, 1996), p. 582.

111 IVVM poll, in *Právo*, 17 February 1998.

112 *Kurier*, 4 March 1994, in FBIS, 7 March 1994, pp. 8–9.

113 Gita Bisschop, 'Reviving the Environment's Political Role', *Transition* (Vol.2, No. 16, 9 August 1996, pp. 42–43 & 64.

114 *World Development Report 1993: Investing in Health* (New York: Oxford University Press, 1993), cited in Alexander S. Preker and Richard G. A. Feacham, 'Health and Health Care', in Barr, p. 304.

115 Alexander S. Preker and Richard G. A. Feacham, 'Health and Health Care', in Barr (ed.), p. 299.

116 Nicholas Barr, Stanislaw Gomulka and Igor Tomeš, 'Constraints on Change', in Barr (ed.), p. 104.

117 Nicholas Barr, 'The Role of Government in a Market Economy', in Barr (ed.), p. 44.

118 *Mladá fronta dnes*, 31 March 1998.

119 *Mladá fronta Dnes*, 24 March 1998.

120 ČTK, 23 July 1998

121 *Hospodářské noviny*, 3 March 1998.

122 EIU, *Country Report: The Czech Republic* (2nd Quarter 1997), p. 18. See also table 4.1 at the end of this chapter for an overview of the Czech trade balance between 1990 and 1998.

123 *Ibid.*, p. 14.

124 RFE/RL Newsline No. 39, 27 May 1997.

125 Reuters, 23 March 1998.

126 László Csaba, *The Capitalist Revolution in Eastern Europe: A Contribution to the Economic Theory of Systemic Change* (Aldershot: Edward Elgar, 1995).

127 *The Economist*, 12 April 1997.

128 EIU, *Country Report: The Czech Republic*, (1st Quarter 1996), p. 5.

129 *Hospodářské noviny*, 9 January 1998.

130 EBRD, *Transition Report, 1998*.

131 *Mladá fronta Dnes*, 3 March 1998.

132 *Hospodářské noviny*, 9 March 1998.

133 *Hospodářské noviny*, 11 February 1998.

134 EIU, *Country Report: The Czech Republic*, (2nd Quarter, 1998), p. 8.

135 *Hospodářské noviny*, 18 February 1998.

136 *Lidové noviny*, 5 March 1998.

137 Petr Mareš, Libor Musil and Ladislav Rabušic, 'Values and the welfare state in Czechoslovakia', in Bryant and Mokrzycki, p. 82. (Emphasis in the original).

138 Václav Havel, *Letní přemítání*, (Praha: Odeon, 1991).

139 Radiozurnal, 4 April 1993, in FBIS, 5 April 1993, p. 16.

140 *The Economist*, 22 October 1994, p. 25.

141 ČTK, 15 January 1993

142 EIU, *Country Report: The Czech Republic*, (No. 1, 1993), p. 6

143 *Právo*, 28 August 1997.

144 *Právo*, 30 March 1998; and Reuters, 27 March 1998.

145 *Hospodářské noviny*, 30 March 1998.

146 *Právo*, 5 February 1998.

Chapter 4

The Czech Republic's foreign policy is not merely a set of relations with external entities; it is an export of Czech values and a representation of its place in Europe and the world. Czech foreign policy after 1993 shares qualities and characteristics with post-communist Czechoslovak foreign policy, but is able to achieve its overarching foreign policy aims better as the Czech Republic, and indeed better than at any time in modern Czech history.

The defining feature of Czech foreign policy is summarized in the slogan 'Back To Europe'. As with other Central and Southeast European states and the Baltic Republics, a strong assertion, grounded in a mix of myth and fact, has been advanced by Czech leaders that their people are not only part of the European fold but that they are also contributors to the totality of European culture and history. The Czechs may believe this even more forcefully than their neighbours. The content and aims of Czech foreign policy reflect the distinctiveness of the new Czech nation. This chapter will consider the themes of Czech foreign policy before turning to specific areas of Czech foreign relations, namely with Slovakia, Central Europe, Germany, the European Union (EU) and the North Atlantic Treaty Organization (NATO).

To be sure, other geographic areas or actors are important to the Czech Republic, such as the United States and Russia. Relations with the former can be summarized as exceedingly good, typified by the coincidence that Czech-born Madeleine Albright, daughter of diplomat-historian Josef Korbel, is now US Secretary of State. President Clinton even joked to Havel that, when Albright was serving as US Ambassador to the UN, the Czech Republic was singular for having two ambassadors in that global body. Czech relations with Russia are generally good, largely because Russia has now become less of a tangible threat to the country. Part of Prague's thinking regarding NATO membership is motivated by the general post-Cold War security vacuum in Europe; but, as shall be discussed presently, Czech policy on NATO is only partially influenced by considerations of Russia. Instead, Russia is seen, as mentioned in Chapter 3, as a potential market for Czech goods. The areas of Czech foreign policy that will be considered in more detail present challenges to the Czech Republic and are liable to significant fluctuations.

In this way the content of the Czech Republic's foreign policy was a continuation of the post-communist foreign policy of the federation between 1990 and 1992. That foreign policy contained large strands of what might be called idealism. The driving forces behind post-communist foreign policy were Havel and his long-time friend and fellow dissident Jiří Dienstbier. Just as Havel envisaged a new type of domestic politics, he and Dienstbier both sought to reinvent the rules of world politics.[1] Even though Dienstbier was only a year younger than Havel, he had had a very different career. Unlike Havel, Dienstbier enjoyed University education, studying philosophy at Charles University. He was also a KSČ member and a Czechoslovak radio journalist; his foreign postings included Washington and the Far East. He became a dissident, however, after expulsion from the Party following the Prague Spring and was a signatory of, and a spokesman for, Charter 77. His dissident work considered alternatives for world politics and was reflected in his editing the underground international relations journal *Čtverec* and authoring a collection of *samizdat* essays entitled *Snění o Evropě*, or tellingly, *Dreaming about Europe*.[2] While he said after the revolution that those writings were dated he also admitted that they provided the basis for 'discussion' of post-communist foreign policy possibilities.[3]

Nevertheless, specific aspects of dissident writings and proclamations foretold and even guided post-communist Czechoslovak foreign policy, particularly the notion of overcoming geopolitics in Europe and reuniting the divided continent. Once in power Dienstbier pursued these aims by launching in April 1990 his 'Memorandum on European Security'. The proposal suggested that, rather than disbanding the Warsaw Pact and NATO, they should evolve into strictly political organizations that could then be collapsed into a pan-European collective security system, effectively a revamped Helsinki process that had brought the two European military blocs into sustained dialogue in the 1970s.[4] The realities of post-communist European security—including the resistance of Western leaders to contemplate changes to NATO's mission and worrying developments in the Soviet Union—brought Prague to seek NATO entry within a year. But Charter 77's 1985 'Prague Appeal', calling for German unification, seemed borne out in the course of 1990. Havel's first foreign policy act was to visit the two Germanies, and unlike West European leaders in early 1990, he not only called for unification but said that the quality of

Germany's democracy, rather than its size, would make it a reliable, peaceful European state.

Post-communist Czechoslovak foreign policy was also realistic. A foremost aim was to regain national sovereignty. This was obtained particularly by the new Czechoslovak government's success in achieving the agreement of the Soviet Union to withdraw its military forces by June 1991.[5] While aspects of the withdrawal remained disputed, such as claims by Prague against Moscow for environmental damage caused by the Soviet military presence and Soviet counterclaims for the value of buildings left behind, the withdrawal ensured the removal of a foreign physical presence that had both symbolically and actually undermined the sovereignty of the country.

Czechoslovakia's post-communist regional relations perhaps best indicated the mix of idealism and realism in its foreign policy. Havel travelled to Poland and Hungary in January 1990 and spoke to each Parliament. He stressed the common history and experience of the three countries and even alluded to shared common values, but foremost emphasized their need to cooperate on their 'return to Europe'. To this end he convened a summit of regional Presidents in Bratislava in April 1990, and while largely unsuccessful, this meeting began a process of Central European regional cooperation that was fostered by the need to coordinate policies towards both the East and the West. The killing of nationalist protestors in Latvia and Lithuania in January 1991 was followed by a meeting a month later of the three Central European leaders in the Hungarian town of Visegrad where a firm, common policy was adopted to terminate the Warsaw Pact and to intensify efforts to gain entry into the European Community. A second Central European summit followed in October 1991 in Krakow, Poland, as the disintegration of the Soviet Union intensified.[6] The three countries signed separate Association Agreements with the European Community in December 1991 that would eventually lead to tariff-free trade. A third summit in Prague in July 1992 was called the most significant to date and saw the launch of the Central European Free Trade Area (CEFTA). But it was precisely at this time, perhaps the pinnacle of the blend of pragmatism and idealism of Czechoslovak foreign policy, that the Federation itself was disintegrating. The overall aims of Czechoslovak foreign policy—reorienting the country's orbit from East to West—not only had been started but already had achieved concrete results, providing an auspicious inheritance for Czech foreign policy.

THE PRINCIPLES OF CZECH FOREIGN POLICY

To fulfil national interests is generally the purpose of any country's foreign policy. The foreign policy of the Czech Republic was more hard-headed and realistic than its Czechoslovak predecessor. But still, Czech foreign policy assumed larger proportions than merely an expression of national interests. Early in the life of the Czech Republic Havel even said that '"Czech interests" appeared too often in official statements about Czech foreign policy'. Rather, he said, Czech foreign policy was one of global responsibility and it should serve global interests. Indeed, Havel saw Czech interests as best being served by demonstrating 'that we are not indifferent to what is happening around us'.[7]

Such statements may be a veneer for the achievement of national interests. Adopting the language of universal responsibility may also be a way of conforming to any prevailing international ethos. Many acts of Czech foreign policy suggested such conformity. The first trip abroad by Foreign Minister Josef Zieleniec was to Paris to sign a 120-country convention outlawing chemical weapons. But, where it had the resources or will, the Czech Republic sought to distinguish itself in contributing to and upholding international standards. The Czech Republic also sought to sustain its modest but notable contributions to peacekeeping operations. Federal Czechoslovakia had supplied a 500-man battalion to the UN Protection Force (UNPRO-FOR) deployed in former Yugoslavia. With the breakup, each Republic said that it sought to provide the same. The Czech Republic also planned to send 20 peacekeeping observers to Mozambique and the Czechoslovak mission in Iraq was to be replaced by Czechs. Prague spoke out against human rights violations, such as in Cuba, North Korea and China. This was not merely rhetoric; national interests, particularly trade, were jeopardized. Relations with North Korea deteriorated so badly that it disallowed the Czech Republic from acting as successor to Czechoslovakia on the Neutral Nations Supervisory Commission which maintains the Korean armistice. This breakdown prompted the Czech Republic to recall all of its embassy staff and to expel 13 of the 16 North Korean diplomats accredited to Prague.[8] These are but small expressions of the values and aims of Czech foreign policy; when necessary, Czech idealism challenged existing international values and risked immediate Czech national gains. Czech foreign policy meant to contribute to and shape international political thinking and not merely to conform to it.

But as much as Czech foreign policy contained noble aims, it was not naive. The Czech Republic was a non-permanent member of the UN Security Council when that body debated its response to the 1994 massacres in Rwanda. While Prague pressed for intervention, its UN ambassador, Karel Kovanda, later recounted that his government must have received pressure from 'elsewhere', intimating major powers, to modify its position.[9]

The Czech Republic never relied entirely on moral persuasion or international institutions. On a practical, operational level, the Czechs challenged the provisions made for its personnel participating in the UN peacekeeping missions in former Yugoslavia. Jaromír Novotný, head of the Foreign Relations Section of the Defence Ministry, expressed concern that the Czech battalion was insufficiently armed and said that heavier equipment, including anti-tank missiles, would be made available.[10] In 1994, Novotný also saw the appointment of a Czech officer as commander of the South Sector of UNPROFOR as recognition of the work of Czech peacekeepers who had been deployed since its outset.[11] In the larger picture, Prague endorsed international measures against Iraq. Post-communist Czechoslovakia was one of the few coalition armies that entered Iraqi territory during the war to restore Kuwaiti independence, an act that France, for example, refused to undertake. Thereafter, the Czech Republic supported legal measures to curb Iraq. Klaus saw the sanctions as 'principled', and Havel reiterated Czech support for the use of force against Iraqi non-compliance with UN resolutions. Internally, while slimming down its armed forces, Prague was still committed to developing the country's defence. More importantly, it combined support of consensus agreement in international affairs, such as the Organization for Security and Cooperation in Europe (OSCE), with the desire for a workable, meaningful security guarantee: NATO membership.

The morality of Czech foreign policy was also, perhaps predictably, contradictory, for example, in the area of arms sales. The Czech Republic possessed an advanced industrial base that included sophisticated military production. It simultaneously sought to curb the supply of arms to questionable regimes while ensuring that the lucrative arms industry continued. Havel called new legislation regulating the foreign sale of arms 'a very good law, a very strict law.' He was realistic enough to add:

> By itself, a law is not sufficient to improve the image of our country. What is important is the practice and the application of the law. However, the law is an important precondition. It seems to me that this whole area will become more transparent now. It will become clear what the state did allow

and what it did not allow, why it allowed it and why it did not allow it. Of course, there is no law that cannot be bypassed by inventive people. It will be important that the law is really functional and not bypassed. That will be fundamental in securing a good image of our state.[12]

In pursuing this strict application, the Czech Department of Trade and Industry (DTI) refused a license for the sale of Czech-made gas masks to Croatia, which the Croatian Ministry of Labour and Social Affairs claimed were for use primarily by firemen and a few by civilians.[13]

The Czech ammunitions manufacture Sellier & Bellot, which extensively supplied Warsaw Pact armies, announced that it would no longer aim to sell abroad and had not applied for export licences from the DTI. A spokesperson said that the company would focus on munitions for sport, and that military production had ceased to be a priority. Speculation was rife, however, that the company decided to stop foreign sales because a subsidiary had earlier been denied an export license by the DTI.[14] If this is the case, then the Czech government could be seen to be restricting sales even of ammunition. But in the same year, the Czech Republic exported weapons to 52 countries, the value of which had increased 16 percent over the previous year. Of the 558 applications for export licenses, only 16 were rejected.[15]

Often the end-users of Czech arms were unknown, as consignments were sold on by middlemen. It was rumoured in September 1994 that the Israeli firm Elbit purchased Czech warjets at $1.3 million each, added $600,000 of equipment and resold them to Thailand for $4.5 million.[16] While Israel may have resold Czech weapons, Prime Minister Yitzhak Rabin asked the Czech Republic to stop exporting nuclear technology to Iran via Russia. The Czechs denied the charge.[17] Two Russians and a Czech nuclear scientist were arrested by Czech police in December 1994 for attempting to smuggle enriched uranium; this was probably the largest attempt to do so in world history.[18]

The Foreign Ministry authorized the sale of 40 T-55 tanks and other military vehicles to Cambodia in November 1994. The tanks were to have been destroyed under the terms of the Conventional Forces in Europe Treaty that stipulated conventional force reductions throughout Europe. Plans to sell tanks to Algeria, in the throws of a murderous struggle, not only prompted criticism from the opposition ČSSD but also risked breaking apart Klaus' coalition government.

The inconsistency of aims illustrated by arms sales is one example of competing tendencies within Czech foreign policy; a problem common to the foreign policy of many countries. In fact, at times and in certain policy areas, actual divergences appeared within Czech foreign policy. While the new Czech Constitution reduced the powers of the President domestically, the office retained a large influence over foreign policy, a capacity which Havel tended to exercise. The coalition politics of the Klaus government resulted in ministries being apportioned to parties which then ran them as fiefdoms and increased the scope for partisan politics. This was true of the Foreign Ministry which went to Klaus' ODS[19]. The Cabinet often took views opposing the President on foreign policy and pursued what might be considered a less idealistic and more 'practical' line. Havel was even publicly critical of what he saw as a 'lack of coordination' between his Office and the Foreign Ministry in early 1993.[20] Political parties also took competing positions on key issues, including the question of NATO membership and how EU accession should be decided.

Despite some fragmentation of foreign policy making, the process has been fairly consistent because of a general agreement of aims and the continuity of Foreign Ministers. Josef Zieleniec held the post for five years, from the inception of the Czech Republic to his resignation in 1997 in protest to Klaus' leadership style. He was succeeded in November 1997 by Jaroslav Šedivý. The appointment of this respected dissident historian had, from a policy-making viewpoint, the advantage that he had served in the post-communist Foreign Ministry consistently since the Velvet Revolution. It was on him and two other personal acquaintances that Dienstbier called to reorganize the Foreign Ministry with him.[21] This was an environment in which only communist-appointed bureaucrats worked and in which, as Dienstbier explained, he needed people he could trust utterly.[22] Šedivý was appointed ambassador to France in June 1990 and returned to Prague for home duty in 1995, heading the Ministry's Policy and Planning Division. At the end of that year he was named the Czech Republic's ambassador to Belgium and Luxembourg and its representative to NATO and the WEU.[23] He remained Foreign Minister until Tošovský's interim Cabinet dissolved after the June 1998 elections.

Jan Kavan became the Czech Republic's third Foreign Minister, named to the post on 19 July 1998 as part of Zeman's Social Democrat government. Kavan was unjustly accused under lustration of collaborating with the StB while in exile in the United Kingdom, where his support for dissidents still in Czechoslovakia included founding the *samizdat* publishing house Palach Press in 1974 and running *East European Reporter*. These activities helped Kavan to establish strong contacts in the West which continue to assist Czech foreign policy after 1998. Kavan's aims as Foreign Minister very much continued those before him: the pursuit of what he called Czech national interests but in the context of international cooperation and the upholding of human rights.[24] Thus, Czech foreign policy has never been strictly idealistic; rather, it sought to combine the observance of international law and morality with military preparedness, the managed use of coercion and formal military alliances. In these ways, the foreign policy of the Czech Republic resumes the foreign policy of interwar Czechoslovakia. International circumstances now, however, allow the Czech Republic a much greater opportunity to fulfil its aspirations in the global sphere. This is not least because of its geographical relocation after the Velvet Divorce.

Indeed, it is imperative to note that the most striking feature of the foreign policy of the Czech Republic was its new geographic context. In contrast to the slender, elongated Czechoslovakia which stretched from Germany to Ukraine, the new Czech state became much more spherical and compact. Reduced from 127,896 to 78,864 sq. kms, the Czech Republic exceeds in territorial space only Albania and Slovakia among its regional neighbours. The breakup also relocated the country more westward. The dissolution of the Soviet Union in December 1991 distanced Czechoslovakia from Russia by the creation of a band of independent states, including Ukraine, whose sovereignty Czechoslovakia was among the first to recognize. With the Czechoslovak breakup a year later, the Czech Republic was removed even further from the Russian orbit by the statehood of Slovakia. As a result, the Czech Republic was repositioned relatively further West as three-quarters of its borders were now shared with EU-member states Germany and Austria, with only a northeastern and shorter eastern border fronting Poland and Slovakia respectively.

In January 1993 Zieleniec made explicit the significance of the country's new geography to its foreign policy: 'It is clear that the change in our geopolitical location must result in a change in our foreign policy, because the geopolitical location is an essential, if not the most essential, factor of foreign policy'.[25] The clearest expression of that new geographic location was the need to create relations with a new neighbour: Slovakia.

RELATIONS WITH SLOVAKIA

After affecting a peaceful and rational separation, relations could have been expected to be good between the Czech Republic and Slovakia after 1993. Many Czechs and Slovaks share personal connections; Klaus is married to a Slovak. Economic connections also remained strong, with each being the other's primary trading partner. Officially, Prague embarked on a 'special relationship' with Slovakia and Havel called bilateral relations a 'priority' and planned to make his first formal state visit abroad as Czech President to Slovakia. Slovak President Michal Kováč acknowledged this, noting that, for example, the Czechs were assisting the Slovaks in setting up a Presidential office. Havel added that he was pleased that Kováč kept his promise that the Czech Republic would be his first foreign official visit.[26] Immediately thereafter differences arose in bilateral relations, and Prague began to introduce measures that not only made relations more formal but that also distanced Slovakia both physically and psychologically from the Czech Republic.

Havel had called for completely free movement across the new Czech-Slovak border; but he then asked Slovaks to understand the necessity of having a formal border between the two countries. A dispute arose as to the documents required to cross the border. Havel repeatedly said that this was merely a technical question, but also insisted that passports be used. He qualified this by saying that passports were not discriminatory against Slovaks. Kováč, however, opposed the introduction of passports, partly, he said, because it would be embarrassing for those who did not possess them.[27]

The division between the Czech Republic and Slovakia became more formal in other realms. The preceding chapter on the Czech economy reviewed the establishment of a customs union and the creation of separate currencies. Slovak Prime Minister Mečiar commented that Slovaks had not expected a new separate currency, or that the border would go up so quickly or to have to face such 'excessive' border checks. He also objected to the division of assets and the claim by the Czech Republic that Slovakia owed Prague money and, asserted that private Slovaks who invested in what became privatized Czech assets were now deprived of their assets. Bratislava also accused Prague of stealing the former federal flag (which both republics agreed in November 1992 not to use) and demanded compensation for the post-World War II trade of Polish Těšín to the Czech Lands in exchange for part of Slovakia. But early plans to coordinate Czech and Slovak foreign policy were most damaged by the inalterable influence of geography. As Zieleniec explained: 'I do not think that we will coordinate our foreign policy because Slovakia has different neighbours from us, which naturally means that they will place a different emphasis on their foreign policy'.[28]

To be sure, official Czech rhetoric spoke of wanting good relations and of assisting Slovakia to gain NATO and EU membership. But between 1993 and 1998 the Czech Republic pursued a foreign policy often at odds and even hostile towards Slovakia. And differences between the Czechs and Slovaks could not strictly be attributed to the governments of each. Many of the bilateral problems were attributable to Mečiar's confrontational style. Even Jozef Moravčík, Slovak Prime Minister for over a year after Mečiar's government fell in March 1993, who was seen as amenable to listening, saw Czech-Slovak relations as unequal.[29] But personality did exacerbate relations. Havel publicly questioned Mečiar's sanity, while Mečiar insulted Czech leaders by proposing a new Czech bank note which would feature on one side Havel and wife 'Daška' in bed while on the other Klaus with a Czech banknote lodged in his posterior.

Overwhelmingly, however, Czech relations with Slovakia were conditioned by Czech aspirations to join the EU. Deputy Foreign Minister Pavel Telicka said that the Czech Republic's 'special relationship' with Slovakia would probably cease upon Czech accession to the EU. He added that the Czech Republic wanted Slovakia included in the accession talks but if that did not occur, then the Czech Republic would have to follow EU practice and secure its frontier with Slovakia.[30] Similarly, the prospect of EU membership only heightened the need to tighten borders. Interior Minister Cyril Svoboda proposed tightening the Czech-Slovak border in 1998 to reduce refugees coming into the Czech Republic in order to meet expected EU requirements.[31]

A potential strain on relations occurred from Havel's efforts to encourage democratic development in Slovakia prior to the October 1998 elections, diverting from the diplomatic practice of non-intervention in internal states' affairs. While Kováč attended the January 1998 summit of 11 regional leaders at Levoca, Slovakia, Prime Minister Mečiar did not. Havel met with people from the Slovak opposition and the Hungarian minority and announced that Czechs desired improved relations.[32]

The opportunity for better relations arose in October and November 1998 after Mečiar was defeated in the Slovak parliamentary elections and, despite expectations, withdrew from politics. Prague promptly and categorically issued its congratulations to the coalition government of Mikuláš Dzurinda. Havel visited Bratislava shortly thereafter; Czech newspapers featured photographs of Slovaks waving a tricolour flag to welcome him. The question rightly posed was whether the flag was the Czech or the Czechoslovak. Regardless, Czech-Slovak relations can now be expected to improve, not least because Bratislava can regain some of the distance lost by the Mečiar government in complying with requirements of the EU and NATO for the establishment of full democratic practice in the country.

REGIONAL RELATIONS

The breakup of Czechoslovakia not only prompted the establishment of formal diplomatic relations between the two constituent republics but also changed the pattern of regional diplomacy. Since the inception of post-communist Czechoslovakia's foreign policy, Havel fostered Central European relations. As mentioned, he initiated the 'Bratislava process' which led to the Visegrad Group.[33] The Group proclaimed a new form of relations in the region and pledged multilateral consultation and coordination on foreign policy, particularly in their efforts to secure European integration. Similarly, Czechoslovakia became a member of the *Pentagonale*, a loose grouping that included Italy, Hungary, Yugoslavia and Austria. The *Pentagonale* lost salience with the violent demise of Yugoslavia, although it also expanded to become the *Hexagonale* with the admission of Poland, and was rechristened the Central European Initiative following the admission of Slovenia, Croatia and Macedonia. That grouping aside, the Visegrad Triangle, as this core of Central European cooperation became known, seemed to continue promisingly, particularly with its July 1992 Summit in Prague. But it was exactly at this time that the consequences of the June 1992 Czechoslovak elections would be felt by the country and the region.

Assuming the post of Czech Prime Minister, Klaus gained a vehicle with which to exercise his views on regional cooperation. Regional cooperation may have occurred in part because of the absence of other options and because of perceived needs to meet outside expectations, particularly that of the European Community.[34] But this was insufficient justification for Klaus, and he, unlike Havel, saw no benefit to developing a Central European identity. He even referred to the Visegrad Group as 'an artificial process' created by an anticipated regional desire of such behaviour by the European Community. At most, Klaus reduced Central European cooperation strictly to the economic, and tended to refer to the Visegrad countries only as CEFTA. When Klaus attended the 25 November 1994 meeting of CEFTA

Prime Ministers at Poznán, Poland, he reaffirmed his opposition to the 'political interdependence' of Visegrad countries and said that Czechs were only willing to cooperate on trade matters within CEFTA. At the meeting's final press conference, he went as far as to say: 'Now the Czech Republic, in its dictionary, literally translates "Visegrad" as "CEFTA"'.[35] Klaus denied non-cooperation in the region; instead, he contended that the Czech Republic was the 'driving force' behind the economic cooperation embodied in CEFTA.[36] But what trade liberalization occurred never exceeded the requirements expected under the Association Agreements, signed with the EC in December 1991. In diplomatic terms, the Klaus government broke protocol by sending inappropriately low-ranking officials to ministerial-level meetings. When Klaus did seem to be involved in the region, he was accused by Polish President Lech Wałęsa of elevating Czech interests over those of the Visegrad Group.[37]

After Klaus' prime-ministerial resignation the prospects for regional relations improved, but still remained on a practical and functional level. Regional relations were expanded to include Slovakia more fully, with all three Central European states pledging to assist Bratislava in accelerating its efforts to gain entry to the EU and NATO after Mečiar's defeat. As at the beginning of the decade, so towards its end, the countries of Central Europe pursued similar foreign policies and cooperated closely in their integration into Western institutions.

CZECH-GERMAN RELATIONS

The Czech Republic's relations with Germany are its most ambiguous and difficult. It was no understatement when Havel called Germans and Germany 'part of Czech destiny and identity' and 'an inspiration and a pain'. He added that some now saw Germany as the Czech nation's greatest hope while others perceived it as their greatest risk.[38]

Germany remains essential to Czech foreign policy for several reasons. As discussed previously, it is the largest foreign investor in the Czech Republic and (inter-republic trade with Slovakia notwithstanding) by far its largest trading partner. Prague also hopes, as do other Central Europe states, that Germany will continue to lobby for early Czech accession to the EU. But, in addition to these important practical considerations, that history makes Germany central to Czech foreign policy.

Perhaps the most challenging and contentious issue in Czech foreign policy has been reconciliation. This is not simply a moral issue, although righting historical wrongs has been important as well. Indeed, some on the Czech side, notably Havel, believed that proper bilateral relations could not begin without mutual apologies: the Germans for their wartime behaviour towards Czechoslovakia; the Czechs for the post-war expulsion of the Sudeten Germans. While statements of contrition have appealed to some Germans, such as President Richard von Weizsäcker, it did not satisfy the powerful Sudeten German expellee lobby, based largely in Bavaria. This group, whose members have included the Premier of Bavaria, insist on the restitution of their Czechoslovak (or, after 1993, their Czech) citizenship and their property. In addition to presenting untenable problems to the restitution and privatization programmes, this suggestion has been morally unacceptable across the Czech political spectrum.

Historical claims have resulted in deadlock in several aspects of Czech-German relations. Negotiations on bilateral relations have been stalled by demands of the Sudeten Germans for representation in German diplomatic and negotiating teams. While the Klaus government agreed in late May 1993 to 'dialogue' with the *Landsmannschaft*, the organization representing Sudeten German expellees, it rejected its inclusion in official negotiations. Bonn eventually came to this position as well although it continued to be sensitive to this highly organized and vocal lobby based in Germany's richest *Land*.

German leaders set out conditions for relations on this historical matter. German Chancellor Helmut Kohl announced on 3 September 1993 that Czech dialogue with the Sudeten Germans was a precondition to Czech integration into Europe. Bavarian Premier Edmund Stoiber even intimated that his support for the construction of an urgently needed oil pipeline for the Czech Republic should be reciprocated by dialogue with the Sudeten Germans.[39]

The signing of a new treaty between post-communist Czechoslovakia and Germany was delayed until February 1992 because of domestic Czechoslovak objections and even then protests and newspaper letters condemned the deed. While small gestures, such as 'Reconciliation 95' were made, the drawing of the proverbial line in the sand of Czech-German history was delayed effectively several years. When negotiations began in earnest, over a year was required before a Declaration would be signed. On the popular level, Czechs generally viewed Sudeten German claims as motivated by financial considerations rather than historical redress, and 37 percent of Czechs in a 1995 survey said they feared the aim was to reannex Sudeten land.[40] The

Czech public also felt that historical guilt overwhelmingly rested with the Germans. On a practical level, Czech politicians stress that Czechs are alone among Germany's wartime victims in not yet having received compensation. But they explained that relations with Germany should not hinge on history and, instead, the two countries should allow their coexistence to lead to a future in an integrated Europe.[41] For his part, Havel, who had been thoroughly conciliatory towards the Germans, maintained that commencing discussions with the Sudeten Germans was not a precondition for expediting compensation of Czechs.

On 20 January 1997, Kohl made what was called an 'historic' visit to Prague to sign the Czech-German Declaration of Historical Reconciliation.[42] The Czech government understood the agreement finally to preclude the issue of property rights for expelled Sudeten Germans. Shortly after the signing, Kohl announced that the property issue remained undecided. In addition, the powerful Christian Social Union in Bavaria, sister party of the nationally ruling Christian Democratic Union, came out against the agreement. Ratification of the Declaration also produced acrimony in the Czech Parliament. The Communist and Republican parties were united in opposition to the agreement, the latter charging the government of being composed of 'foreign elements' such as Jews, Poles and even Germans and of selling out the country. Republican leader Sládek declared his regret that not more Germans were killed during the Second World War, a statement that resulted in his arrest on charges of racist provocation. Even the Social Democrats were split, with only 31 of their 50 MPs voting to accept the Declaration because they refused to accept the notion of Czech guilt towards the Germans. The ČSSD also wanted inclusion in the Declaration of a clause stipulating that that German government agreed that these historical issues were now closed.

The Declaration was intended to put an end to historical disputes and facilitate new relations in Czech-German affairs, but the matter was not settled. Even Kohl indicated in a 30 January 1997 Bundestag speech that the property issue was not closed and a resolution by the German Social Democrats recognizing the Declaration as ending discussion on historical issues was defeated. The Declaration included an agreement to create a Reconciliation Fund to compensate Czech victims. But this was delayed because of disputes over the composition of its membership. In the end, the Declaration was not legally binding, and Sudeten Germans resumed their drive for Czech citizenship and property restitution.

In March 1998 the German Secretary of State for Foreign Affairs Hans-Friedrich von Plotz said that Germany would not connect Czech (or Polish) entry into the EU to matters dating from the Second World War. But at the same time Sudeten German leader Franz Neubauer reiterated his opposition to Czech membership of the EU until the Czech Republic disassociated itself from the post-war 'persecution' of the Sudeten Germans and also affirmed their right to return to their homeland.[43] After the Czech Republic began membership talks with the EU, Bavarian Premier Stoiber said at a Sudeten German celebration in Nuremberg that the talks provided an opportunity to seek a repeal of Beneš' decrees and other laws considered discriminatory against Sudeten Germans.[44] Czech-German relations on this issue continued to be sensitive under Zeman's premiership. He opposed the inclusion of *Landsmannschaft* in the Czech-German Discussion Forum, provoking criticism from German Finance Minister Theo Waigel and Foreign Minster Klaus Kinkel.

Outside of historical differences, both the Czech and German governments proclaim their relations to be excellent. Already in 1994 the two countries held joint military exercises at Janovice nad Uhlavou. And despite threats from specific interests in Germany to the contrary, Prague continues to hope for German goodwill in its efforts to secure full membership of Western institutions. Such hopes were strengthened following the election of Gerhardt Schröder as German Chancellor. Unlike other German politicians, Schröder has opposed postponement of EU enlargement until outstanding German issues with both Poland and the Czech Republic are definitively settled. It is to Western integration that the chapter now turns.

WESTERN INTEGRATION

While Western integration has been the cornerstone of Czech foreign policy, both the Klaus government and the Czech people have exhibited ambiguous tendencies towards the process. Herein we find distinctive Czech traits. On the military security front, one would expect that the Czech experiences of 1938–39 and 1968 would have driven the population to seek a firm security guarantee. That such a guarantee could simultaneously mean that the country was connected to democratic countries through a multilateral forum should have made the prospect of joining NATO all the more attractive. In the realm of the socio-economic, the Czech Republic's market and trade reforms should have dictated unquestioned entry into the world's largest single market. Similarly, cultural affinity that underscored 'back to Europe' suggested an immediate and uncompromising desire for full institutional membership of the Western world. As Zieleniec affirmed in the first week of the Czech Republic's existence, European integration was the country's 'main political goal'.[45] Yet the Czech approach to both organizations was distinctive: on NATO, both the Czech public and many politicians were sceptical of membership at all; on the EU, the population was ambivalent, while the position of the Klaus government was that the Czech Republic was in some respects superior to the EU and could instruct it on the management of a large supranational bureaucracy. This section will consider in turn the paradoxes of Czech policy towards the EU and NATO.

EUROPEAN UNION

Czech membership of the EU was meant to signal the recognition of Czech values as fundamentally European. As Zieleniec explained again in mid-January 1993, central to Czech foreign policy was 'the fact that we share the same values as Western Europe and that we want to bear joint responsibility for it'. He added that now that it was independent this was even more 'consequential' for the policy of the Czech Republic.[46] But the approach of the Klaus government towards gaining EU membership was one of self-confidence. In January 1993 Dlouhý said that the Czech Republic would be ready for EU membership in two years, citing its 'democratic system, economic stability, low unemployment rates, and satisfactory balance of payments'.[47] Similarly, Czech leaders pronounced on 8 January 1993 that within two to three years the Czech Republic would be ready to 'march into the EC'.[48] The Klaus government's view remained unchanged even though Brussels continued to impose standards on potential applicant countries. While Central European states were generally unsatisfied with the outcome of the 9–10 December 1994 Essen European Council meeting that deliberated a pre-accession strategy, Klaus said it was irrelevant that little aid was promised and no accession schedule forthcoming because the country was progressing towards membership on its own.

To be sure, this confidence was moderated over time. Czech television political analyst Zdeněk Velíšek put it in 1995: 'When we were told by Western politicians five years ago that it would take us a decade or more to become part of their world, we considered it a misjudgement or, worse, an outrageous brush-off. When those politicians tell us today that the most optimistic predictions are that our integration into Western institutions will come around the end of the century, we welcome it with something close to relief'.[49] But even his caution dissipated into calls for full expansion of Western institutions and to the making of the Czech Republic into the heart of this new institutional Europe.

While Czech policy became more practical in having to meet accession terms it still offered its own caveats to a process over which it was not meant to have any control. When, for example, Hungary announced its decision to apply for full EU membership on 3 March 1994, a Czech Foreign Ministry spokesman said that the country would apply when it was fully ready.[50] Klaus said that the Polish and Hungarian applications would 'lie around' and that an interim stage between associate and full membership would be necessary.[51] That aside, policy began to take concrete shape. An Association Agreement with the EU, replacing one signed with post-communist Czechoslovakia in December 1991, was formalized on 4 October 1993 and on 1 February 1995, the Czech Republic became an associate member of the EU. But its leaders again overestimated the significance of these steps. Zieleniec pronounced the measure irreversible and that the country would definitely enter the EU.[52] The Klaus government also believed it had lessons for Brussels. Klaus cautioned about the bureaucracy and lack of democratic accountability in the EU and even likened it to Soviet control over Eastern Europe. Zieleniec spoke of Europe being formed of many nations, each contributing ideas. One of the ideas from the Czechs, he explained, similar to Klaus, was the warning to be drawn by the excessive bureaucracy of communist rule. This 'warning', Zieleniec elaborated, informed Czech discussions of the future form of the EU.[53]

As we saw in Chapter 3, the success of the Czech economic miracle has since been questioned, if not entirely deflated. Entry into the EU was also not unconditional. The European Commission assessed the suitability of the 10 applicant countries for accession talks (which in themselves were not a guarantee of membership). Known as Agenda 2000, the Commission's report was issued on 15 July 1997 and judged applicants on their political and democratic development, their ability to meet competition from EU economies, and their readiness to fulfil EU obligations, including the common law or *acquis communautaire*. The Czech Republic was among five post-communist countries (as well as Cyprus) deemed advanced enough for detailed membership negotiations. But while the Commission found fundamental freedoms to be assured in the Czech Republic, Prague was criticized nevertheless for what was deemed its discriminatory treatment of its Romany population. It must also have come as a blow that, having previously been the golden economic success of the post-communist world, the Czech Republic was surpassed in some of the economic indicators by Estonia and Slovenia. KSČM leader Miroslav Grebeníček, a politician ideologically intent on attacking Klaus, nevertheless offered perception when he pronounced that officials in Strasbourg saw the situation in the Czech Republic more realistically than the government.[54]

Despite the expression of a distinct Czech view of membership of the EU and of how the organization should operate, inclusion remained the priority. The practical question became whether there should be a referendum on membership, a move which interim Prime Minister Tošovský proposed but was unable to enact and which now seems unlikely. This may be just as well: in advance of Agenda 2000 only 43 percent of Czechs supported EU accession, well below the average of 61 percent in favour among all post-communist applicant countries.[55] Accession talks with the EU are proceeding under the ČSSD government. The key issue for the Czech Republic is no longer advocating a particularist position; it will now be a matter of painstaking preparation of bureaucratic and legislative detail to ready the country to meet the requirements of the *acquis communautaire*. Czech views on NATO, however, illustrate Czech ambiguities on Western integration.

NATO AND EUROPEAN SECURITY

The leadership of the Czech Republic views membership of NATO not simply as a security alliance or guarantee but, like the EU, as an affirmation that Czech values are European. This view led Prague to advance a cultural and even a moral argument for its inclusion. Havel consistently spoke of the right of entry into NATO of like-minded democratic countries and of the civilizational values to which the Czechs subscribe. Defence Minister Vilém Holáň regarded membership not only as practical means of defence, but also as a part of Czech duty to contribute to Europe, particularly in protecting its broader values.[56]

The history of Czechoslovakia would lend argument to the Czech case for inclusion. The betrayal of Czechoslovakia by Britain and France at Munich and its abandonment by the West during the 1968 Warsaw Pact intervention could be expected to give ammunition to

Czech leaders in their claims for NATO membership and to bolster public desire for inclusion, at last, in a credible, democratically multilateral security arrangement.

But neither of these developments occurred. Czech politicians who advocated NATO membership tended not to refer to such historical claims; and the public remained sceptical of membership. 3 of 4 Factum polls in 1997 showed that between only 39.9 and 42.8 percent of the public supported membership. Only one poll showed interest over 50 percent, and then by only one-tenth of one percent.[57] With membership talks confirmed at the July 1997 NATO Madrid Summit, support increased, but only modestly. A January 1998 poll by the Czech public opinion research institute IVVM found 54 percent of Czechs supported membership over 43 percent in November 1997, while those in favour climbed to 60 percent in March.[58] This more supportive result was taken after several initiatives which would almost certainly have increased support for membership. These included a television campaign by the Ministry of Defence to enlighten the population on NATO membership; the establishment of a Euroatlantic Forum by Zieleniec; and a billboard campaign featuring an impersonation of Brezhnev thanking the Czechs for not entering NATO. By contrast, a November 1997 referendum in Hungary returned 85 percent in favour while a comparably-timed survey in Poland found 80 percent in favour.[59] As Table 4.1 shows, a Eurobarometer study of popular support for entry into NATO among all candidate countries published in March 1998 showed Czech support to be well below the average:

TABLE 4.1   REFERENDUM ON NATO MEMBERSHIP[60]
Question: If there were to be a referendum tomorrow on the question of (our country's) membership of NATO, would you personally vote for or against membership?

COUNTRY	% IN FAVOUR	% UNDECIDED	% AGAINST
Romania	67	11	9
Poland	61	18	4
Candidate Countries	**52**	**18**	**11**
Hungary	47	22	15
Slovenia	45	13	23
Bulgaria	37	22	14
Czech Republic	**36**	**21**	**22**
Estonia	32	37	12
Lithuania	31	28	16
Slovakia	31	24	27

The Czech Republic's attitude towards NATO presents a paradox. This was a country which, from its history, should want NATO membership. Its mainstream political leadership vigorously pursued that aim abroad and Czech diplomacy had an added advantage in the appointment on 5 December 1996 of Madeleine Albright as US Secretary of State. Born Marie Korbelová, having fled Czechoslovakia and spending the war in British bomb shelters, she was expected not only to be sympathetic to Czech security needs specifically but also to the principle of NATO expansion generally. She explained that the historical reference points that framed her foreign policy thinking were different from other current leaders. As she pronounced, 'my mindset is Munich—most of my generation's is Vietnam'.[61] Her approach to Central Europe became unambiguous: the region was to be admitted into NATO. However, the Czech population was relatively unenthusiastic about NATO membership. While on fertile ground for membership, Czech politicians had to present a view that was unrepresentative of public opinion and downplayed the extent of popular ambivalence. When, for example, the Chairman of Belgium's Chamber of Representatives asked Chairman of the Chamber of Deputies Milan Uhde whether entry into Western institutions was supported just by the Czech government, Uhde replied that this was a 'majority view', save for what he called a segment of the opposition.[62] Throughout the Klaus government no effort was made to inform the population of the advantages of membership and the security it would provide.[63]

A second irony of Prague's approach to European security is that the Czech government's campaign for NATO membership was based on logical strategic calculations. It did not accept security offerings from the West that was short of full NATO membership. But, at the same time, the Czech government undertook exceedingly few measures domestically to assist the country's entry into NATO.

Insistent on NATO membership, Prague carefully avoided what it—and objective strategic analysts—would consider insufficient substitutes. One such issue was membership of the West European Union (WEU), the embryonic military wing of the EU. But the structure of the WEU prevents it from providing a meaningful security guarantee. It has no standing army and is hampered in its decision-making, not least because its membership does not coincide with that of the EU. It is also the only military organization to which both the United States and Russia agreed that Central European states could join; where these two powers disagreed on the composition of other institutions, such consensus on the WEU almost certainly signalled to Central Europe that membership was trivial. The Czech Republic certainly accepted, along with eight other post-communist countries, associate partnership on 9 May 1994, but this was of limited significance. True, Russia was not included. But the associate member states are unable to invoke meetings of the WEU, a crucial requirement should a response be needed to a crisis. Appropriately, Klaus downplayed WEU membership, especially because of its lack of troops. Only after NATO accession was assured and the Czech government was run by the Social Democrats did Prague begin to pursue WEU membership seriously. Foreign Minister Kavan announced in November 1998 that he intended for the Czech Republic to enter the organization by the middle of 1999.[64]

The WEU was insufficient in itself and NATO membership, therefore, remained Prague's primary goal. Understandably, NATO strategists had to weigh the gains of increased security of some European states by the expansion of the Alliance against the costs of alarming Russia with that same act. NATO's general response since the early 1990s was to offer talking shops that included almost all post-communist countries, including the one which former socialist bloc states feared most, Russia. Post-communist Czechoslovakia accepted participation in such organizations as the North Atlantic Cooperation Council even though it provided no real security guarantee and accorded to Russia the same status as itself.

NATO continued its overtures to the former Soviet bloc with its Partnership for Peace (PfP). Again, no Central or East European state could be fully satisfied with that proposal as a final arrangement for European security. PfP was meant as a practical military cooperation that might eventually contribute to participating states obtaining NATO membership. But PfP was extended to almost all post-communist states. The attitude of the Czech leadership towards PfP was cautious. Zieleniec said that PfP did not constitute an alliance but simply military and political cooperation. He also acknowledged that there was 'a tacit part of the agreement' that PfP would intensify if the situation in Eastern Europe deteriorated. He said that NATO signified joint guarantees for similar interests and ways of life but also that the opening of NATO to all of the East would be risky.[65] Zieleniec was judicious in assessing the meaning of PfP as a selection process for full NATO membership. While he said it was impossible to set criteria for membership, precisely because doing so would identify some countries as members and others as not, he also said that is was possible to envision who could fulfil criteria.[66] After returning from a March 1995 visit to NATO Headquarters, Holáň commented that Czech participation in PfP could be so high as virtually to equal actual membership.[67] On a practical level, the Czech Republic participated in bilateral exercises with NATO-member countries and multilateral NATO military exercises. It was using the avenues open to it.

Czech thinking on European security was conditioned by awareness of the necessity of not provoking Russia. Chairman of the Chamber of Deputies Uhde explained in 1994 that he understood that Russia would not appreciate if security structures were designed against it. Havel consistently wanted to keep Russia as part of Europe, advising 'It is in the interest of the whole world and in the interest of peace that the West should have the best possible relations with Russia, anchored in some system of treaties'. But such thinking was tempered by realistic analysis. Havel also rationalized that Russia should not get membership of NATO on the grounds that it cannot simultaneously want the same type of membership as small, non-nuclear Central European countries and allow its military to submit to external command, while still claiming to be a superpower.[68]

Similarly, Uhde wrote that the Czechs understood that militarily underdeveloped countries could not immediately be admitted into the Alliance but that they sought a guarantee that entry was not closed to them. He also acknowledged that Russia could not be provoked and said that PfP allowed European structures to be fluid. At the same time, he warned against solutions based entirely on avoiding incitement of a particular state, again insinuating Russia, and invoked the example of Yalta and the Soviet intervention of 1968. He explained that the influence states wielded in Europe would derive from its domestic democratic arrangement, its adherence to the principles of the rule of law and its observance of human rights and by respecting the freedom guaranteed by a market economy, a freedom he called a 'spiritual and cultural symbolization'.[69] Similarly, some columnists expressed concern that NATO, because of its acquiescence of Russian behaviour in former Soviet republics, would also not 'confront' Russia over Central Europe.[70]

The achievement of Czech foreign policy was securing, along with Poland and Hungary, a statement from NATO at its July 1997 Madrid

Summit that accession talks would begin with the three countries. But with that achievement in hand, the question turned ever more to what preparation the Czech Republic was undertaking to fulfil NATO membership requirements. In this, much more than in the internal dynamics of NATO, could the Czech Republic have had decisive influence; but it was in this area that Prague did least to secure its ambition for NATO membership.

The Czech Republic was singled out by NATO in January 1995 for being unable to protect classified information. The measures taken to secure information were even considered insufficient by a Czech Interior Ministry spokesman and the Defence Minister also conceded that the maintenance of secrecy and the screening of personnel in the armed forces was also inadequate.[71] And even though the Czech Republic became the first post-communist country to implement an agreement with NATO on the safeguarding of classified material,[72] problems remained with securing state secrets as late as 1998. Senate Foreign Affairs Committee Chairman Michal Žantovský and NATO Security Office Chief Peter Gallant agreed on 10 March 1998 that a new law was necessary 'immediately'.[73] Perhaps even more significantly, civilian control over the military—an essential requirement of NATO membership—has been criticized as lax and observations have been made that the Czechs simply expect democratic values to replace Marxist-Leninist ideology in the armed forces.[74]

Domestic politics also shook NATO confidence in the Czech Republic. The low public interest in membership, the outright opposition to joining the Alliance by the Republicans and Communists, and the insistence by the ever-stronger ČSSD on a referendum suggested to Brussels that the Czech Republic was a domestically-divided prospective partner. NATO Secretary-General Javier Solana sought to keep the Czechs from scuttling their own entry into NATO. He applauded the progress the country was making towards entering the alliance, an improvement on suggestions from NATO officials the year before that the country trailed Poland and Hungary. But he still said, probably due to the ČSSD's demand for a referendum on membership, that it would 'strange' for aspiring members to ratify the accession agreement but then to annul it because of the prospect of an opposing referendum.[75]

The perceived cost of membership has tempered preparations for accession. While overall integration into Western institutions remained the priority of foreign policy, Pilip's state budget of 1997 did not plan to meet the increased defence spending expected as part of entry into NATO. The Finance Minister declared that safeguarding domestic economic and social stability was more important than budgeting a 0.1 percent annual increase in defence spending.[76] The Defence Ministry announced that it would reconsider its plan for arming the military. It budgeted 150 million crowns in 1998 but this was to be revised to 50 million.[77] Concern regarding Czech military readiness was expressed by Žantovský, in his role as ODA chairman, who opposed the sale of 100 T-72 tanks to Algeria partly on the grounds that the army would require all of its 541 main battle tanks for accession to NATO. Similarly, when Zeman's government developed interest in WEU membership, his Defence Minister Vladimír Vetchý said that Czech military spending would have to increase by as much as 70 percent to meet the organization's standards.[78]

In addition to funding, the Czech military has been criticized for matters that would seemingly be easily rectified, including insufficient training of officers in the English language. The armed forces have also had problems retaining their best soldiers. The first Czech officer to graduate from the US military academy West Point returned to resume his duties in the Czech Republic only to chastise the military bureaucracy for its hindrance of the provision of key supplies and for preventing basic training from occurring. He and 10 other of the Czech Republic's 75 Western-trained officers have left the Czech military out of dissatisfaction. Czech Defence Ministry's Foreign Relations Department Head Novotný dismissed the comments and instead offered a rationalization based on the whole of NATO's operations: 'If NATO is today capable of deploying troops on Norway's northern frontier or Turkey's eastern frontier, why shouldn't it be capable of deploying troops in Poland or the Czech Republic, which are closer? We will have to make improvements, but nothing here has to be built on a green field'.[79]

Despite concern, and even criticisms, from NATO of Czech readiness for membership, since the Madrid Summit NATO officials have largely undertaken to reassure the Czech Republic (and perhaps themselves) that it was doing enough for membership. Visiting Prague in February 1998, NATO's Supreme Commander in Europe, General Wesley Clark, said that Czech defence spending was appropriate and commended the work of Czech forces serving in the Stabilization Force in Bosnia. But he also added that the country trailed Hungary and Poland in preparations for membership.[80] NATO confirmed on 20 March 1998 that Poland, Hungary and the Czech Republic were proceeding satisfactorily with their military preparations for membership. 70 percent of their 'force' goals had already been achieved.[81]

In spite of ambivalence among Czechs for entry in NATO and questions of military and financial preparedness, the Czech Republic entered the Alliance officially on 12 March 1999. The limitations to entry were counteracted by Havel and the respect he carried in NATO's circles.

In the entirety of the goals of the Czech transformation its foreign policy is of unambiguous success. The country has been removed from the East and fully reoriented towards and even integrated into the West. And while Hungary and Poland have achieved the same goals, the Czech Republic has done so with particular flair and against perhaps greater, if somewhat self-imposed restraints. It is perhaps representative of Havel's immense, even unparalleled stature in the West that it is his comments on the meaning of NATO that are selected from those of every member leader and the heads of the EU, OSCE, and the UN, to close the Alliance's commemorative publication for its fiftieth anniversary. He said: 'NATO membership amounts not to the mere protection of one's own state security, paid for by the obligation to assist some other country now and again—that is to say, by our readiness to protect others in exchange for their preparedness to protect us. Rather, it is the manifestation of a certain spirit: the spirit of the love of freedom, the spirit of solidarity, the spirit of the will to protect, together, our common cultural wealth, the alliance spirit which is not opportunistic but which—if I may use the expression—is moral'.[82]

At the end of the 1990s, then, the overall aims of Czech foreign policy goals were being fulfilled. NATO accession is not only an achievement in itself but also testimony to the recognition given by the Euroatlantic community to the values expounded by the Czechs, particularly through the personality of their President. But the EU accession process, quite apart for eventual institutional membership, will change Czech foreign policy thinking. The tendency of Czech foreign policy has been towards exceptionalism, even arrogance, and with that, the intimation that the Czech Republic does not follow, let alone conform to, the Western example. The Czech Republic has been criticized both by NATO and particularly by the EU, the latter on issues which Prague least expected: political and human rights. Czech self-satisfaction in foreign policy is indicative of some of the frayed edges of this Velvet Nation.

1. See Rick Fawn, 'Symbolism in the Diplomacy of Czech President Václav Havel', *East European Quarterly* (Vol. XXXIII, No. 1, March 1999), pp. 1–19; and *Matter over Mind: Revolutionary Idealists and the Civic Foreign Policy of Post-communist Czechoslovakia* (forthcoming).
2. Jiří Dienstbier, *Snění o Evropě* (Praha: Knihovna lidovech novin, 1990).
3. Interview with the author, September 1995.
4. See 'Memorandum o evropské bezpečnostní komisi', in *Československá zahraniční politika* (Dokumenty, 4/1990), pp. 155–57.
5. Jiří Šedivý, 'Odchod sovětských vojsk z Československa', *Mezinárodní vztahy* (3/1993), pp. 40–52.
6. Rudolf L. Tőkés, 'From Visegrád to Kraków: Coup, Competition, and Coexistence', *Problems of Communism* (Vol. XL, No. 6, November–December 1991), pp. 100–14.
7. *Mladá fronta Dnes*, 1 February 1993.
8. *The Korean Herald*, 5 March 1995, in Foreign Broadcast Information Service, *Daily Report: East Europe* (hereafter cited as FBIS), 6 March 1995, p. 4.
9. Stated in 'Panorama', BBC1, 7 December 1998, 10.00pm.
10. *Mladá fronta Dnes*, 28 February 1994.
11. *Český deník*, 1 March 1994.
12. Prague Radiozurnal, 20 February 1994, in FBIS, 22 February 1994, p. 4.
13. *Mladá fronta Dnes*, 1 March 1994.
14. *Mladá fronta Dnes*, 3 February 1995.
15. *Respekt*, 15 February 1995.
16. *Economist*, 22 October 1994.
17. *Mladá fronta Dnes*, 30 January 1995.
18. Maggie Ledford Lawson, 'Czechs and Russians Forge New Nuclear Ties' *Prague Post*, 3 January 199; Maggie Ledford Lawson and Jan Stojaspol, 'On a Prague Street, Hot Uranium' *Prague Post*, 10 January 1995.
19. Jiří Pehe, 'Souvislosti domácí a zahraniční politiky', *Mezinárodní politika* (1/98), p. 7.
20. Sharon L. Wolchik, 'The Czech Republic: Havel and the Evolution of the Presidency since 1989' in Ray Taras (ed.), *Post-Communist Presidents* (Cambridge: Cambridge University Press, 1997), p. 183.
21. *Jana Klusáková a Jiří Dienstbier rozmlouvají* (Praha: Primus, 1993), p. 12.
22. Author's interviews with Jiří Dienstbier and Jaroslav Šediv, September 1995.
23. Šedivý's personal account is given in his *Černínský palác v roce nula* (Praha: Ivo Železný, 1997).
24. Jan Kavan, 'Zahraniční politika České republiky', *Mezinárodní politika* (9/98), p. 4.
25. *Hospodářské noviny*,19 January 1993.
26. Radiozurnal, 31 March 1993, in FBIS, 1 April 1995, 8.
27. CTK, 31 March 1993, in FBIS, 5 April 1993, 14. Havel claimed the Czech insistence on the use of passports, rather than simply identity cards, was meant to prevent those awaiting trial from fleeing as their passports are held by the authorities.
28. *Hospodářské noviny*, 19 January 1993.
29. *Lidové noviny*, 20 April 1994.
30. RFE/RL Newsline Vol. 2, No. 42. 3 March 1998.
31. *Mladá fronta Dnes*, 2 March 1998.
32. Genieve Zalatorius, 'The Levoc Summit', RFE/RL Newsline, 28 January 1998.
33. The Hungarian spelling of Visegrad, which has generally been adopted internationally, is used here.
34. See generally Milada Anna Vachudová, 'The Viesgrad Four: No Alternative to Cooperation?' RFE/RL Research Report (Vol. 2, No. 34, 27 August 1993).

35. Vladimir Todres, 'Czechs Reject Political Ties Within Free-Trade Agreement', *Prague Post*, 6 December 1994.
36. *Denní telegraf*, 19 January 1995.
37. *Lidové noviny*, 10 January 1994.
38. Speech to Charles University, 17 February 1995, in *Lidové noviny*, 18 February 1995.
39. CTK, 20 October 1993, in FBIS, 25 October 1993, p. 9.
40. Carol Skalnik Leff, *The Czech and Slovakia Republics* (Boulder: Westview Press, 1995), p. 169.
41. See, for example, Foreign Minister Zieleniec's comments in *Lidové noviny*, 24 February 1995.
42. Ian Traynor, 'Good old days fail Kohl', *The Guardian*, 30 January 1997. See also Andrew Stroehlein, *Czechs and the Czech-German Declaration: The Failure of a New Approach to History* (The Glasgow Papers, No. 1) (Glasgow: IREES, 1998).
43. RFE/RL Newsline Vol. 2, No. 56, 23 March 1998.
44. *Právo*, 1 June 1998.
45. *Telegraf*, 12 January 1993.
46. *Hospodářské* noviny,19 January 1993.
47. Radiozurnal, 21 January 1993, in FBIS, 22 January 1993, p. 20.
48. Oesterreich Eins Radio, 8 January 1993, in FBIS, 11 January 1997, p. 17.
49. Zdeněk Velišek, 'Now is the Time to Recognize Europe—In Its Entirety, *Prague Post*, 3 January 1995.
50. Radiozurnal, 4 March 1994, in FBIS, 7 March 1994, p. 8.
51. *Denní telegraf*, 9 April 1994.
52. See, for example, *Hospodářské noviny*, 1 February 1995.
53. *Lidové noviny*, 24 February 1995.
54. *Lidové noviny*, 18 July 1997.
55. *Central and Eastern Eurobarometer No. 7* (Brussels: European Commission Directorate-General, Information, Culture, Audiovisual, 1997).
56. *Mladý svět*, 19 January 1995.
57. Jane Perlez, 'Despite Havel, It's Check, If Not Mate, on NATO', *International Herald Tribune*, 24–25 December 1997.
58. *Mladá fronta Dnes*, 28 January and 3 March 1998.
59. Elizabeth Gleick, 'Are they up to it?', *Time*, 15 December 1997.
60. *Central and Eastern European Eurobarometer No. 8* (Brussels: European Commission Directorate-General, Information, Culture, Audiovisual, 1998).
61. Martin Walker, 'Albright makes history', *The Guardian*, 6 December 1996.
62. Rudé právo, 24 February 1994.
63. Milada Anna Vachudová, 'The Czech Republic', in Jan Zielonka and Alex Pravda (eds), *Democratic Consolidation in Eastern Europe: The Influence of International Factors* (Florence: European University Institute, forthcoming).
64. ČTK, 18 November 1998.
65. Prague Radiozurnal, 24 January 1994, in FBIS, 24 January 1994, p. 12.
66. *Reflex*, 28 February 1994.
67. Radiozurnal, 6 February 1995, in FBIS, 7 February 1995, 5.
68. 'President Václav Havel Interviewed by Jacques Rupnik', *Perspectives*, No. 3, Summer 1994, *passim*.
69. Denní telegraf, 28 February 1994.
70. See, for example, *Český deník*, 2 March 1994.
71. *Mladá fronta Dnes*, 16 January 1995.
72. *Respekt*, 15 January 1995.
73. *Mladá fronta Dnes*, 11 March 1998.
74. Marybeth Peterson Ulrich, 'U.S. Assistant and Military Democratization in the Czech Republic', *Problems of Post-Communism* (Vol. 45, No. 2, March/April 1998), pp. 22–32.
75. *Lidové noviny*, 6 March 1998.
76. *Mladá fronta Dnes*, 1 September 1997.

77. *Mladá fronta Dnes*, 25 March 1998.
78. ČTK, 18 November 1998.
79. Elizabeth Gleick, 'Are they up to it? *Time*, 15 December 1997.
80. RFE/RL Newsline Vol. 2, No. 23; and Central Europe On-line, 4 February 1998.
81. RFE/RL Newsline Vol. 2, No. 56, 23 March 1998.
82. *NATO Review*, Commemorative Issue 'NATO 1949–1999, 50th Anniversary', 1999, p. 50.

Chapter 5

A NATION OF VELVET?
TOWARDS A NEW CZECH NATIONAL IDENTITY

When Václav Havel was sworn in as the first President of the Czech Republic on 2 February 1993, he noted the creation of a new Czech state but also stressed its lineage:

> The horizon of what we call homeland has thus been significantly narrowed. No one is easily coming to terms with this change, but we have not lost our homeland because of this. On the contrary, its new state image represents for us an appeal for new thinking about its very essence and identity, its possibilities and prospects, its hopes. It is, at the same time, an appeal for truly creative work. We must arrange our transformed homeland so that we can live in it as well as possible and be respected by others.[1]

The meaning of Czech history and the question of the Czech identity arose in the Czech national revival of the mid-nineteenth century and have filled Czech intellectual debate since. Today, Czech doctoral students in the social sciences and philosophy prepare for comprehensive exams on the works of František Palacký and Tomáš Masaryk. Bookshops carry titles by political thinkers and activists such as Petr Pithart, asking 'After 1989: Who Are We?',[2] and a television series is devoted to examining the nature of Czech national identity.

In some senses, Czech identity can be readily defined. Bounded by mountains, the current territory of the Czech Republic has, the Sudeten annexation notwithstanding, remained the same for centuries. Czech language was eroded under Austrian rule since 1620 but made a substantial recovery in the nineteenth century. Despite plans under Nazi and Soviet rule to erase or Russify Czech language and culture, today Czechs absorb Western commercialism in their diction as an indication of world membership rather than as a menace to their national identity. The new Czech Republic appropriated existing Czechoslovak symbols, particularly the tricolour flag; its new currency continues to herald Czech figures such as the ancient and mediaeval Czech monarchs Wenceslas, Otakar and Charles IV and the scientist-philosopher Comenius. With these symbols and personalities, so readily accorded to (non-communist) Czechoslovak history, the Czechs are able to give themselves, or rather sustain, a sense of a long national pedigree.

The Czech Republic has many traditions on which to draw its contemporary creed. Whether these traditions, as ever in the study of nationalism, may be partially or wholly false is irrelevant. Instead, the Czechs take the glory of their history as an indicator of their future. The success of interwar Czechoslovakia is a particular case: a stable, democratic political system with an advanced, successful economy providing a high standard of living, and an egalitarian ethos among nations and classes, the latter aided in the Czech Lands by the loss of the indigenous aristocracy to the victorious Austrians, and supplemented by an extensive social welfare system. The egalitarian streak is identified by Klaus and Ježek who commented that Czech was the first language into which José Ortega y Gasset's *Revolt of the Masses* was translated from Spanish.[3]

The Czech Republic has been viewed as liberal, partly for its interwar values that reflect in its contemporary political culture and distinguish from those of neighboring post-communist states. It is observed, for example, that Czechs are much less likely than people in Hungary, Poland, and Slovakia, to hold anti-Semitic views, that litmus test of Central European tolerance, and are 'also more likely to favor compromise to solve political issues'.[4]

Czech politics may indeed be inclusive and consensual at the level of political parties. It was argued in the politics chapter, contrary to other views, that the end of Klaus' coalition did not constitute a 'crisis'. Instead, it demonstrated the routinization of politics; and with that routinization comes the return of negotiation and compromise. What is striking in recent Czech politics is not Klaus' demise but that his coalition lasted so long and that compromise could again be made among politicians and parties with substantially different personalities and agendas.

In other, very difficult aspects of Czech political life inclusiveness has also been evident. The Czechs could easily assume a position of outright victim of Nazi Germany. Instead, efforts were made, not least but not only by Havel, at recreating bilateral relations on the basis of apology, forgiveness and reconciliation. The Czech leadership apologized for historical injustice to the Germans for the postwar expulsion. Where contemporary Sudeten German demands have not been met is due more to practical considerations than vindictiveness: returning property is too disruptive to the recreation of the Czech economy. The Czech population, especially older generations, tend to disagree with Havel's conciliatory attitude towards the Germans; his views, therefore, many not be fully representative, but it is still a striking feature of Czech society that it has leaders who adopt such an overtly and arguably unnecessary moral stance.

The treatment of communists also suggests a high degree of forgiveness and accommodation. While the Czechs pioneered the systematic removal of communists from high office after 1989, extending that ban for a further 5 years, no real or wholesale punishment was inflicted. The ban itself can be interpreted again as pragmatism to ensure the unfettered development of democratic political institutions.

Cracks in Czech political inclusiveness and liberalism appear in their attitude to minorities. The Czech Republic is now overwhelmingly an ethnically homogenous state. The Czech Republic is unusual, and by most standards fortunate, in its ethnic composition. It inherited a situation whereby it could be nation-state, namely, that every member of the nation is within the borders of the state and all those living within the borders are of that state. Excluding Czech émigrés no more than 1 percent of those considering themselves Czech were living in Slovakia after 1992. In addition, the non-Czech population of the Czech Republic amounted to no more than about 6 percent of its population. About half of these were Slovaks and their families who had come to work in the federal bureaucracy who would have been discounted by Slovaks as no longer being 'Slovak'. The Czech Republic's largest minority is the Roma, or Gypsy population.

To be sure, an ethnically 'pure' state contradicts Havel's creed. He repeatedly cautions that efforts to make ethnically homogenous states in Yugoslavia negate the fundamental values of European integration.[5] For Havel, those who had some ethno-linguistic connection to the country deserved atypical attention. Interviewed on how the Czech Republic should treat Czechs in Kazakhstan, he said

> Although our state cannot be built along purely ethnic lines and although we cannot elevate the feelings of Czech national identity above everything else, I still think that, regardless of these people being rich or poor, we should have and we should demonstrate stronger feelings for those who originate from this country, who speak this language, and who feel some bond with this country.[6]

The bond must be strong, and on terms decided by the Czech Republic. Citizenship is the prerogative of the state. But the Czech Republic has not been liberal in this regard. Refusing to allow dual citizenship presented dilemmas not only for Slovaks but for Czech émigrés. Most significantly, it disenfranchised and marginalized thousands of Romanies who tend to have, after 1993, Slovak passports, but who live in the Czech Republic. In addition to lacking Czech citizenship, Romanies have been targets of beatings and murder and receive less tuition than Czechs. Czechs generally accuse Romanies of a parasitic, even criminal lifestyle. Western reports demonstrating that Romanies are socially ghettoized by lack of educational opportunities and that challenge Czech claims that Romanies commit disproportionate amounts of crime are dismissed by Czechs. Tension between Czechs and Romanies was highlighted by the acts of municipal officials. In northeastern Moravia, a mayor offered prepaid one-way airtickets to local Romanies on condition they never return. When criticized for similar actions, the mayor of Mariánské Hory Liana Janačková explained 'We're only helping our fellow citizens fulfil their wishes. What can be wrong with that?'.[7] In northern Bohemian the town council of Ustí nad Labem proposed the fencing off of tower blocks inhabited by Romanies.

While these acts were undertaken by some Czech officials, others attempted to counteract measures against the Romanies. From the outset of the Czech Republic, upwards of 20 million Crowns have been allocated for minority publications, with the Romany community receiving the largest share.[8] Havel and to some extent Klaus have defended Romanies. The President pardoned two Romanies when they assaulted Republic leader Miroslav Sládek following characteristic racist remarks made at the party's rally on 9–10 May 1997. Following the Prague murder of a Sudanese student by Czech skinheads, bedridden Havel deplored the Czech 'government's obvious deficiency in paying insufficient attention to the problem' of racism.[9]

Czech antipathy towards Romanies, regardless of the grounds, indicates a taint of intolerance and a hole in the velvet of the new Czech political creed. Fortunately, several Czech leaders are using their authority to counteract in practice some of the official and unofficial acts made against the Romanies. But this episode nevertheless illustrates that Czech velvet values of tolerance and inclusiveness do not extend throughout society.

Klaus said early in the life of the new Czech Republic that there was no intention to create prematurely a new Czech statehood and aiming to do so was 'childish'.[10] Instead, he emphasized that the goal was to complete the transformation begun after November 1989. He may discount the need to create a Czech identity, his statement nevertheless reveals the priority of economy to that identity, and it is perhaps in this realm that the emergence, or reemergence, of Czech identity is most clear.

That identity takes two forms—the nature of the economy itself, and the economic nature of the people. The economy, as noted in Chapter 3, is overwhelmingly market-driven, even if large industry and the financial sectors remain disproportionately in state hands. Despite setbacks, the Czech Republic was an economic frontrunner among post-communist states, both in terms of the aims and methods of its economic transformation and in the tangible results. The reforms also sought to change the economic nature of the people. The privatization process was devised to prevent anyone from having advantage. Restitution, particularly of family dwellings, has been as 'the replication of pre-communist patterns of ownership instead of the continuation of communist patterns of privilege'.[11] Some enterprises remain in state hands, but in other sectors like agriculture, communist-era organizations like cooperatives were excluded in order to prevent property from returning to state hands. In addition, the reformers sought to transform Czechs into little capitalists through voucher privatization. The concentration of vouchers in investment funds was an unintended and unpredicted outcome. The objective was egalitarian capitalism, a resumption of the First Republic.

A successful market economy alongside a social safety net and relatively egalitarian wealth distribution was the hallmark of interwar Czechoslovakia. Klaus' mixed economic programme, right-wing rhetoric but centrist policies, should be seen as political expediency; it was not a departure from Czech traditions but a return to them. The failure of aspects of the reforms brought greater social pressure in the form of strikes and the exponential growth of support for the ČSSD. These political developments will mean a convergence of ideology and practice: the Czech economy, regardless of a centre-left or centre-right government, can henceforth be expected to enjoy a mix of market and state.

A new Czech national identity is also contoured by external developments and Prague's response to them. Czech foreign policy has capitalized on changes in Europe; it has pursued what it sees as the right of Czechs to reintegrate themselves in their cultural historical fold. The success for several years of the Czech economy and the stability of its government, and a centre-right one nonetheless, was meant to prove the Czech Republic's unique return to European values. But, as the Czech-born social anthropologist Ladislav Holy observes, many Czechs do not see themselves as being in the West:

> They talk about a trip to Austria, Germany, France or Britain as visiting the West; they talk about 'Western cars', 'Western goods', 'Western films'.... They talk similarly about the 'East'—Russia, Romania, and other countries of the former socialist bloc. They see themselves as belonging to neither the East nor the West—as standing in between.[12]

Other Czechs may disagree; what is clear of Czech foreign policy is that the country is seen in exceptional terms. While cooperating on practical issues with it Central European neighbours, it is also distinct; while desiring EU and NATO membership, they want them largely on Czech terms. As Klaus and Zieleniec emphasized, they felt it was the Czech Republic that had something to teach European institutions.

Ultimately, the future of Czech society comes down to its people. As cautioned in the preface, one need not be a Czechophile to acknowledge the contributions that this small nation has made to world technology, political thinking and culture. True, Czechs will refer to the stereotype of the bumbling Švejk; but the Czechs also have a confident view of themselves. These are the people whose inventions include contact lens and the world's leading plastic explosive, Semtex. The Czechs draw pride from the international successes of their own nationals, be they tennis stars such as Ivan Lendl, Martina Navrátilová and Jana Novotná; the model Eva Herzigová who projected awareness of the Czech Republic on the world stage in another manner; the Oscar-winning film director Miloš Forman; or a series of novelists. To reinforce this image with a technical note, a Czech economist observed that 'the inherited human capital is perhaps the most important building block in the transition process'.[13] Unsurprisingly, Czechs also laud their successes in education; after worldwide exam results were published, Czech newspapers proclaimed 'The Czech Lion is like an Asian Tiger: Our students rank among the best in the world in maths and science'.[14] The geostrategist Halford Mackinder observed back in 1919 that the Czechs were a talented people endowed with 'the most extraordinary political capacity'.[15] Now, for the first time in modern Czech history, circumstance may allow Czechs simply to be able to rely on themselves; if so, the next century promises to fulfil the hopes that were denied fruition in the last century.

1. Radiozurnal, 2 February 1993, in Foreign Broadcast Information Service, *Daily Report: East Europe* (hereafter cited as FBIS), 3 February 1993, p. 10.

2. Petr Pithart, *Po devětaosmdesátém: kdo jsme?* (Bratislava: Kalligram, 1998).

3. Václav Klaus and Tomáš Ježek, 'Social Criticism, False Liberalism, and Recent Changes in Czechoslovakia', *East European Politics and Societies* (Vol. 5, No. 1, Winter 1991), pp. 26–40.

4. Sharon L. Wolchik, 'The Czech Republic and Slovakia', in Zoltan Barany and Ivan Volgyes (eds), *The Legacies of Communism in Eastern Europe* (Baltimore, MD and London: The Johns Hopkins University Press, 1995), p. 169, citing 'Attitudes towards Jews in Poland, Hungary, and Czechoslovakia: A Comparative Survey' (American Jewish Committee and Freedom House, January 1991).

5. See for example, Havel's interview with Jacques Rupnik, *Perspectives*, (No. 3, Summer 1994), p. 6.

6. Prague Radiozurnal, 20 February 1994, in FBIS, 22 February 1994, p. 4.

7. Quoted in Kate Connolly, 'Canadian vision leads Czech Gypsies astray', *The Guardian*, 14 August 1997.

8. *Lidové noviny*, 6 May 1994.

9. RFE/RL Newsline II, No. 157, 11 November 1997.

10. *Ekonom*, 1–6 January 1993.

11. Hilary Appel, 'Justice and the Reformulation of Property Rights in the Czech Republic', *East European Politics and Societies*, (Vol. 9, No. 1, Winter 1995), p. 33.

12. Ladislav Holy, *The Little Czech and the Great Czech Nation: National Identity and the Post-Communist Social Transformation* (Cambridge: Cambridge University Press, 1996), p. 182.

13. Jan Svejnar, 'Introduction and Overview', in Jan Svejnar (ed.), *The Czech Republic and Economic Transition in Eastern European* (San Diego: Academic Press, 1995), p. 3.

14. *Respekt*, No. 50, 9 December 1996. Such successes may still be a result of the communist-era education system. But education faces financial cuts and with teacher/student ratios in Eastern Europe as low as 3:1, the Czech Republic has considered the mandatory retirement of teachers. Bruno Laporte and Julian Schweitzer, 'Education and Training', in Nicholas Barr (ed.), *Labor Markets and Social Policy in Central and Eastern Europe: The Transition and Beyond* (New York: Oxford University Press, 1994), p. 272.

15. Halford L. Mackinder, *Democratic Ideals and Reality* (New York: W. W. Norton, 1962, originally published 1919), p. 159.

BIBLIOGRAPHY

A vast literature on the Czechs, Czechoslovakia, and increasingly on the Czech Republic, is available. The following is only a brief selection, limited to books available in English.

Garton Ash, Timothy, *We the People: The Revolutions of 1989* (London: Granta, 1990). Vivid first-hand account of the Revolutions, including events in Prague.

Hašek, Jaroslav, *The Good Soldier Švejk*. A famous anti-war novel in its own right, the fictional protagonist is often taken as a characterization of Czech national tendencies.

Havel, Václav, *Living in Truth* edited by Jan Vladislav (London & Boston: Faber & Faber, 1986). An anthology including Havel's seminal and other works, and commentaries on the playwright from leading artists.

Havel, Václav, *Summer Meditations* (London & Boston: Faber & Faber, 1992). English translation updated to 1992 of Havel's 1991 reflections of his own values in practice in post-communist change in Czechoslovakia.

Heitlinger, Alena, and Trnka, Susanna, *Young Women of Prague* (London: Macmillan, 1998). A collection of interviews offering female perspectives on the Czech transformation.

Holy, Ladislav, *The Little Czech and the Great Czech Nation: National Identity and the Post-Communist Social Transformation* (Cambridge: Cambridge University Press, 1996). Highly insightful study of parochial priorities of individual Czechs against the larger, loftier aims of the nation, written by a Czech-born anthropologist.

Korbel, Josef, *Twentieth-Century Czechoslovakia: The Meaning of Its History* (New York: Columbia University Press, 1977). Readable survey of twentieth-century Czechoslovak history to the mid-1970s by anti-communist émigré historian and diplomat.

Krejčí, Jaroslav and Machonin, Pavel, *Czechoslovakia, 1918–92: A Laborartory for Social Change* (London: Macmillan, 1996). Historical overview with extensive use of statistics by two leading Czech sociologists.

Leff, Carol Skalnik, *National Conflict in Czechoslovakia: The Making and Remaking of a State, 1918–1987* (Princeton: Princeton University Press, 1988). Detailed study of the political expressions of the Czech-Slovak relationship from the inception of the country to late communism.

Leff, Carol Skalnik, *The Czech and Slovak Nations* (Boulder: Westview Press, 1995). Historical overview followed by detailed and thematic account of the transformation of the two republics until 1994.

Lewis, Paul G. (ed.), *Party Structure and Organization in East-Central Europe* (Cheltenham: Edward Elgar, 1996). Development of post-communist political parties in the region, including chapters on the Czech Republic.

Mamatey, V. S. and Luža, Radomír (eds), *The History of the Czechoslovak Republic 1918–1948* (Princeton: Princeton University Press, 1973). A major edited collection covering an extensive range of issues in the first three decades of Czechoslovakia.

Musil, Jiří (ed.), *The End of Czechoslovakia* (Budapest: Central European University Press, 1995). Czech, Slovak and foreign academics provide a multifaceted if also divergent collection of accounts of the breakup.

Myant, Martin, *The Czechoslovak Economy 1948–1988: The Battle for Economic Reform* (Cambridge: Cambridge University Press, 1989). Thorough account of economic change in the communist period.

Pynsent, Robert B., *Questions of Identity: Czech and Slovak Ideas of Nationality and Personality* (Budapest: Central European University Press, 1994). Literature specialist offering multidimensional assessment of Czech and Slovak identity through a study of intellectual figures, including Havel.

Sayer, Derek, *The Coasts of Bohemia: A Czech History* (Princeton: Princeton University Press, 1998). A provocative cultural interpretation of Czech history from its mythological inception to the communist era.

Shandor, Viktor, *Carpatho-Ukraine in the Twentieth Century: A Political and Legal History* (Cambridge, MA: Ukrainian Research Institute, Harvard University, 1997). A personal and historical account of Czechoslovakia's understudied eastern region by an interwar representative.

Shawcross, William, *Dubcek: Dubcek and Czechoslovakia 1918–1990* (London: The Hogarth Press, 1990). Acclaimed journalist's biography of the reformer, including personal accounts of the Prague Spring and Velvet Revolution.

Skilling, H. Gordon, *Charter 77 and Human Rights in Czechoslovakia* (London: Allen and Unwin, 1981). Major study of the crystallization of Czechoslovak dissident movement, with key documents.

Skilling, H. Gordon, *Czechoslovakia's Interrupted Revolution* (Princeton: Princeton University Press, 1976). At almost 900 pages, the volume is likely to remain the definitive account of the Prague Spring and Soviet intervention.

Skilling, H. Gordon and Wilson, Paul (eds), *Civic Freedom in Central Europe: Voices from Czechoslovakia* (London: Macmillan, 1991). Timely collection of statements by leading Czech and Slovak dissidents, many of whom entered public office after the Velvet Revolution.

Svejnar, Jan (ed.), *The Czech Republic and Economic Transition in Eastern Europe* (San Diego: Academic Press, 1995). Extensive economic study by Czech economists, although occasionally technical.

Teichova, Alice, *The Czechoslovak Economy, 1918–1980* (London and New York: Routledge, 1988). Short, accessible and informative economic history.

Večerník, Jiří, *Markets and People: The Czech Reform Experience in Comparative Perspective* (Aldershot: Avebury, 1996). Readable economic overview with substantial statistical detail.

Wheaton, Bernard and Kavan, Zdeněk, *The Velvet Revolution: Czechoslovakia, 1988–1991* (Boulder: Westview Press, 1992). Colourful account of the November Revolution and immediate political developments, informed by on-ground research and observation.

Wightman, Gordon (ed.), *Party Formation in East-Central Europe: Post-communist Politics in Czechoslovakia, Hungary, Poland and Bulgaria* (Aldershot: Edward Elgar, 1995). Contains analytical chapters on political parties in the Czech Republic and Slovakia and their impact on the breakup of the federation.

Williams, Kieran, *The Prague Spring and its Aftermath* (Cambridge: Cambridge University Press, 1997). Updates the study of 1968 with access to new documents and offers a useful survey of events and interpretations, with its own conclusion.

Wolchik, Sharon L., *Czechoslovakia in Transition* (London: Pinter, 1991). Partly as a result of the book's inception before 1989, it usefully bridges thematically the communist legacy and developments in post-communist Czechoslovakia to 1991.

Index